The Mirror in the Roadway

"A novel is a mirror carried along a roadway."—*Stendhal*

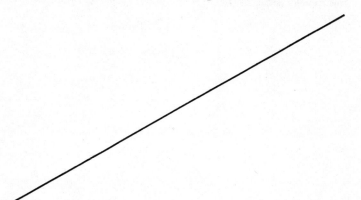

The Mirror in the Roadway

A Study of the
Modern Novel by

Frank O'Connor

Alfred A. Knopf 1956 New York

Acknowledgment is made to the *Yale Review*, in which the chapter on Jane Austen first appeared.

L.C. catalog card number: 56-8926

© *Frank O'Connor, 1956.*

●

THIS IS A BORZOI BOOK
PUBLISHED BY ALFRED A. KNOPF, INC.

●

FIRST EDITION

Introduction

This book is substantially a series of lectures delivered at Harvard Summer School in 1953 and 1954. I have published them because it seems to me that, whatever their faults, they fill a gap and attempt to cover a great art otherwise covered only in sections, as in the little book which I might describe as my inspiration for attempting the subject at all—Lord David Cecil's Early Victorian Novelists. I should have similarly exploited Walter Allen's English Novel if it had been available at the time.

Like the critical judgment, the psychology, I am afraid, is all my own. For some years I have been working on the problem of dream language, not as a psychologist, but as a writer interested in the problem of language. This study seemed to me to support none of the existing psychoanalytical theories. Instead, it seemed to emphasize the classical distinction between judgment and instinct, which in dreams is represented by the metaphor of father and mother.

Naturally, I have no desire to take sides in the eternal dialectic. The purpose of dreams is mainly to keep these two forces in balance, and conflict occurs only when one or the other is threatened. It helps us to understand certain writers in whom the conflict is visible—for instance, Jane Austen and Turgenev —and has no other importance.

As I concluded the book, I found myself listening to a Russian lady complaining indignantly that in her house—in her house!—a German visitor had dared to say that Jane Austen was a better novelist than Dostoevsky. I hope I smiled, but it made me realize again the magnitude of the job I had set myself. Literature, I can only repeat, is a very impure art. It could scarcely be otherwise, since it carries such a cargo of com-

munication, and—in the novel, at least—of information. But I do not abandon hope that in heaven we shall hear lectures that will once for all settle the problem of Jane Austen and Dostoevsky.

Contents

Contents

part **I**

Forerunners

chapter 1

Preliminary

To have grown up in an Irish provincial town in the first quarter of the twentieth century was to have known the nineteenth-century novel as a contemporary art form. The suburban road where we took our walks was the Nevsky Prospekt; Madame Bovary lived across the way. The great Celtic scholar Osborn Bergin used to quote another scholar friend, Joseph O'Neill, who had grown up in Galway, as saying: "For me, literature means three names—all Russian." I do not remember that I ever made so sweeping a statement, but I do remember that when Bergin told me the story, my immediate thought was "Which three?" When I was taken prisoner during the Irish Civil War, it was with a copy of Dostoevsky's *Idiot* in my pocket; and the first person I met in Cork Gaol was obviously Baburin, straight out of Turgenev's story.

It is a background I have never regretted, because the nineteenth-century novel still seems to me incomparably the greatest of modern art forms, greater even than the symphony with which it has so much in common; greater perhaps than any other popular literary form since the Greek theater. Merely to call that great roll of names: Jane Austen, Stendhal, Dickens, Thackeray, Balzac, Turgenev, Tolstoy, Dostoevsky, Flaubert, Trollope, which one could make twice as long without any perceptible lack of quality, should satisfy us that we are deal-ing with a literary universe. The nineteenth-century novel was what the drama was to the Athenians and the Eliza-bethans—a great popular art, shared by the whole com-munity in a way inconceivable in either the eighteenth or the twentieth century.

There is a moving story of Kuprin's which tells how an old deacon of the Orthodox Greek Church is called on to take part in the excommunication of Tolstoy. Since the name at first means nothing to him, he practices his curses in the manner of an operatic part. But then things begin to come back to him—little scenes from *The Cos-sacks*, for example—and he realizes who the man is that he is required to anathematize, and when the moment comes he bursts into an exultant *Ad multos annos*. Of course, this is not criticism, any more than Bret Harte's poem describing the miners in camp weeping over the death of Little Nell is criticism; popularity is not enough; but popularity in a popular art form is also part of the story, and Tolstoy's novels are addressed more directly to the deacon than they are, say, to Mr. F. R. Leavis.

2.

Our way of writing literary history by countries in-stead of by periods makes it hard for us to appreciate what the nineteenth-century novel really was. Dickens, Thackeray, and Trollope tend to get dwarfed in histories of English literature; Jane Austen turns up as a minor and, of course, quite charming figure, like Mrs. Gaskell;

while I know at least one history of French literature from which anyone might reasonably deduce that Stendhal and Flaubert were minor writers quite unworthy of comparison with great poets like Leconte de Lisle.

In studying the novel it is necessary to remember that the only natural classification of European literature is by periods, and that any English novelist is likely to have more in common with a French novelist of his own period than with an English novelist of a different period. This does not mean that all the novelists of one period are equally influenced by one another. The Russians are immediately influenced by the English, but the influence of the Russians on English fiction does not come until much later. All it means is that the influences are there to unite the novelists, and that we must never forget that the nineteenth-century novel is a nineteenth-century art and a European art, and that all its variations are merely local and relatively unimportant. I once printed a list that I jotted down from books on my own shelves in the space of a few minutes. I print it again because it taught me more about the novel than any work on the subject I had read.

1850	Dickens, *David Copperfield;* Hawthorne, *Scarlet Letter*
1851	Hawthorne, *House of the Seven Gables*
1852	Tolstoy, *Childhood;* Thackeray, *Esmond*
1853	Dickens, *Bleak House*
1854	Dickens, *Hard Times*
1855	Trollope, *The Warden;* Tolstoy, *Sebastopol*
1856	Turgenev, *Rudin*

1857   Flaubert, *Madame Bovary;* Trollope, *Barchester Towers*
1858   Turgenev, *A Nest of Gentlefolk;* Eliot, *Scenes from Clerical Life*
1859   Tolstoy, *Family Happiness;* Turgenev, *On the Eve;* Meredith, *Ordeal of Richard Feverel*
1860   Tolstoy, *Cossacks;* Eliot, *Mill on the Floss*

It does not take great critical perception to see that here we are dealing not with three arts, but with one art, and that its origin, development, and decline must be traced to common sources.

Its origin seems almost certainly to be among the European middle classes, released by the French Revolution from their intellectual dependence on the aristocracy. Though the form spread to America, Spain, and Italy, it is mainly the product of England, France, and Russia. Germany seems never to have produced a novelist of the first rank. The only reason which I have seen suggested for this is that of a critic in the *Times Literary Supplement,* who argued that the teaching of philosophy in the German universities made educated Germans unfit for the plastic, concrete form of thought required by the novel. In support of this theory one might instance Turgenev, a student of philosophy who seems to have had the greatest difficulty in shaking off its effects, if indeed he ever did so.

It is convenient for certain scholars to argue that the novel is really a very old form, and to speak of "the Hebrew novel" and "the Greek novel," and people who accept this view naturally tend to regard E. M. Forster's definition of the novel as reasonably complete. Mr.

Forster's definition is a borrowed one—*une fiction en prose d'une certaine étendue*—"and that," he adds, "is quite good enough for us, and we may perhaps go so far as to add that the extent should not be less than 50,000 words. Any fictitious prose work over 50,000 words will be a novel for the purposes of these lectures, and if this seems to you unphilosophic, will you think of an alternative definition which will include the *Pilgrim's Progress, Marius the Epicurean, The Adventures of a Younger Son, The Magic Flute, The Journal of the Plague, Zuleika Dobson, Rasselas, Ulysses* and *Green Mansions,* or else give reasons for their exclusion."

We do wrong to offer Mr. Forster even the show of violence, but I am afraid that his definition *is* unphilosophic, and that his limitation of length only makes it more so by excluding what Biblical scholars call "the Hebrew novel." After all, the *Book of Tobit* has as much claim to be called a novel as *The Pilgrim's Progress* has. The trouble with Mr. Forster's definition is that it takes over a whole mass of existing narrative forms which antedate the novel and differ not only from the novel but from one another— prose translations of epic, medieval romances, medieval sagas, Biblical sagas, religious allegories, and satires—and re-defines them as novels. If *The Pilgrim's Progress* is a novel, then the *Visio Tundalis* is equally one, and if *Zuleika Dobson* is a novel, then anything on earth is a novel and Mr. Forster's own admirable discussion of characters in novels is entirely irrelevant, since characters have no necessary place in the novel—as, indeed, one whole group of modern critics maintains.

In my youth it used to be an axiom of criticism that the novel was a comparatively late form that becomes recognizable only with *Don Quixote*, and it seems hard luck if we are now asked to admit that *Don Quixote* and the medieval romance it makes fun of are equally novels. I do not think they are, and I believe there is a perceptible difference of temper between *Don Quixote* and *Diana Enamorada*, a difference of temper similar to that we find between Jane Austen's *Northanger Abbey* and *The Castle of Otranto*. I believe that this difference of temper is the key to the novel, and that it becomes more marked with the development of scientific thought, the improvement in communications, and the growing popularity of the printed book, and that by the time we reach the nineteenth century it has become an essential and obvious element in the novel and is so recognized by the novelists themselves, even though to this day their admirers among the critics may dissociate them from all connection with it.

The nineteenth-century novel became the great thing it was largely because it was the form in which the scientific temper of the modern world could best act as control. When Trollope criticizes Dickens, it is for his lack of verisimilitude, but when Dickens defends himself, it is not on the ground that verisimilitude is of no importance; on the contrary. Lord David Cecil may tell us that "exaggeration is a sign that Dickens' imagination is working," which is true enough so far as it goes, though it would not be much recommendation in a police court. But what Dickens himself tells us is that "Everything set forth in these pages concerning the Court of Chancery is substantially true and within the truth" and that "Mr. Squeers and his school are faint and feeble pictures of an existing reality, purposely subdued and kept down lest they be deemed impossible."

The curious relationship between imagination and truth, recognized by nineteenth-century readers as well as nineteenth-century novelists, is summed up neatly in Trollope's amusing description in *Phineas Finn* of his own trouble in getting his facts right, and represents the groans of generations of suffering storytellers and of readers with specialized knowledge and critical minds.

> The poor fictionist very frequently finds himself to have been wrong in his descriptions of things in general, and is told so roughly by the critics and tenderly by the friends of his bosom. He is moved to tell of things of which he omits to learn the nature before he tells of them—as should be done by a strictly honest fictionist. He catches salmon in October or shoots his partridges in March. His dahlias bloom in June, and his birds sing in the autumn. He opens the opera houses before Easter, and makes Parliament sit on a Wednesday evening. And then, those terrible meshes of the Law! How is a fictionist in these excited days to create the needed biting interest without legal difficulties; and how again is he to steer his little bark clear of so many rocks—when the rocks and the shoals have been purposely arranged to make the taking of a pilot on board a necessity? As for those law meshes, a benevolent pilot will, indeed, now and again, give a poor fictionist a helping hand—not used, however, generally with much discretion. But from whom is any assistance to come in the august matter of a Cabinet assembly?

Trollope is making fun of the rules of the game that he plays, though he still recognizes that there are rules, but when Dickens protests against the charge of inaccuracy in his description of the Court of Chancery and Balzac cries in the first chapter of *Père Goriot* that "Everything is true," they are not making fun of the rules, and it is simply not good criticism to maintain that they mistook the rules. When Trollope tells us how he lived for years with his characters, grew to love and admire them, and parted from them with regret, it is not good criticism to say that the characters are merely his "verbal arrangements." Truthfulness with regard to facts and truthfulness with regard to characters are inherent elements in the nineteenth-century novel, and any criticism which disregards them, disregards the conventions on which it is based, and as close as makes no difference condemns itself to irrelevance.

3.

As an art form, the novel is really a development of the abortive comedy of trades and humors of Shakespeare's day. "I will have a citizen and he shall be of my own trade. I will have a grocer and he shall do admirable things." Beaumont thought his merchant funny, and history seems to have thought so too, for the movement appears to have been politically premature. Even the plays themselves have largely disappeared, and it is only in our own time that Professor Sisson has uncovered the legal documents and revealed a theater that in its outlook was very like the nineteenth-century novel, with a shrewd eye on the newspapers for the "good story" of the unhappy marriage and the unreasonable will.

At any rate, it is hard to see how the theater could ever have become the great middle-class art, for the middle classes were carriers of puritanism, and while they distrusted most arts, they detested the theater. Mr. Collins in *Pride and Prejudice* may have boasted that "he never read novels," but Jane Austen's own tone when she deals with amateur theatricals is scarcely less discouraging. The great middle-class art could only be a private one, and this fact alone makes for an enormous difference in the writer's approach. In a public art like the theater, illusion is created by the audience in a common consent to the conventions. In an art that depends exclusively on the printed page and the solitary reader, no convention can be taken for granted, and the element of illusion has to be supplied by the writer. Shipwrecked mariners who turn out to be long-lost sisters produce too many lifted eyebrows among the initiated. The fact that the intelligence of the reader has time and scope to function implies an increasing appeal to it, either in the form of a narrative which is demonstrably based upon the reader's experience or, in another way, in one which deliberately sets out to flout the element of probability. The decline of romance means the re-emergence of nonsense.

This is one main reason for the set of realistic rules which Trollope, in the passage I have quoted, writes of. His reader is trying to catch him out. This has its drawbacks, though they are not the sort of drawback that people who dislike the form of the novel generally attribute to it. The principal drawback, as I see it, is that, by appealing to the intelligence instead of to the imagination, it tends to break down the old classical division of comedy and tragedy, and that because comedy is so very much the art of the intelligence, it weights the scales in favor of the comic writer. It is not for nothing that Jane Austen is probably the greatest of English novelists, or that a real tragedy is an exceedingly rare thing in the novel form. Most novels which aim at this effect—*Wuthering Heights* is an example—are more romances than novels. A great poet or dramatist may be all the better for lacking a sense of humor, but a novelist who lacks it—as I think Lawrence and even Tolstoy do—begins under a handicap.

It was in the Lowlands rather than in England that the middle classes established themselves politically, and pictorially their attitude was fully expressed in Dutch genre painting. Except for the moral passion which is literature's main contribution to the arts, a Dutch interior might be chosen as the ideal of the nineteenth-century novelist. Dutch painting clarifies what we can already discern in the remains of the middle-class Elizabethan theater. The novel, when it came, would be primarily domestic and civic, would concentrate on the study of society and the place of the individual in it, and on the structure of the classes, professions, and trades rather than on the mythological or historical past.

And partly because of the nature of the subject, partly because of the technique imposed on the writer by the printed page and the solitary reader, the treatment would be realistic rather than romantic, prosaic rather than poetic. Some of the greatest moments of the nineteenth-century novel are little genre scenes of this sort which might have come to us from a Brueghel painting: a view of Dorchester seen from afar in the evening light; a hay-cart lurching down the street of a country town in sunlight, and painting yellow the walls of a sitting-room as it passes; a troop of lancers bobbing to battle down a tree-shadowed lane. This is what critics of the novel mean when they refer to the "domestication of literature," and what one critic means when he speaks of the novel as "a decline from the heroic and romantic."

The novel is not only limited in material, but is also limited in outlook. The middle classes had been largely responsible for the simplification of religious issues embodied in Protestantism, and the morality that motivates the nineteenth-century novel is largely that of the merchant classes, and it has suffered by it in more ways than the obvious one of having been subjected to the intensest form of censorship. The middle classes were interested in money rather than in rank; in character rather than in breeding; in honesty rather than in honor; and—except in Stendhal's work, with its angry revolt against the money mania of the time—the crises of the nineteenth-century novel tend to take place within a very narrow moral range. Sometimes the range is too narrow. A scruple about holding a clerical sinecure dating from the Middle Ages—the middle classes hated medieval sine-cures—or a misunderstanding about a check for twenty pounds is all the motivation Trollope needs for a crisis, and as far as the free discussion of sex goes, *Anna Karenina* and *Tess of the D'Urbervilles* show us the limits. Yet it is precisely this simple, clear, workmanlike ethic—as simple as a schoolboy's code of honor—that gives the nineteenth-century novel its characteristic note of deep human feeling, as satisfying to our unspoiled moral sense as is the gleam of tiles in a Dutch painting to our unspoiled æsthetic sense, and that saves it from the fate of Elizabethan tragedy as a whole, which has sunk in the bog of its own moral anarchy.

It is, in spite of its limitations, a profoundly serious art. Sometimes, as in Tolstoy's *Sebastopol*, we get the impression that never before has the subject of war been adequately dealt with; it is respectful of human life and dignity, and is the normal medium for the expression of humanitarian sentiment. One of the most fruitful approaches to the subject is through the novelists' reaction to executions and floggings, for all of them were haunted by these things, from Dickens and Turgenev to Chekhov and Hardy, and nothing so clearly reveals a man's ultimate attitude to human life. When Swift howls for Defoe's ears, we are before the period of the novel; when Lawrence angrily demands the hanging of some poor Italian criminal whose face has failed to take Lawrence's fancy, we know the period of the novel has gone by. In studying it we are studying history.

Consider *Sebastopol* itself, for instance. For the first time war was being described by young Tolstoy, not as it appeared to the excited poetic imagination, but as it appeared to the intelligence. On the English side, the first

war correspondent, W. H. Russell of *The Times*, was
doing the same thing, though with a different object and in
a different way. At the same time English lads, dying of
exposure and starvation, were being carried down to
Scutari to be nursed by a young Englishwoman, no older
than Tolstoy himself, who was trying to prove that
women nurses need not necessarily be the drunken and
ignorant sluts described by another novelist under the
general name of Sairey Gamp. When the war was over,
her biographer Miss Woodham-Smith tells us, that young
woman would stamp her room all night in an agony of
self-reproach. "Oh, my poor men," she wrote in her
journal, "I am a bad mother to come home and leave you
alone in your Crimean graves—73% in 8 regiments in
6 months from disease alone—who thinks of that now?"

Who, I wonder, thinks of anything else in connection
with Sebastopol except of a young Russian officer and a
young English nurse? A nurse who inspired much poetry
in others, but who in that Shakespearean cry of anguish
talks in percentages, as well she might, since she was the
inventor of statistical diagnosis. "A decline from the
heroic and romantic"? But is it?

In fact, I am afraid that the truth is that I am not only a
nineteenth-century realist, but also a nineteenth-century
liberal. I am not sure that either realism or liberalism is a
good thing in itself, but at least I believe that they are
aspects of the same attitude of mind. I have an idea that
conservatism and romanticism may be aspects of the same
attitude of mind. I even fancy that symbolism and naturalism in literature, fascism and communism in politics,

represent substantially similar attitudes. And being, as I am, a realist and liberal, I must maintain in my mild, muddled, liberal way that, on the whole, they seem to me bad attitudes.

It is a great mistake to abolish the death penalty. If I were dictator, I should order the old one to be hanged at once. I should have judges with sensitive, living hearts; not abstract intellects. And because the instinctive heart recognised a man as evil, I would have that man destroyed. Quickly. Because good warm life is now in danger.*

Forgive an old-fashioned liberal, and bear with him a little, but I do not like that tone. I do not like it at all. As a liberal, I hate to raise my voice, but I really must say that I think, in the words of Mr. Woodhouse in Jane Austen's novel, that "that young man is not quite the thing."

---

*D. H. Lawrence: *Sea and Sardinia*.

chapter 2

Jane Austen: The Flight from Fancy

Any timetable showing what went on in the English novel during the decade after 1810 reveals an extraordinary fact—the fact that, though Jane Austen was a strict contemporary of the most popular novelist who ever lived, Sir Walter Scott, and though, at the time it was published, her work was overshadowed by his and his imitators', the novel did not go his way; it went her way. By 1850 scarcely a trace was left of Scott and the cult of the historical novel. I am not, of course, suggesting that her influence accounted for this; on the contrary, I am convinced that it had nothing to do with it. What I do mean is that it took considerable astuteness on her part to recognize her own proper direction, and that it was not merely modesty which impelled her to decline the Prince Regent's proposal that she should write a historical novel dealing with the House of Coburg.

This is one of the things that critics fail to recognize about Jane Austen, and it makes much of the criticism that deals with her meaningless. She was a deeply literary woman, and her work from her girlish efforts up to *Sanditon* is filled with references to literature that show how widely she had read and how much she had brooded on her reading. She brooded in the way of a creative writer rather than in that of a scholar: that is, she read her own problems into the work she studied in a way that

any academic critic would properly shun, but precisely
because of this her criticism has to be understood if we
are to understand her creative work.

Her early work is as much literary criticism as fiction.
It sets out to make fun of certain types of literature of
which she disapproved, particularly fiction, and particularly those types of fiction which indulge the imagination
and sensibility. Her first important work, *Northanger
Abbey*, though revised in her maturity, still suffers as a
novel from this element of literary criticism, for we no
longer read the Gothic romances she was criticizing and
we miss the points she makes. The situation is a recurring
one in the history of the novel. The temper of the true
novelist is always reacting against romanticism in fiction,
and Jane Austen is only reacting against the Gothic romance as Cervantes did against the medieval romance,
and with similar results. The thing against which they
react disappears, and with it disappears the very reason
for the reaction. And the reason for the reaction is never
quite the simple matter it appears to be from histories of
literature. Cervantes did not parody medieval romance
merely because he disliked it. It would probably be truer
to say that he liked it far too well for his own comfort.

Catherine Morland in *Northanger Abbey* is one of a line
of Jane Austen heroines who indulge their imagination at
the expense of their judgment, and the author criticizes
her strictly in terms of what she herself knows to be
true. Now, the extent of what a young lady could know
to be true was considerably enlarged during Jane Austen's
lifetime—that is, between 1775 and 1817—even though,

from our point of view, it may still appear excessively narrow. Largely, this had been the result of a considerable improvement in transportation, which plays more part in the history of the novel than critics have yet realized. Jane Austen was well aware of this. "And what is fifty miles of good road?" asks one of her characters in *Northanger Abbey*. "Little more than half a day's journey. Yes, I call it a very easy distance."

That is more than a novelist of the early eighteenth century would have called it, but it was still strictly limited, and beyond those limits Jane Austen refused to go. To do so, she would have had to put herself into the position of the characters she criticized, would have had to make use of her imagination. So much for the critics who complain of her narrow range. This was determined by the limits of her own observation. It has been shrewdly remarked that she never describes a scene in which two men have a discussion without a woman's being present, since she did not know how men might speak under such conditions. It has not, I think, been remarked that though Edward Ferrars and Mr. Darcy are both in very unusual situations, situations of far greater interest to the novelist than those the author deals with, we never see them in those situations. We have only their own descriptions of the situations as given to Elinor and Elizabeth.

The reason for this was not primarily artistic. It was because the author's subject—her obsession, one might say—was the imagination, and she could observe this only by isolating it in the manner of a scientist. Her verisimilitude is of an entirely different kind from that of any other great novelist, for it has something about it that is reminiscent at the same time of a scientific technique and of a ritual. Truth as it is perceived by the judgment is her aim, and everything that would disturb this is eliminated. I believe I am correct in saying that, for all the feminine qualities of her women characters, none of them ever tells a lie—which is magnificent, but not realism.

We lose a lot of the fun in the opening chapters of *Northanger Abbey* through our ignorance of contemporary fiction, but the fun holds good for a great deal of fiction which had not even been written at the time—the novels of Dickens, for instance. In everyday life, the author notes, all the props of romantic fiction are missing.

There was not one lord in the neighbourhood; no, not even a baronet. There was not one family among their acquaintance who had reared and supported a boy accidentally found at their door, not one young man whose origin was unknown. Her father had no ward, and the squire of the parish no children.

But this playful analysis is not merely the reaction of a high-spirited girl to Mrs. Radcliffe. It is something more, for it serves to introduce Jane Austen's own standards, which are never entirely left out of the picture. Take, for instance, the description of Catherine's departure for Bath.

When the hour of departure drew near, the maternal anxiety of Mrs. Morland will be naturally supposed to be most severe. A thousand alarming presentiments of evil to her beloved Catherine from this terrific separation must oppress her heart with sadness, and drown her in tears for the last day or two of their being together; and advice of the most important and ap-

plicable nature must, of course, flow from her wise lips in their
parting conference in her closet.

Not a bit of it!

Everything indeed relative to this important journey was done
on the part of the Morlands with a degree of moderation and
composure which seemed rather consistent with the common
feelings of common life than with the refined susceptibilities,
the tender emotions which the first separation of a heroine from
her family ought always to excite.

"The common feelings of common life"—these are
Jane Austen's standards of what is proper to the novel, and
these can be gathered only from close observation of a
society one knows and understands—in fact, a society
bounded by "fifty miles of good road." For it is to be
noted that not only will she not make a guess at what men
say when they are together in the absence of women, or
how they behave in delicate personal situations like those
of Darcy and Ferrars, but also she will not even make a
guess at what goes on beyond those "fifty miles of good
road." Though Catherine Morland's summing-up of her
own situation at the end of the book is outrageously funny,
it is all the funnier because it is a complete reply to those
critics who would have had Jane Austen write about the
Napoleonic wars. Catherine Morland *is* Jane Austen, and
her discoveries of what may pass for truth describe the
limits that her creator imposed upon her own imagination.

Charming as were all Mrs. Radclyffe's works, and charming
even as were the works of her imitators, it was not in them perhaps that human nature, *at least in the midland counties of England*
was to be looked for. Of the Alps and the Pyrenees with their

pine forests and their vices, they might give a faithful delinea-
tion; and Italy, Switzerland and the South of France might be as
fruitful in horrors as they were there represented. Catherine
dared not doubt beyond her own country, and even of that, if
hard pressed, would have yielded the northern and western
extremities. But *in the central part of England* there was surely
some security for the existence even of a wife not beloved, in
the laws of the land and the manners of the age.

The italics are mine, and they reveal something much
more than urbane literary fun. They are Jane Austen's
Que scay-je? Men *may* be the same when there is no
woman round to observe them; human nature *may* be
much the same in the North of England as in Buckingham-
shire; but this is something the author can take only on
trust, and her compact with herself is to write of nothing
but what she has herself observed. It might almost be
described as an art of testimony, an art in which the
writer calls on God to witness that what she says is true.

2.

It was not only that Jane Austen had a fanatically
serious approach to the difficult problem of verisimilitude
in fiction; she had also what so many novelists have
lacked, a profound respect for the art she practiced. At a
time when the novel was regarded by serious people as
being no better than card-playing, she took it seriously,
and resented all criticism of it. Even through her stiff
prose one can feel the throb of a passion that is not in the
least urbane.

Although our productions have afforded more extensive and

unaffected pleasure than those of any other literary corporation in the world, no species of composition has been so much decried. From pride, ignorance or fashion, our foes are almost as many as our readers. And while the abilities of the nine-hundredth abridger of the History of England, or the man who collects and publishes in a volume some dozen lines of Milton, Pope or Prior, with a paper from the Spectator and a chapter from Sterne are eulogized by a thousand pens there seems almost a general wish of decrying the capacity and undervaluing the labour of the novelist and of slighting the performances which have only genius, wit and taste to recommend them. "I am no novel reader—I seldom look into novels—Do not imagine that I often read novels—It is really very well for a novel." Such is the common cant— "And what are you reading, Miss—?" "Oh, it is only a novel," replies the young lady while she lays down her book with affected indifference or momentary shame. "It is only Cecilia or Camilla or Belinda"; or in short, only some work in which the greatest powers of the mind are displayed, in which the most thorough knowledge of human nature, the happiest delineations of its varieties, the liveliest effusions of wit and humour are conveyed to the world in the best chosen language. Now had the same young lady been engaged with a volume of the Spectator instead of such a work, how piously would she have produced the book and told its name, though the chances must be against her being occupied by any part of the voluminous publication of which either the matter or manner would not disgust a young person of taste: the substance of its papers so often consisting in the statement of improbable circumstances, unnatural characters, and topics of conversation which no longer concern anyone living; and their language too, frequently so coarse as to give no very favourable idea of the age that could endure it.

We must not be misled by Jane Austen's urbanity or even her occasional insipidity into regarding her as anything but a young woman with a formidable critical intelligence. Nor is her attitude to romanticism anything like so simple as it is made to appear. Is it merely from literary good manners that she describes Mrs. Radcliffe's novels as "charming"? Or is it that she found them so? For, as I have said, Catherine Morland is Jane Austen, and I suspect that in real life she knew herself to be a creature of mood and fancy. For that is her one subject: the conflict between the imagination and the judgment, and she returns to it again and again in *Sense and Sensibility*, *Emma*, and even in *Pride and Prejudice* and *Sanditon*, until at last she calls a weary armistice in *Persuasion*.

Like *Northanger Abbey*, *Sense and Sensibility* is one of the works of her girlhood revised in maturity, and has the same strongly literary atmosphere. *Northanger Abbey* attacks the imagination; *Sense and Sensibility* attacks emotionalism as an aspect of the imagination. Marianne Dashwood is the romantic young lady who, through her addiction to romantic literature, particularly poetry, makes all the mistakes her sensible sister avoids. It is an English version of *Madame Bovary*, with the typical English sense of proportion and the typical English approach to the novel as something intended to give delight rather than instruction. It is not altogether satisfactory as a work of art because, however misguided Marianne may appear in her liking for natural beauty, we find it easier to sympathize with her than we do with the characters who are set up in antithesis, particularly Edward Ferrars, who says:

24

I call it a very fine country—the hills are steep, the woods seem full of fine timber, and the valley looks comfortable and snug—with rich meadows and several neat farmhouses scattered here and there. It exactly answers my idea of a fine country, because it unites beauty with utility.

Edward exactly answers my idea of a prize bore, and, indeed, this was not Jane Austen's own view of scenery, for she makes Edmund in *Mansfield Park*, her most serious book, express pity for those who have not been taught in early life to appreciate nature. It is hard to understand the book unless we assume that Elinor and Marianne represent Jane Austen drunk and Jane Austen sober; unless we understand that Marianne's passion for natural beauty and poetry were both shared by the author. Years later, when she was already dying, Jane Austen was to make one of her characters say that "It was the misfortune of poetry to be seldom safely enjoyed by those who enjoyed it completely; and that the strong feelings which alone could estimate it truly were the very feelings which ought to taste it but sparingly." If the tone of a sentence means anything, those are not the sentiments of a woman who did not enjoy poetry, but of one who loved it too well for her own peace of mind. And it is not more certain that the girl who made such fun of romantic literature was steeped in it than it is that she who made such fun of romance was chock-full of it. If I read her rightly, she was a woman afraid of the violence of her own emotions, who rode the nightmare and sometimes rode it on too tight a rein.

2 5

For it is this fear of herself that makes her the moralist she is, and that very often weakens her finest work. It weakens *Sense and Sensibility* because we cannot really sympathize with the figures in it who represent sense, and so have to fall back on poor Marianne, of whom we are asked to disapprove. And here we come to the characteristic form of Jane Austen's fallibility, for whenever she does fail, it is because she produces an effect that is the very opposite of what she sets out to do. She does so because the moralist and the artist, the judgment and the instincts, are always at war in her, and she never really distinguishes between respect, which is the goal of the moralist, and affection, which is the goal of the artist. In art, knowledge can reach us only through our emotions.

This is particularly obvious in the drawing of her heroes. When she wished to draw a hero, she tended to draw upon the masculine side of her own character, the side she respected. Her heroes too evidently represent judgment in spite of the fact that in real life they too must have had instincts and fantasies to contend with. The result is that all of them, sooner or later, turn into what modern psychologists call "father figures." Every man falls in love with Elizabeth Bennet. I have yet to meet a woman who fell in love with Mr. Darcy or Mr. Knightley.

Jane Austen's first mature book is *Pride and Prejudice*, a novel so impeccable that it is hard to say anything new of it. That household of girls is part of one's experience, like some family one was attracted to in adolescence and which in maturity still continues to haunt one with the feeling that this, at least, was real. Jane Austen's own criticism of the book is still the best.

It is rather too light, and bright and sparkling; it wants shade; it wants to be stretched out here and there with a long chapter of sense, if it could be had; if not, of solemn, specious nonsense, about something unconnected with the story; an essay on writing, a critique of Walter Scott or the history of Bonaparte, or anything that would form a contrast and bring the reader with increased delight to the playfulness and epigrammatism of the general style.

The young lady had, as I say, a formidable critical intelligence. The brilliance and lightness that she admires are obviously the result of very careful writing and rewriting. Most readers fail to notice the technical tour de force of the opening chapters, in which the material is organized in dramatic form so as to combine exposition and development. "My dear Mr. Bennet," the first scene begins, and we gather only from casual indications in the dialogue that Mr. and Mrs. Bennet have children; that a girl called Lizzy is the father's favorite; that there are at least two others—Jane, who is handsome, and Lydia, who is good-natured; then that there is a fourth called Mary, who is studious; and finally that Mrs. Bennet has five daughters in all, and all unmarried. In narrative this is an extraordinarily difficult thing to do, because the attention of the reader is never focused as it would be in the theater, but here the writing is so amusing that we never notice at all how we are being played with, and we wake up, six full chapters later, not only having acquired all the essential information without having been made aware of it, but also ready to take sides between husband and wife.

Another device used here is equally effective and equally daring. Most critics and all novelists know the troubles of the "point of view," which kept Henry James awake at night, and even masterpieces of fiction like *Wuthering Heights* remind them of the penalties to be paid if the wrong point of view is chosen and essential matters have to be seen through the eyes of a narrator who, by the nature of things, could not have been present. This classic problem is magnificently solved by Jane Austen, who merely ignores it altogether. Because Elizabeth Bennet is the heroine, most readers will tell you offhand that the story is told from her point of view, but in fact the narrative moves freely in and out of the minds of most of the characters, and merely lingers more on her than on the others. The result of this is that a whole mass of detail is kept moving under our eyes without its ever wearying us. Consider, for instance, a passage like this:

The evening altogether passed off pleasantly for the whole family. Mrs. Bennet had seen her eldest daughter much admired by the Natherfield party. Mr. Bingley had danced with her twice, and she had been distinguished by his sisters. Jane was as much gratified by this as her mother could be, though in a quieter way. Elizabeth felt Jane's pleasure. Mary had heard herself mentioned to Miss Bingley as the most accomplished girl in the neighbourhood; and Catherine and Lydia had been fortunate enough to be never without partners, which was all they had yet learned to care for at a ball.

So brilliant is the book that it conveys an impression of complete objectivity. In fact, we are never far away from

Jane Austen's central theme, the only difference being that here she handles it with detachment. Jane and Elizabeth are the same pair of girls we find in *Sense and Sensibility*, and their future husbands, Darcy and Bingley, are masculine equivalents of the antithesis between them. The real difference is that, exceptionally and providentially, Jane Austen walks out on moralizing and permits the judgment to have faults of its own, as with Darcy's pride, which causes as much tribulation as though it had been a fault of the imagination, and Elizabeth's fancifulness, which is reinforced with so much wit and charm that it seems only another form of intelligence. We are allowed to overlook Elizabeth's errors; we are never allowed to overlook Marianne Dashwood's, while as for Mary Crawford's! . . .

For if in *Pride and Prejudice* Jane Austen the moralist was given a holiday, in *Mansfield Park* she was given a field day and wreaked absolute havoc on the book. This is not, as with *Sense and Sensibility*, the relative failure of a minor masterpiece; it is the absolute failure of a major one. It could almost be described as an artistic comedy of errors, all of them the author's, for here we find in perfection that weakness of hers I have already referred to of producing precisely the opposite effect from that she sets out to produce.

What she tries to do is to make us respect Fanny Price and Edmund Bertram and dislike Henry and Mary Crawford. Edmund is in love with Mary, which is natural enough, as she is the only woman in the book whom any sensible man could be in love with. But she and her brother have a passion for amateur theatricals which ultimately leads to the seduction of Edmund's married sister and Edmund's disillusionment with Mary Crawford. This Jane Austen obviously considers a desirable result, like the reformation of the wastrel brother, Tom. "The self reproach arising from the deplorable event in Wimpole Street, to which he felt himself accessory by all the dangerous intimacy of his unjustifiable theatre, made an impression on his mind which at the age of six-and-twenty with no want of sense or good companions, was durable in its happy effects. He became what he ought to be—useful to his father, steady and quiet, and not living merely for himself." One searches vainly for a grin on the narrator's face.

The result is that we detest Fanny Price and Edmund Bertram and give our affections entirely to the Crawfords. If we continue to enjoy the book, it is only because we read it in a sense quite contrary to that in which the author wrote it. Anyone who agrees with Lord David Cecil that Jane Austen never wrote outside her artistic range should study *Mansfield Park*. With the exception of the amusing scenes in which Lady Bertram and Mrs. Norris appear, it is all written well outside her range. If one glances through the pages, the rancorous, censorious tone becomes apparent in the words with which the author tries to batter our moral sense. "Disapprove," "censure," "corrupted," "evil," "wrong," "misconduct," "sin," "crime," "guilt," "fault," "offence," "abhorrence" are only a few of the words that shriek at the reader with a sort of moral hysteria that stuns and bewilders him. And the morality itself is of a pretty low order. Fanny Price's attitude when she returns to her parents' wretched home in Portsmouth is not remarkable for decent feeling.

No doubt there is some explanation for all this, but it is hard to see what it is. As Lionel Trilling points out, it is not that Jane Austen was not familiar with amateur theatricals, for she had had them in her own home. No, theatricals here, like landscape and poetry in the earlier books, are not things the author dislikes, but things she likes far too well. It is as though at some time that gifted girl with her passion for the arts had had ducks and drakes played with her feelings by some talented hanger-on of literature and the theater. For me, the most revealing passage in the book is that in which Henry Crawford, whom Fanny dislikes, reads Shakespeare to her, dramatizing as he reads, and gradually captures her entire attention.

Whether it were dignity or pride, or tenderness or remorse, or whatever were to be expressed, he could do it with equal beauty. It was truly dramatic. His acting had first taught Fanny what pleasure a play might give, and his reading brought all his acting before her again.

Edmund watched the progress of her attention, and was amused and gratified by seeing how she gradually slackened in the needlework, which at the beginning seemed to occupy her totally; how it fell from her hand while she sat motionless over it; and at last, how the eyes which had appeared so studiously to avoid him throughout the day were turned and fixed on Crawford, fixed on him in short, till the attraction drew Crawford's upon her, and the book was closed and the charm was broken.

"It was the misfortune of poetry to be seldom safely enjoyed by those who enjoyed it completely. . . ." The repetition is too pronounced to be an accident. Jane Austen saw the arts as a means of seduction. I get the impression that in *Mansfield Park* she was attempting a different sort of novel, a realistic treatment of her obsession. Her technique is different, and in the description of Portsmouth she tried her hand at something she had never tackled before and never tackled again: local color in the manner of Scott. But if so, she entirely failed to see that her theme was not suitable for realistic treatment; that the presentation of poetry, drama, or love of natural beauty as though they were really faults of character could produce nothing but a caricature of herself.

3.

Emma, *Persuasion*, and *Sanditon* are already the work of a sick woman. The sick woman would not have been Jane Austen unless she had seized on illness, too, as an aspect of the erring imagination, and the three stories are filled with imaginary invalids airing their ailments, being enthusiastic about their doctors, and comparing the air of their favorite health resorts. That is the real reason for what is frequently described as her unusual choice of a theme in *Sanditon*.

"Mr. Wingfield most strenuously recommended it, sir, or we should not have gone. He recommended it for all the children, but particularly for the weakness in little Bella's throat—both sea air and bathing."

"Ah, my dear, but Perry had many doubts about the sea doing her any good; and, as for myself, I have been long perfectly convinced, though perhaps I never told you so before, that the sea is very rarely of use to anybody. I am sure it almost killed me once."

Emma is Jane Austen's last bold fling at the imagination. As with Catherine Morland, everything unusual sets Emma's imagination to work, and her imagination always functions inaccurately. Naturally, she tends to describe her imagination as "penetration." She befriends an illegitimate girl called Harriet Smith, who has not had the "penetration" to discover her father, and within two pages Emma has established that he was "a gentleman," and within thirty that he was "a gentleman of fortune." Mr. Knightley, her admirer, tells Emma's old governess what Emma's principal fault is, and it is much the same as with all Jane Austen's heroines. "She will never submit to anything requiring industry and patience, and a subjection of the fancy to the understanding." (It was the psychology of the period, and a similar statement was made about Stendhal by his father.) In Emma's lucid moments she even recognizes this and makes good resolutions about the duty of "repressing imagination all the rest of her life."

But her resolutions rarely last long, and, having almost ruined Harriet's life by opposing her marriage with a respectable young farmer and encouraging her to set her cap at the rector, Mr. Elton, Emma goes on to apply her "penetration" to the mysterious gift of a piano to a girl called Jane Fairfax, invents an affair between her and her employer, and rounds off her romances with one about herself and Frank Churchill, who is secretly married to Jane, before admitting her errors and marrying the man she really loves, and who has always loved her—Mr. Knightley.

Emma has nothing of the brilliance of *Pride and Prejudice*, but this difficulty was inherent in the material. The subject of *Emma* is a bad one, for it is a closed circuit; everything of importance takes place within the mind of the principal character, and this mind is a fantastic one, incapable not only of seeing events accurately, but also of judging itself and its own motives. Everything depends upon the reader's ability to perceive immediately when Emma starts to go wrong. The story has to be told with the minimum of externalization, and the technical devices by which the author manages to conceal the awkwardness of her subject make the book a delight and a flattery for the knowing type of reader.

Jane Austen seems to have been so amused by the technique she invented that she applies it to characters other than Emma. By the fourth chapter we get our first hint of Emma's real love, when she remarks to Harriet that "You might not see one in a hundred with *gentleman* so plainly written as in Mr. Knightley," and this prepares us for the great passage that occurs later when Mrs. Elton discovers that he is a gentleman. But Mr. Knightley himself is not really much more perceptive, for not only does he tell Mrs. Weston that "I have no idea that she has ever yet seen a man she cared for," but he also refers to a reading list that Emma had drawn up at the age of fourteen and adds "I remember thinking it did her judgment so much credit that I preserved it some time." This is delightful.

Neighborly interest never yet made a man preserve the reading list of a girl of fourteen!

By the time the book develops, it acquires a particular interest for readers of our own time because Jane Austen has had no choice but to discover and interpret the unconscious for herself ninety years before Freud. By prodigies of technique she explores Emma's self-deceptions, and the task proves so interesting that she applies the technique to characters like Knightley and Harriet. Here is Emma, having satisfied herself that Knightley is in love with Jane Fairfax.

Her objections to Mr. Knightley's marrying did not in the least subside. She could see nothing but evil in it. It would be a great disappointment to Mr. John Knightley, consequently to Isabel. A real injury to the children—a most mortifying change and material loss to them all—a very great deduction from her father's daily comfort—and as to herself she could not at all endure the idea of Jane Fairfax at Donwell Abbey. A Mrs. Knightley for them all to give away to! No—Mr. Knightley must never marry. Little Henry must remain the heir of Donwell.

In fact, the one notion that never crosses Emma's fanciful mind is that Mr. Knightley must not marry because she is in love with him herself. In the great passage in which Mrs. Elton calls Mr. Knightley "Knightley," we see Emma in the grip of the unconscious, entirely unaware of what she is doing and thinking, and literally, in the Freudian sense to which we have accustomed ourselves, not responsible for her actions. Because I sometimes wonder how many readers grasp the implications of Emma's outburst, I have italicized the significant sentences.

"Insufferable woman!" was her immediate exclamation. "Worse than I had supposed. Absolutely insufferable! *Knightley! I could not have believed it. Knightley—never seen him in her life before and call him Knightley and discover that he is a gentleman.* A little upstart vulgar being with her Mr. E. and her *caro sposo* and her resources, and all her airs of pert pretension and underbred finery. *Actually to discover that Mr. Knightley is a gentleman.* I doubt whether he will return the compliment and discover her to be a lady. I could not have believed it! And to propose that she and I should unite to form a musical club! One would fancy we were bosom friends! And Mrs. Weston! Astonished that the person who brought me up should be a gentlewoman. Worse and worse! I never met with her equal. Much beyond my hopes. Harriet is disgraced by any comparison. Oh, what would Frank Churchill say to her if he were here? How angry and how diverted he would be. Ah, there I am, thinking of him directly. *Always the first person to be thought of! How I catch myself out! Frank Churchill comes as regularly into my mind—!*

The effect of this extraordinary technique is to make a passage like this almost identical with similar passages in James Joyce, where the fact that the author is trying to express something that has not yet reached the conscious mind compels him to express it symbolically. The principal passions of Emma's life are set out as they present themselves to the author's mind: they are Mr. Knightley, Mrs. Weston, and the fancied attachment to Frank Churchill. The last and least important Emma exaggerates into a principal one. She may imagine that she really catches herself out, but her self-knowledge is of much the same kind as Stendhal's.

It is still more interesting when Jane Austen dramatizes those unconscious predilections. A good example occurs when the two brothers Knightley discuss the handwriting of Emma and her sister, Isabella. John thinks them much alike. "Yes," said his brother (George) hesitatingly, "there is a likeness. I know what you mean—but Emma's hand is the strongest." An even better example is the delightful scene in which Harriet abandons her hopes of Mr. Elton—or tries to.

"I do remember it," cried Emma; "I perfectly remember it. Talking about spruce beer. Oh, yes! Mr. Knightley and I both saying we liked it and Mr. Elton's seeming resolved to learn to like it too. I perfectly remember it. Stop—Mr. Knightley was standing just here, was not he? I have an idea he was standing just here."

"Ah, I do not know. I cannot recollect [said Harriet]. It is very odd but I cannot recollect. Mr. Elton was sitting here, I remember, much about where I am now."

It is almost as hard to criticize *Persuasion* as it is to criticize the two great fragments of *Sanditon* and *The Watsons*, for, whatever we may feel about them, they are unfinished work and there is no knowing what an implacable and resourceful artist like Jane Austin would have done with them before they were published.

Apart from its own great virtues, *Sanditon* is remarkable for the light it throws on Jane Austen's aversion from poetry. I have said that she saw the arts as a means of seduction. Sir Edward is the prize literary seducer, who relies upon poetry to affect what he cannot himself affect by charm. Charlotte is a girl who approaches it with proper circumspection. Her words should be noted. "I have read several of Burns' Poems with great delight, but I am not poetic enough to separate a man's poetry entirely from his character; and poor Burns' known irregularities greatly interrupt my enjoyment of his lines. I have difficulty in depending upon the truth of his feelings as a lover. I have no faith in the sincerity of the affections of a man of his description." Once more, I can only say that these are not the sentiments of a woman who did not enjoy poetry. I might even say they are not the sentiments of a woman who did not enjoy "irregularities."

The style of *Persuasion* is patchy, and indulges to the full the author's greatest stylistic weakness, a passion for the habitual tenses that were all the rage in Regency times. It is full of the melancholy of a sick woman seeking for health at watering-places and brooding on the full life that might have been hers if only she had taken a different course in youth. All the repressed passions, for romance and poetry and natural beauty, emerge with a sort of Keatsian regret for what might have been.

Its form, too, makes for a certain languor and monotony because once again that astonishing woman invents an entirely new technique, and this time it is closer to Virginia Woolf than to Joyce. The whole story is composed as a sort of Air and Variations, and consists of a series of eerie echoes of a central situation. It even has a Jamesian symbol, for the sea is a symbol of the full life that Anne Eliot rejected out of prudence—"an unnatural beginning," as the author grimly adds. We recognize it in that most moving scene when her absurd father, Sir Walter Eliot, asks his lawyer: "Who is Admiral Croft?" and the reply comes unexpectedly from his daughter: "He is rear-admiral of the White." A single sentence gives us the effect of years of brooding. Everyone she meets and everything that happens to her merely bring back the thought of her own folly, whether it is the parody of the situation in her father's views of sailors' complexions or Mrs. Croft's reminiscences of life aboard ship. Almost everything in this strange, lonely, beautiful book is overheard, as when Anne hears Louisa Musgrove say of Mrs. Croft: "If I loved a man as she loves the Admiral, I would be always with him, nothing should ever separate us, and I would rather be overturned with him than driven safely by anyone else" or Captain Wentworth say: "Woe betide him and her too when it comes to things of consequence, when they are placed in circumstances requiring fortitude and strength of mind, if she have not resolution enough to resist idle interference in such a trifle as this." Everything is remote, allusive, symbolic. Even the presence of Wentworth's friends evokes in Anne only the thought that they might have been hers. Captain Benwick's loss of his young wife merely makes her think that he can still get another companion, while she is doomed to live with her regrets. No drama is ever allowed to interrupt the long soliloquy of the intimate voices, and even the crisis, in which Anne and Captain Harville argue about fidelity in men and women, is only overheard by Wentworth, and the only intimation Anne has that he has been affected by it is the sound of his pen falling to the floor.

One flash only reveals the old Jane Austen. Captain Benwick, the widower, is devoted to poetry, which she felt must infallibly be the sign of a weak character, and we do not need to be told that anyone capable of being consoled by such silly stuff will not be long without a silly woman to complete his comfort.

Apart from this, the crisis of the book is never really resolved. Its emotional effect comes from the overflowing of the instinctual side of the author's character, from the realization that this time it was not fancy, but judgment, that had put Anne Eliot's life astray. "She had been forced into prudence in her youth, she learned romance as she grew older—the natural sequel of an unnatural beginning." But when she comes to the last pages, all Jane Austen can do is return to her original position.

"I was right in submitting to her [says Anne, referring to her mentor, Lady Russell], and . . . if I had done otherwise, I should have suffered more in continuing the engagement than I did even in giving it up, because I should have suffered in my conscience. I have now, as far as such a sentiment is allowable in human nature, nothing to reproach myself with; and if I mistake not, a strong sense of duty is no bad part of a woman's portion."

After the passion of regret in the story, one can but wonder with how much conviction Jane Austen wrote the last words. They are so different in tone from everything that has preceded them. Certainly there was something unnatural in her own beginning; and if *Persuasion* has always been a favorite with her admirers, it may well be less for the sake of its literary merits than for the feeling that it was a natural sequel to the restraints she had imposed on herself in youth, the revenge of her imagination on her judgment.

chapter 3

Stendhal: The Flight from Reality

In the sense that Stendhal's novels are contemporary
with those of Dickens and Balzac, they should perhaps be
considered with these. In the sense that his work has
nothing whatever in common with Dickens's and Balzac's,
and in spirit and style is so close to Jane Austen's, he is
best considered with her. The literary peers of Stendhal
and Jane Austen were Turgenev and Tolstoy, and the
Russian writers are because of their background what
Stendhal and Jane Austen were in fact: children of the
eighteenth century. They were alike in their ideas of style
and in their utter integrity. Integrity is not a word one
thinks of in connection with Dickens or Balzac.

Otherwise, it would be hard to think of two writers
more different. Stendhal had been everywhere and
experienced everything, while Jane Austen remained
chained to her fifty miles of good road and her innocence
of the great world. She dreaded the imagination as the
source of all evil, while Stendhal remained wedded to his
and, whenever he escaped for a little while from it, wondered what had gone wrong with him. "My physical well-
being with Angeline has robbed me of a lot of my imagination," he confesses regretfully. In life he was everything
she most disapproved of: he was Marianne Dashwood,
Catherine Morland, the two Crawfords, and Emma all

4 2

rolled into one. Mr. Knightley's complaint of Emma, that she would "never submit to anything requiring industry and patience and a subjection of the fancy to the understanding," was exactly his father's complaint of Stendhal, of whom he said that "if ever he learned to subordinate his fancy to his reason he would become a most successful man." Of himself in youth Stendhal could only write regretfully that "my judgment was absolutely the sport of my emotions."

And yet, while the game of imaginary matches yields no fit mate for Jane Austen among the Dickenses and Balzacs, it is pleasant and rewarding to think of a match between herself and Stendhal. It would probably have been violent and brief, and might even have ended in the criminal courts with a charge of homicide against one or the other, but its offspring would have been highly interesting. As the poet-hero of an Irish romance says to his poet-mistress, "A child of us two should be famous."

It is characteristic that we should know little or nothing of her, and that we cannot even begin to understand him except through his journals and autobiographies, as numerous and frank as Boswell's. She is nothing if not a novelist, but he came late to the form as that which most closely approximated to what he wished to do. At the same time, what he wished to do is only very doubtfully the business of the novelist, since he looked on the novel merely as an extension of his journals and autobiographies, a new means of exploring his own ill-balanced character. "In order to mend my ways I had been counselled to know

myself," he says. In literature he comes closest to
Montaigne, though he has a lot in common with Boswell,
Rousseau, and Pepys.

He was born in 1783, the son of Chérubin Beyle, to be
known henceforth as "The Bastard," and Henriette
Gagnan. His mother died when he was seven, and because
he loved her very dearly he credited her with a possible
Italian ancestry. He fell into the hands of his Aunt
Séraphie, whom he loathed, but received affection from
his grand-aunt Elisabeth, to whom he accordingly attributed Spanish blood—one of "the vile self-deceptions of
noble Spanish ancestry into which I fell during the first
thirty years of my life," as he puts it. There was nothing
in the least vile about it. It is part of the fantasy of illegitimacy known to every misunderstood child in the world
(does this mean every child?). What is interesting about
the fantasy is that it goes on so long and, above all, that it
is associated with Italy and Spain. Nobody who has
written about Stendhal seems to have realized that his
rancor against France is due to the fact that he associates
it with the paternal side of his character. The later flight
to Italy was something more than a quest for love and art.
It was also the resolution of a boyish conflict in which
Italy represented his mother.

Many of his later difficulties can be traced to his
mother's death, for it threw the responsibility of his
upbringing on people whom he hated. He indulged himself in fantasies of illegitimacy and in adolescent self-
abuse, neither of which would have done him much harm
but for the extraordinary sensitiveness of his character.

For a nature like his, the consequence of an overindulgence in fantasy is an acute and almost feminine sensibility, and when in 1799 he came to Paris with the intention of becoming a playwright, we may be sure it was "with the air of a nun" and "too scared even to use a pocket handkerchief." He bought himself a pair of pistols, and these become almost a symbol in his life. Even in later life when he had nerved himself to go with prostitutes, he scared the wits out of a gentle little English girl by putting the pistols beside her bed. He was always prepared to sell his life dearly to any group of assassins which might try to take it, and went through life wondering at the pacific, almost cowlike nature of the vast majority of his fellow creatures. It was the same with love, for though his imagination drew maddening pictures of its delights, it also drew terrifying ones of its terrors and humiliations, and this, for the most part, reduced him to a state of stuttering imbecility. "I was always like a restive horse," he wrote, "who does not see things as they are, but shies off constantly at imagined obstacles or perils. The good side of it was that my courage usually rose to the test and I proudly faced the greatest dangers." This was very far from being "the good side of it." When his will triumphed over his imagination, there was, of course, nothing in nature to correspond with the ordeals he had endured, and afterward there came an overwhelming sense of anti-climax and boredom till the imagination got to work again. For, as he noted with his usual clarity, "people with this temperament live in terror of being bored." "And is Paris nothing but that?" he asked himself, the same question he was to ask himself after every great event of his life, the question he was to make his heroes and heroines ask.

In 1800 he set off with the Army of Italy, wore a sword that was too big for him and that he did not know how to use, got run away with by his first horse, and found himself under fire. He also, aged seventeen, contracted the syphilis that plagued him for the rest of his life and ultimately killed him. It was hard luck on a dreamy, ugly, romantic boy. In Italy he also fell in love with Angela Pietragrua, the first of his three great loves, though it was not till 1811 that she became his mistress. Love was the great business of his life, but he continued to be hampered by his excitable temperament. "One step further and I would have blown out my brains rather than tell a woman who perhaps loved me that I loved her. And yet I am twenty-eight and have travelled the world and have some character." But even when the women were accommodating, his imagination continued to play the deuce with his happiness. As became a man of honor with the noblest blood of Spain in his veins, he handled his love affairs as though they were military campaigns, but, the resemblance between love and war being exceedingly remote, he only brought misery on himself and the women he loved.

Your love [wrote one of his mistresses] is the most terrible misfortune that can happen to a woman; if she has happiness, you take it from her; if she has health, you make her lose it: the more she loves you, the harsher and more brutal you are to her; when she says 'I adore you,' you put to work the system that will refine her misery as far as she can bear, or more.

The letter has the ring of absolute truth; and, indeed, it could not have been otherwise, for, with Boswell, Stendhal is the most self-conscious of all writers, endlessly watching the effect he is creating, always acting and never being himself, and almost as incapable as Boswell of the patient exploration of a situation or a character. He is never without that infernal brace of pistols in his hands, heroically rushing out at two o'clock in the morning to search the living-room for the Black Hand Gang, congratulating himself upon his courage in doing so, and then, as he declines into boredom, denouncing the century for its lack of enterprise. His prose, too, is like that: electric with nerves and exploding constantly in little unexpected spasms of sensibility and mockery. Even his diaries are full of mystifications—bastard English and Italian, false names and misleading clues that may or may not have been intended to deceive the spies who would or would not read them the moment his back was turned. On this subject his editors are endlessly gullible, and if Stendhal ever did fall under suspicion, it can only be because he would keep on donning disguises and inventing codes. Spy mania was only part of his general self-consciousness. He is never for a moment free of the idea that someone may be looking over his shoulder, and he bursts into appeals to any honest man who may happen to find his diaries, not to read them. Hence, too, his frequent appeals from his own generation to the generation of 1880, 1900, or 1935. To Stendhal, history itself was a spy.

There has been a tendency on the basis of his originality,

which is as great as Boswell's, to elevate him into a novelist of unique gifts, but Stendhal's gifts as a novelist are more limited than his worshippers realize. He remained to the day of his death the prisoner of his imagination, an obstreperous, unsubduable prisoner whose struggles are far more entertaining than the behavior of most of those at liberty, but a prisoner all the same, without the intellectual detachment of the really great novelist.

In 1802 he returned to Paris, and from 1803 to 1809 was an administrative officer in Brunswick. He served in the Russian campaign and took part in the retreat from Moscow. After the fall of Napoleon he returned to Italy and began the career of a literary man. He published in 1830 the first of his two great novels, *The Red and the Black*, and in 1839 *The Charterhouse of Parma*, which, but for Balzac's unsolicited and noble praise, went almost unnoticed. He died in 1842, leaving a mass of unpublished manscripts, including a very interesting unfinished novel, *Lucien Leuwen*, and the sketch for another.

Contemporary memoir-writers describe him in his later years, and we see that the gross clumsiness of the imaginative boy had mellowed into a blasting irony that put pious people to rout. His friends loved him, and to those who appreciate his work, he remains the most lovable of authors; one of those who, in Goethe's words, "forever seek a death of flame"; a man, like Yeats's beloved:

> *Whose soul could not endure*
> *The common good of life.*

2.

In 1828 Stendhal read a newspaper account of a murder committed by an ecclesiastical student named Berthet from Stendhal's native town, Grenoble. Berthet had seduced the wife of his employer while acting as tutor in the house; he had then seduced the daughter of a second employer and got himself expelled from the seminary, and, finally, blaming the wife of his first employer for his downfall, had shot her in church.

Excited, as any novelist would be by the fact that the events had taken place in his own town, Stendhal read the story in a typically romantic way, identifying himself with the ecclesiastical student. By this time Napoleon, of whom he had earlier been very critical, was beginning to play in his work the same part Parnell plays in Joyce's. The magnificence of the Imperial regime was beginning to display itself by contrast with the seedy, greedy inertia of reaction that followed it. France after Napoleon was like Ireland after the Revolution, and Stendhal felt that his youthful energy, which had driven him to Italy, Germany, and Russia, would now have had to make its way through the Church—the Red giving place to the Black. It was quite clear. Berthet was what Henri Beyle would have been had he grown up in the Grenoble of his day; he too would have had to subdue his imagination, sensibility, and pride, be meek and hypocritical and conceal his adoration of the Emperor; he too might have ended his days on the guillotine.

It says a lot for Stendhal's imagination that he was able

to identify himself with a character like Berthet, and before the novel was finished he found himself in grave difficulties because of it. The fact, of course, is that Stendhal was not interested in Berthet; he was interested only in Stendhal, and the actual events that he followed closely in the construction of his novel were entirely beyond the capacity of his own character. Otherwise, it represents what might be described as the perfect fusion of subject and object in the novel. The object itself had been treated by others, most notably by Balzac in *The Vicar of Tours* and elsewhere, but Balzac—it is part of his peculiar genius—transects it from a position not far removed from that which he is describing. Stendhal, with his romantic notions of eighteenth-century "honor," hits it at right angles like a truck involved in a collision with an express train.

Stendhal never understood the merchant code of the later novelists. He never realized that the sexual attitudes of the nineteenth century, though they had much puritanism in them, were also a revolt against the whole feudal conception of honor and an attempt at applying to human relations the mercantile ideal of honesty. He would have been quite incapable, for instance, of seeing why Caesar Birotteau in Balzac's novel, as well as regarding bankruptcy as an intolerable stain, is also faithful to his wife; but the European middle classes found it hard to distinguish between deceiving a tradesman and deceiving a wife or husband. Nor in his contempt for the money mania which swept Europe after the industrial revolution did he ever realize that "honor" was as securely based on landed property as "honesty" was on money; that war was the nobleman's trade as trade was the merchant's war.

This was something of a danger to him as a novelist because his position is so far removed from what he describes that his work sometimes tends to degenerate into satire, more reminiscent of Anatole France or Norman Douglas than of a great novelist. But this is true only when he is describing the *general* thing, as for instance the Besançon chapters of *The Red and the Black* and the Nancy chapters of *Lucien Leuwen;* never that I know of when he is describing the particular reactions of Julien and Lucien, since these are so largely himself and he was too unusual a character to be typical of anything.

Like Stendhal, Julien Sorel, the woodcutter's son, is "timid, proud, and misunderstood." Unlike the author, but very like the author's pet idea of himself, Julien has for father a brutal and avaricious man, and the suggestion is frequently made that Julien is a bastard of noble family. Stendhal never seems to have shaken off the fantasy of illegitimacy.

It might be said that Julien suffers from an inferiority complex that drives him on to actions of the most unexpected and exaggerated kind. When he first comes to the house and sees Mme de Renal, "the bold idea at once occurred to him of kissing her hand. Next this idea frightened him; a moment later he said to himself 'It would be cowardly on my part not to carry out an action that may be of use to me and diminish the scorn that this fine lady probably feels for a poor workman, only just taken from the sawbench.' " But if so, we must also admit that the inferiority complex has been very loosely described. Julien's, like Stendhal's, reads more like the despairing attempt of an almost entirely subjective nature to make contact with external reality. "The hand"—this is later in the first part—"was hurriedly withdrawn; but Julien decided that it was his *duty* to secure that the hand should not be withdrawn when he touched it. The idea of a duty to be performed, and of making himself ridiculous, or rather being left with a sense of inferiority if he did not succeed in performing it, at once took all the pleasure from his heart." He drives himself to his task only by the thought of those pistols upstairs—though we have not been told that Julien has pistols or knows how to use them. "At the precise moment when ten o'clock strikes, I shall carry out the intention which, all day long, I have been promising myself that I would fulfil this evening, or I shall go up to my room and blow my brains out."

This is an inadequate substitute for real contact because the effort it requires diverts the impulse from the real object, which is no longer the enjoyment of an external good, but the cessation of an internal conflict. "His heart was flooded with joy, not because he loved Mme de Renal but because a fearful torment was now at an end." As a result, Julien sometimes attains his goal only by accident; as, for instance, when he plans to seduce Mme de Renal in a way that would certainly have resulted in failure and scandal but for the fact that at the moment of crisis his overcharged sensibility breaks down and he bursts into tears at her feet. Further, the relief occasioned by the cessation of the ordeal leaves no room in him for the ordinary human reactions. He feels it merely as anti-climax.

"Heavens! Is to be happy, to be loved, no more than that?" Such was Julien's first thought on returning to his own room. He was in that state of astonishment and uneasy misgivings into which the heart falls when it has just obtained what it has long desired. It has grown used to desiring, finds nothing left to desire, and has not yet acquired any memories.

Julien is condemned by his own nature never to experience any real happiness. It is in the past (his heart "had not yet acquired any memories"), in the future, in some extension of his ambition, or else someone else enjoys it. "Happiness is where I am not," as Stendhal wrote of himself.

One could explain it by saying that Julien, like him, was a complete romantic, but *The Red and the Black* is anything but a romantic book. It is too full of bewilderment and pain. One winces for Julien's clumsiness and scowls at his heartlessness. It is, as no romantic novel was, an exploration of reality by means of the romantic temperament, and it tries to explain the failure to make contact with reality, either by reason of Stendhal's temperamental incapacity or by reason of the century in which he lived, which had no use for his like. Perhaps the truest thing we can say of the author is that in the conflict between instinct and judgment which he endured, his judgment constantly tended to take the form of irony, as in that last passage when Julien asks: "Is to be happy, to be loved, no more than that?"

He had made a bad error in identifying himself so

closely with his original, and this great novel begins to collapse precisely where the identification has to be made complete. A romantic like Julien or Stendhal could no more have attempted to murder a mistress in church than he could have flown. Berthet's behavior was not that of a romantic hero, but that of a man with a sense of grievance operating on a limited intelligence. "There's a big difference between a gallus story and a dirty deed." At a stretch, Julien or his creator might have killed a mistress if he had found her deceiving him with someone else, but on the one occasion when it happened to Stendhal he did nothing of the sort. With those two pistols always on the bedside table, either of them might easily have committed suicide. But not the sneaky sort of murder here described. Significantly, Stendhal rattles through it at the rate of a mile a minute.

The unfinished *Lucien Leuwen* is a significant stage in Stendhal's development. Lucien is Julien all over again with a large independent income. Unlike Julien, he has a worldly-wise and cynical father who is not an independent character, but Stendhal himself twenty years older, almost (not quite) Count Mosca of *The Charterhouse of Parma*, the accumulated disillusionment of a lifetime. In Stendhal's novels after *The Red and the Black*, the growth of irony is remarkable, and it tends to rob the books of their emotional impact. Also, we notice that the characters are richer, freer. Though Lucien is separated from his beloved Bathilde by an ultra-Royalist intrigue that beats anything in medieval farce for improbability, Stendhal definitely intended to reunite his lovers and carry them off to Italy with himself. At the same time he realized that his own flight to Italy was also a flight from his material. "Perhaps it is harmful to my talent to live far from my disgusting models," he wrote.

Emotionally, it was a refusal to integrate himself fully. "Sensibility applied to the blackguards who surround me, beginning with the Bastard, is the one and only cause of my griefs. Being in the midst of people unknown to me, this superfluous, inconvenient sensibility will not have to be exercised." But, however we regard it, it was only a step from Lucien with his millions and his prepared escape route to the perfect escape—into history.

The Red and the Black is a great novel that has continued to grow on me from the days when I found it almost too painful to read. I cannot say the same for *The Charterhouse of Parma*, though, like Dostoevsky's novels, it was one of my delights in youth and may again become so. The source of the trouble is the source of the novel itself, which is not something that Stendhal found in a daily paper and into which he felt he could read his own life-story, but one of those Italian chronicles of the Renaissance which he worked over without realizing that other romantics had been at them already, and that they were more historical romance than history. His hero for *The Charterhouse of Parma* was Alessandro Farnese, the nephew of Vanozze Farnese, who had been the mistress of Cardinal Roderigo Lenzuoli. Farnese had abducted a woman and killed her servant, so he was confined to the Castle Sant' Angelo, where the Cardinal succeeded in smuggling into him the three-hundred-foot rope by which he made his escape.

Stendhal's biographer Matthew Josephson points out that "Stendhal reverses the procedure of Walter Scott; instead of writing of modern people dressed in antique costumes, he writes of sixteenth century characters and events as if they appeared in his own time." Perhaps it would be more true to say that he wrote of modern people behaving in a sixteenth-century way in a seventeenth-century court surviving into the nineteenth century. The important thing to remember is that the court is made to order—Stendhal's order.

The truth is that he felt he had discovered in the Italian chronicles that had inspired Webster, Tourneur, and Marlowe a real world where his imagination could dwell. He was happy in this imaginative world in which the Black Hand Gang could be endlessly discovered behind the curtains, as he was in the everyday life of Italy, without realizing by what tangled strands he had managed to link it to his childish loss. The identification was too close, and Stendhal was too happy. For whereas in *The Red and the Black* he had collided with contemporary reality with every ounce of his energy, in *The Charterhouse of Parma* he does with historical material what Balzac did with contemporary material: comes at it from an angle so close that we are scarcely aware of an impact. The external reality as described is identical with the imaginative conception of the characters. Fabrizio, though he carries on the fantasy of illegitimacy, has nothing like the intensity of Julien Sorel. While there is something agonizing for the reader in Julien's attempts at imposing his imagination on a life that he does not consider life,

Fabrizio's difficulties are solved for him before the book begins. In this atmosphere heavy with irony there is no particular importance about anything he could do. So he has mistresses, becomes a Monsignore, is imprisoned in the tower, falls in love with Clelia, is rescued, and returns, and so powerful is the author's will that he tears through the cobwebs of fiction which are thrown about him. Everything is too easy; there is no harsh reality that stops anyone dead. Imaginative freedom, the quality for which the dramatist has to struggle, is only a burden to the novelist. His characters are best determined and delimited; his prisons are best bolted and barred.

part II

The Distorting Mirror

chapter 4

The Second Phase

To turn from the world of Jane Austen and Stendhal to that of Dickens, Balzac, and Gogol is a critical nightmare, for it is almost as though the two had nothing in common, intellectually or even technically. We pass from the world of the inspired amateur to that of the professional; from a limited public to a vast and ill-educated one; from ideals of personal conduct to great public issues; and from the passionate quest for objective truth to a sort of mass hallucination.

Even technically, the novel becomes a new thing. Jane Austen and Stendhal added little to the technique of the eighteenth-century novel—little at least, that the popular novelists could make use of—and before it became a great popular art the instrument had to be enlarged and, like the clavichord, given a volume that these two writers had never demanded of it. It had now to find the equivalent for the poetry of Elizabethan tragedy, and this equivalent was local color. In an art so private, so realistic, the characters could not be permitted to speak in the inflated language of verse, so the inflation was added by making them part of their background, as though they were the voices of the great cities in which they lived, like Dickens's, or of nature itself, like Hardy's. Jane Austen, always fascinated by techniques, had tried out the new medium in the description of Fanny Price's Portsmouth home in *Mans-*

field Park and then dropped it, apparently deciding it was no use to her. Stendhal was altogether contemptuous of it. "I have forgotten to describe this sitting room," he says in *Souvenirs d'Égotisme*. "Sir Walter Scott and his imitators would have begun with this; but I myself abhor material descriptions. The boredom of doing them prevents me from writing novels."

The medium, as Stendhal here recognizes, was, to all intents and purposes, the invention of Scott. It is a child of the romantic revival, but, ironically enough, it is also a a child of the Enlightenment, and its aims were basically scientific. It stems originally from the vast interest in folklore that developed in the late eighteenth century. Renaissance classicism was everywhere breaking down. Outside Roman Europe were great tracts of territory inhabited by races who had had little to do with the Empire or the Empire's successors, and people wanted to know how they lived. Not only did the folklorists of the Enlightenment study the manners and customs of the Scots, Welsh, and Irish; they also invented customs for them, and the Welsh, an obliging race, invented a few for themselves. No one wanted to know what Jane Austen's lawyers and gentry were like—obviously they were like everybody else—but Scott's Highlanders were peculiar people who disliked trousers, and to be convincing, they had to be described. Eventually the historical novel turned into a standard method of acquiring information about races remote in time and space.

Scott's imitators began by assuming that in order to use local color you had to have such material, and Balzac and

Gogol duly documented the Bretons and the Ukrainian Cossacks before realizing that one could also use local color in describing contemporary characters and events. Balzac elevated this into a literary theory because he saw that its use could be extended so as to give living characters and events the dignity of history. One could trace the whole development of the nineteenth-century novel in terms of this device. Here, for instance, are four passages: the first by Jane Austen, the second by Stendhal, the third by Balzac, and the fourth by Dickens.

(*1*) As a house Barton Cottage though small was comfortable and compact, but as a cottage it was defective, for the building was regular, the roof was tiled, the window shutters were not painted green nor were the walls covered with honeysuckle.

That is all we ever get to know about the home of Elinor and Marianne Dashwood, and, indeed, Jane Austen was not greatly interested in it except in so far as it permitted her an extra fling at the romantic attitude to architecture as expressed in the *cottages ornées* of the time.

(*2*) A few hundred yards from the picturesque ruins of the old Gothic church M. de Renal owned an old castle with its four towers, and a garden laid out like that of the Tuileries, with a number of box borders and chestnut alleys trimmed twice in the year. An adjoining field, planted with apple trees, allowed the family to take the air. Nine or ten splendid walnuts grew at the end of the orchard; their massive foliage rose to a height of some eighty feet.

The word "picturesque" in reference to Gothic ruins shows that Stendhal has read his Scott, but we can see for ourselves that he does not greatly care for Scott's elaboration of detail, for any real-estate agent worth his salt could give us a clearer impression of the property. But the real-estate agent would have to work very hard to produce anything like this:

(3)   It would be difficult to pass before those dwellings without admiring the enormous joists, with their fantastically carved ends, which, forming a bas-relief, ornament the ground floors of the greater number of them. Here, on the one hand, transverse beams of wood covered with slates trace their blue lines along the frail walls of a house, terminated by a pointed gable, which has yielded to the decay of time, and its shingled roof, completely rotted, has been displaced by the mingled action of rain and sun. There, on the other hand, may be observed the sills of the warped and blackened windows, with their delicate carvings barely distinguishable, and which seem too slight to support the brown earthen pot, gay with the carnations or the rose tree of the poor sempstress girl living there; further on, doors studded with enormous nails, whereon the genius of our ancestors traced certain domestic hieroglyphics, the meaning of which has long since been lost; at one time a Protestant has signed his faith in that way, at another a leaguer has similarly recorded his hate of Henri IV; again a burgess has registered there the badge of his civic dignities, the glory of his departed echevinage. The history of France may be read there in every mark.

In a passage like this, Balzac has taken Scott's local color out of the pages of a historical novel to provide a background for a contemporary miser, and not only does it do this, but it also serves to place the miser in the long history of the French town and to give him something of its significance. That is Balzac's way, and it is sometimes a monotonous way, for, though it is intellectually fascinating, it is emotionally impoverished and tends to present the various objects and details to us rather in the manner of an auctioneer's catalogue. Balzac's local color rarely fails in interest; it frequently fails in beauty because he has not managed to assimilate it to the art of writing. Dickens, on the other hand, with his keen senses and his poetic power of imagery, does really give us local color so that we can at the same time see the object, the lighting, and the general background, as well as hear the noises and even (occasionally) smell the odors. Instead of going through the exhibits with our numbered catalogues, we follow our brilliant showman, who indicates something here, something here, rather like a cinema cutter who juxtaposes a few disparate images or sounds to create a general effect. Dickens always manages to get movement into his local color, and—except for Hardy, the greatest master of the medium—no one ever used it so powerfully.

(4) Presently we lost the light, presently we saw it, presently lost it, presently saw it, and turned into an avenue of trees and cantered up to where it was beaming brightly. It was in a window of what seemed to be an old-fashioned house, with three peaks in the roof in front and a circular sweep leading to the porch. A bell was rung as we drew up, and amidst the sound of its deep voice on the still air, and the distant barking of some dogs, and a gush of light from the opened door, and the smoking and steaming of the heated horses, and the quickened beating of our own hearts, we alighted in no inconsiderable confusion.

Here at last we can see local color absorbed into the narrative art of the novelist, and this is the device that enabled him to give his stories the quality of a Dutch interior, the device by which we can nowadays capture the quality of some book whose very name eludes us by some evocation of place like that produced in Proust at the taste of a pastry dipped in tea, of a troop of lancers bobbing down the light and shadow of a country lane, or the smell of crushed grass in the refreshment tent of a country fair. For it gives the novel a sensual impact, a physical body lacking in the work of Jane Austen and Stendhal. We see, too, that the early nineteenth-century novelists were experimentalists as impassioned as Joyce or Faulkner—and sometimes just as wrong-headed.

"Eve, dearest [says one of the characters in Balzac's *Lost Illusions*, making an impassioned declaration of love], this is the first moment of pure and unmixed joy that Fate has given me. . . . Since the downfall of the Empire, calico has come more and more into use because it is so much cheaper than linen. At the present moment paper is made of a mixture of hemp and linen rags, but the raw material is dear, and the expense naturally retards the great advance that the French press is bound to make. Now, you cannot increase the output of linen rags; a given population gives a pretty constant result, and it only increases with the birth-rate. To make any perceptible difference in the population for this purpose, it would take a quarter of a century and a great revolution in habits of life, trade, and agriculture. And if the supply of linen rags is not enough to meet one half or one third of the demand, some cheaper material than linen rags must be found for cheap paper. . . . The Angouleme paper-makers, the last to use pure linen rags, say that the proportion of cotton in the pulp has increased to a frightful extent of late years. . . ."

Lord, what would they say should their Catullus talk this way! Even a tough-skinned old realist like myself is

bound to admit that there is an occasional decline from
the heroic and romantic.

2.

There is a second way in which the period identifies itself. That is by the admission of a whole mass of romantic
material which Jane Austen and Stendhal deliberately excluded, and which writers of the succeeding period like
Turgenev and Trollope again excluded. It may have been
admitted for different reasons—by Dickens because his
histrionic temperament delighted in it, by Gogol because
he could use it to portray and castigate certain aspects of
his own character, by Balzac because he attributed a certain esoteric importance to it. But, whatever the reason,
late eighteenth-century romanticism, the Gothick castle,
the hermitage, and the ruined abbey all find their way into
the work of those writers, though the realistic background
marvelously disguises the characters, turning them into
lawyers, bankers, or officials. It is these monsters who run
homes and schools for orphaned children; search their
clients' backgrounds for indiscretions that will bring them
to ruin and death; instruct governments; and provoke
wars.

Bound by one and the same interest, we—that dozen men—
meet together one day in every week at the Café Themis near
the Pont-Neuf. There we reveal the mysteries of finance. No
apparent wealth can mislead us; we possess the secrets of all
families. We keep a species of *black book* in which are recorded
most important notes on the public credit, on the Bank, on com-

merce. Casuists of the Exchange, we form an Inquisition where the most indifferent actions of men of any fortune are judged and analyzed, and our judgment is always true. One of us watches over the judiciary body; another the financial body; a third the administrative body; a fourth the commercial body.

The café, the Pont-Neuf, the Exchange are all in the world of Jane Austen and Stendhal; the "casuists," the "Inquisition" are in the world of Mrs. Radcliffe. This is not romance; neither is it realism; it is not romance weighted with realistic detail; it is the realistic novel of the first period using romance as a source of energy. Sometimes the realistic engine breaks down, and then we are aware only of the glowing furnaces of fantasy which drive it.

After the monsters, the freaks. It is the same thing that explains the discomfort we sometimes feel in reading writers of the period that I call the Age of Caricature. Once more we have to distinguish, for all these writers have different reasons for caricaturing, and in Thackeray we find the phenomenon of a caricaturist who is not in any sense driven by romanticism. But what they all have in common is a certain delight in extravagance, in the inflation of everyday reality that sometimes gives us the feeling that it was a period in which there was no such thing as a man or woman of normal dimensions and attributes.

Yet at the same time we are compelled to realize that in many ways these writers give us the true feeling of the period as Jane Austen, for instance, never gives us the feeling of the Regency period. Gobseck and Squeers, for instance, may be no more than figures out of Gothick romances dressed up to take their place in a realistic novel, but they do convey as nothing else could the feeling of what the money mania was like in its heyday, or of what went on in the peculiar institutions of Early Victorian England. Comparing these writers with writers like Jane Austen, we see that they represent another pole of the novel; its realism torn between the scrupulous fidelity of Jane Austen's world, so limited physically, and the charlatanism of Dickens's world, which extends to the last limits of the new coach roads and throws all England open to us: industrial cities, cathedral towns, market towns, villages, old inns, and new roads. Above all, the new roads, which had at last set a whole populace free to travel as it had not done since the days of the Roman Empire. Here it is Gogol who should have the last word.

The highway! And how wonderful that road is in itself. A clear day, autumn leaves, a cool air . . . wrapped more tightly in our travelling coat, with the hat pulled over our ears, we shall huddle more closely and comfortably in a corner! For the last time a chill shudder runs through our limbs and in its place a pleasant warmth steals over us. The horses gallop on. . . . When we wake, five stages have already been left behind and the moon is shining brightly; here is a strange town, churches with ancient wooden cupolas and darkly outlined gables, houses of dark timber and white stone. Here and there the moonbeams look like white linen handkerchiefs hung on walls; on the roadway and in the streets shadows black as coal fall across them slantingly; wooden roofs gleam in the moonlight like glittering metal and there is not a soul about—everything is asleep. . . . O Lord, how splendid that long, long road can be! How often like a drowning man have I clung to you, and every time, great-heartedly you have succored and saved me.

chapter 5

Dickens: The Intrusion of the Audience

It is no use pretending that it is easy to write of either Balzac or Dickens, and it is too much to hope for a critical judgment that will be acceptable to a majority of educated people. Most of us have known homes where Dickens was read and reread, and in France the same sort of thing is true of Balzac. Both are institutions, and the criticism of institutions raises feelings that have nothing to do with literature or art.

Besides, the uneasiness about Dickens is as old as his popularity, and it is not factitious; nor is it to be dismissed as lightly as Dickens's admirers generally dismiss it. Forster, Dickens's biographer and friend, denounced Taine for saying that Dickens takes sides with his subject, "laughs or cries over it, makes it odious or touching, repulsive or attractive, and is too vehement and not sufficiently inquisitive to paint a likeness." Because, according to Taine, it is essential for the novelist, no matter how vile his principal character may be, "to show its education and temptations, the form of brain or habits of mind that have reinforced the natural tendency, to deduce it from its cause, to place its circumstances around it, and develop its effects to their extremes."

This is all finely said, and Forster's attempt to reply is not worth repeating. At the same time, he might have replied that Taine was thinking in terms of the French novel, which aims rather to instruct than to delight, pointed out that the standard Taine is defending is really Balzac, and that Balzac's own performance is open to criticism on grounds not at all unlike those that apply to Dickens.

Trollope took a similar line in criticizing Dickens's character-drawing. Of some of Dickens's most famous characters he wrote that "to my mind they are not human beings, nor are any of the characters human which Dickens has portrayed. It has been the peculiarity and the marvel of this man's power that he has invested his puppets with a charm that enabled him to dispense with human nature."

In our own time Lord David Cecil replies to this:

It is this which led to the old accusation made by Trollope fifty years ago and by less intelligent people since that Dickens is exaggerated. [That, incidentally, is not Trollope's point.] Of course he is; it is the condition of his achievement. It would be as sensible to criticise a gothic gargoyle on the ground that it is an exaggerated representation of the human face as to criticise Mr. Pecksniff, for instance, on the ground that he is an exaggerated representation of a hypocrite. He is meant to be. And this, far from detracting from his vitality, adds to it. For exaggeration is a sign that Dickens' imagination was working.

This is an interesting line of defense, though it is quite as exclusive as the realistic line of Taine and Trollope, and entirely ignores the primary assumption of both, and indeed of Dickens himself, that the novel is intended as a representation of life. Is it, for instance, quite true to say that Dickens meant. Mr. Pecksniff to be exaggerated?

When he has to defend his treatment of Dotheboys Hall or the Court of Chancery, is it on the ground that he meant them to be exaggerated or that "exaggeration is a sign that his imagination was working," or is it not rather on the ground that the statements he has made are, if anything, rather less than the truth? What, indeed, is the purpose of referring to the truth at all in such a context if the only criterion is the imagination?'

I suspect that our real difficulty in dealing critically with Dickens and his contemporaries is that none of our criteria applies. The criterion of realism, which is much closer to my own taste than that of romance, leaves Trollope talking of "the peculiarity and the marvel" of Dickens's power, which really gets us nowhere at all, while the criterion of romance, which is what Lord David is really applying, would suggest that the only English novel of which he could approve would be *Wuthering Heights*.

I think the truth is that neither criterion applies because, in the novel of the second period, we are dealing with a hybrid form, a peculiar blend of romance and novel, the like of which had never appeared before and may never appear again. There is a bogus element in Dickens, Balzac, and Gogol which expresses itself in exaggeration and caricature, and this bogus element comes from a lack of determination between them and their public. This was the great new reading public I have already spoken of, and it did not know its place.

Between Dickens and his public there was what one can only describe as a highly unseemly relationship. An author's public is his patron, the old lady at the manor house from whom he rents his little cottage, and at whose parties he should put in an appearance a couple of times a year. It is a relationship that requires great forbearance on her part and great self-respect on his, but the code of Jane Austen and Trollope provides for this. The author will not willfully insult her, nor will he permit her to dictate to him. But Dickens's patron, though a large and warm-hearted woman, was not a perfect lady, and Dickens himself was a bit of a bounder. The results of their affair—for it was little else—were considerable and magnificent. He may be said to have died in her arms (smothered to death, one suspects), and the colossal monument she erected to his memory is almost as embarrassing as that erected by the other mourning widow to the Prince Consort.

Her pressure was directed in every way, not only on his work but on his life. It was to her that he addressed that shocking statement in which he defends his behavior in separating from his poor silly wife. (When he tells the chaste and censorious Emerson that if he knew his son was a virgin he would assume the boy was ill and send him to a doctor, we know that the old lady has left the table and the gentlemen are at it over their wine.) His most famous novels were serialized, which meant that in fact he was reading them to her as he wrote them, and was subjected to her most pressing entreaties and commands. If she did not like a character, he disappeared very early on, through the window if necessary. She recommended his physically frailer characters to mercy quite in the manner of a jury, and when he proved agreeably ruthless and insisted on reading her the deathbed scenes, she went into happy convulsions. "I am inundated with imploring letters recommending poor little Nell to mercy. Six yesterday and four today." "Paul's death has amazed Paris."

He introduced his friends to the old lady and told them how to behave with her. "Do not be afraid to trust the audience with anything that is good," he told Lever; "though a very large one, it is a fine one." Large and fine the old lady undoubtedly was, but she was also subject to feminine tantrums of a violent and inexplicable kind. "We drop rapidly and continuously with 'A Day's Ride,' " he finally had to tell Lever. "Whether it is too detached and discursive in its interest for the audience and the form of publication, I cannot positively say; but it does not *take hold*."

"Audience" is a revealing word, for it is the actor's rather than the writer's word, and it indicates better than any analysis what Dickens's attitude to the old lady was. In real life as well, he enjoyed reading to her, and she enjoyed being read to, for he began as a good actor and ended up as a superb one. He delighted to act his scenes to his family and friends as they were written, and counted himself fortunate if he drove these into hysterics. "I showed what I have done to Kate last night, who was in an unspeakable *state*, from which and my own impression, I augur well." In later days he did the same thing to whole audiences. "The shrieks of Nancy rang through the hall in a frightening falsetto, and at the conclusion of the episode no one stirred, no one seemed to breathe. It was a searching experience; no one who heard it ever forgot it, and none but the hardiest went a second time."

There was yet a third way in which Dickens fell too deeply under the influence of his public, and that was in his attitude to social reform. He was brave, warm-blooded, and kind-hearted, and, like his patron, he hated the abuses of his time—its materialism, its exploitation of child labor, of illegitimate children and orphans, and its brutal treatment of criminals. He hated cruelty and hypocrisy with a hate that was almost obsessive, and it is no use pretending that he had no abuses to expose or to suggest that Trollope's picture of contemporary England is truer than his. Trollope might make fun of him as "Mr. Sentiment," but beside Dickens he had a cold heart and a not very honest mind. As a novelist he made far better use of his American experience than Dickens did, and managed to isolate the characteristics of the cultivated American long before other writers were even aware that they existed, but one cannot imagine him denouncing the slavery-defending Southern judge as Dickens did, saying that "men who spoke of it as a blessing, as a matter of course, as a state of things to be desired, were out of the pale of reason; and that for them to speak of ignorance or prejudice was an absurdity too ridiculous to be criticised."

Bernard Shaw ascribed his own conversion to socialism to the reading of *Little Dorrit*, and we do not have to search far to find the passage that moved him. It is the superb scene in which the incoherent Pancks receives the gift of tongues to flay the slum landlord alive. It is the finest exposition I know of the principle of tyranny by agent. But it also makes me aware that it is not so easy to dissociate the actor and the humanitarian in Dickens. He liked the subject of the unwanted child because it was theatrical practice. He liked it because he was a big-hearted man who sympathized with the unwanted child of real life. But he also liked it because his public liked it, and as I read him I feel less and less that he himself has the principal say. It is as though it were being evoked from him, and as though the artist, the unique irreplaceable individual, were being smothered in the mob man, the man who does not know how much of what he says comes from within and how much from the outside voices that continue to assail him.

We see Dickens in America, and follow sympathetically whatever process it was that soured America on him. We read *Martin Chuzzlewit* without feeling that any great injustice has been done to that country. But the second American tour and the sudden *volte-face* of his public apology fill me with doubts. Was it really that conditions had changed so much for the better? Or was it that Dickens could not do without America; that it was another part of his public from which he had estranged himself, like the lecture audiences to whom he returned and who finally killed him? How else can we explain the extraordinary public pronouncements concerning his relations with his wife at the time of their separation? These are not the sort of explanation one offers to the old lady at the manor house; they are the sort of thing one says to a sweetheart or a mistress.

2.

What happens to *all* novelists of the second period is clear enough. Their reading public is turning into an audience. What happens to Dickens specifically is that by temperament he was less capable than other novelists of handling the problems raised by the conversion of an extremely private art into a more public one. He was less capable because in fact he was much more skillful than the other novelists in dealing with audiences, present and absent. I say absent because much of Dickens's audience was a secondhand one. Victorian novels were largely bought to be read aloud, and Dickens lent himself magnificently to this. Anyone with the rudiments of a voice can make an effect by merely reading aloud the scene of Jo's death from *Bleak House*. But a novel, after all, is not a play; it is persuasive, not compulsive, and I cannot resist the suspicion that some of Dickens's most fervent admirers are really spoiled actors who revel in his great set speeches.

These minor characters are Dickens's most remarkable achievement, but even they are not above criticism. Proust was deeply influenced by them, and he adopted the Dickens tirade for his own comic characters. But there is a difference, for characters like M. de Charlus are characters of the narrative, while Dickens's great characters are only characters of the dramatization. The novel is a narrative art in which dramatization is used to vary and illustrate the close texture of the narrative. Too much narrative, as in some of Stendhal's work, is wearisome.

Too much dramatization, as in the later Henry James and
Hemingway, can be intolerable because it rapidly ceases to
be dramatic and, like the usual wearisome first ten minutes
of an Ibsen play, turns into an agonizing combination of
exposition and development. Drama belongs to the development, not to the exposition.

But what Dickens does is something else again, for
though he always keeps a fair balance between narrative
and drama, the people he dramatizes are only rarely
characters of the narrative. In a story like *Bleak House*,
for instance, the "given" characters are the Jarndyce
wards and their guardian. In the secondary plot, they are
the Dedlocks, Esther, and Mr. Tulkinghorn. But in fact
the characters by whom we remember the book are Mrs.
Jellyby and her family; Guppy; Krook; Jo; Skimpole;
Mr. Chadband; and the Bayham Badgers. And these we
see only in dramatization. We are *told* that Skimpole is
bribed to betray poor Jo, but nothing he has ever said has
prepared us for such an unusual event. Dickens has not so
qualified the character that we recognize the inevitability
of such conduct. In fact, Dickens is the victim of his own
gift for impersonation, and is incapable of qualifying the
character who exists only when he speaks. The same thing
is true of the Bayham Badgers. They have no life outside
the dramatization, and what they talk of or do when they
are not in company, with Mr. Bayham Badger admiring
his wife's previous husbands, is something neither Dickens
nor we can possibly imagine. Dr. and Mrs. Proudie in the
Trollope saga are an equally comic pair, but they have a
life of their own within the narrative—so intense a life,

indeed, that Trollope can effortlessly, when the need arises, turn them both into characters of tragic power.

This is what Trollope had in mind when he described Dickens's characters as "puppets" and what other critics mean when they speak of "caricatures." Caricature is an art of representation in which the object represented is deprived of objective autonomy. We may for our own purposes and needs prefer puppets and caricatures, but if we are to understand the reaction of Trollope, Turgenev, and Flaubert in the succeeding generation, we must realize that all the art of this period is affected by a sort of distortion. In criticizing Dickens's methods of distortion, it would perhaps be better to use the word "impersonation." Where Balzac distorts in the manner of Daumier, Dickens distorts in the manner of a character actor. The impersonations eventually all turn out to be Dickens himself, Dickens in new disguises, and when the curtain falls and the applause breaks out, it is not Guppy, not Skimpole, not Mr. Chadband who appears, clutching the hands of imaginary leading ladies, but the old magician himself, wiping the sweat from his brow as he gazes lovingly toward the gallery. His impersonations, like a producer's play, a conductor's symphony, most of Dylan Thomas's poetry, are composed with reference to the magnificent instrument and its resources, not to the resources of drama, music, and poetry.

3.

This, then, is the typical Dickens novel: a romance, usually with a romantic sub-plot, the whole thing padded out with scores of supernumeraries. The thinness of the romance is usually concealed by the richness of the different character parts. So, for instance, in *Dombey and Son* we get a straightforward story of a hard-hearted, arrogant business man who pays no attention to his little daughter, Florence, and whose life is bound up with his son, Paul, who he hopes will succeed him in the business. But Paul's mother has died, so he acquires a wet nurse, Mrs. Toodle, who in turn fans out into a number of entertaining characters; while in the sub-plot the hero, Walter, who loves Florence, is the nephew of a wonderful old character called Solomon Gills, and Solomon has as friend an equally wonderful character, Captain Cuttle, who, in turn, has a friend— But the Dickens pattern is clear. In all his work there is a flight to the periphery of the story, a sort of embarrassment with the given material; yet, though this means that almost always the center of a Dickens book is empty or nearly empty, it means, too, that toward the periphery there is always a great sense of crowds and vitality. This explains why, for all its elaboration, *Bleak House* is not so satisfactory a novel as *Nicholas Nickleby*, the central theme of which no one ever bothers to remember, and which is quite frankly a picaresque parade of supernumeraries, a frame of romance filled with novelistic interludes.

Yet one has only to mention *Nicholas Nickleby* to realize that there is a great deal to be said for Dickens's way which is not said by his admirers and which cannot be said at all if one sticks to the strictly realistic approach. To go no further than the superficial level, there is the sense of urgency, the fever pitch at which Dickens must write to keep his childlike audience entertained, the imaginative tension of a modern Scheherazade who lives in fear of his head; and if we are honest, we must admit that a number of highly artistic novelists would not have suffered in the least from the application of such rude sanctions. Art, after all, is delight as well as instruction, and there is a delight in Dickens's work which is too frequently absent from the work of Flaubert and Henry James. These write beautifully; they do now write joyously, as Dickens does even in stray phrases like "The clear cold sunshine glances into the brittle woods," which is as lovely a line as one can find even in Keats. And his dialogue is keyed up in the same way, and even to his comic characters he lends his own eloquence and his own gift for vivid phrase-making, exactly as Shakespeare did. There are characters in Trollope drawn with infinitely more precision than Dickens brought to the description of Sairey Gamp, but none who can enchant us with remarks like: "And as to husbands, there's a wooden leg gone likeways home to its account which in its constancy of walking into wine-vaults, and never coming out again till fetched by force, was quite as weak as flesh if not weaker." Falstaff could have put it no better.

And here we come to what I think is the real virtue of both Dickens and Balzac. They are handling masses of material which no realist could have handled because, in fact, it would have been far too depressing. When Zola, who was incapable of perceiving the fantastic element in Balzac's documentation, did documentation of his own, the results were too painful for any work of art. One can recognize the true realist by the very small area of unpleasant experience which he can comfortably cover. Trollope has a wider range than any other English novelist, but he has not the same sort of range as Dickens or Balzac, for they can distort their backgrounds or introduce into them characters straight out of romance, so that the whole mass of material is fired and we can contemplate it without distress, knowing that with Dickens our Jack can always kill the Giant, and with Balzac that he can at least put up a remarkably good fight. From the realist's point of view, Mr. Squeers is an unbearably painful character and Sairey Gamp not exactly a pleasant one, but in Dickens one can enjoy them both because the romantic imagination has flowed about them and through them and they are half real, half fantastic. Like children listening to an adventure story, we can add just enough incredulity to enable us to enjoy them without being scared by them. In Dickens the fairy tale is being injected into the novel, expanding it to limits it has never reached before and may never reach again. At the same time, to treat him as though he were merely another Hugo, a romancer, is to rob him of half his grandeur.

chapter 6

Balzac: The Boundaries of Science

At first glance a novel of Balzac's seems to have nothing in common with a novel of Dickens's. Even the use of local color seems different, for whereas Dickens's local color is always charged with poetry, Balzac's is like an auctioneer's catalogue.

But mainly they differ in the way in which English and French novels generally do differ. The English regarded the novel primarily as entertainment—it was Jane Austen's complaint—while the French regarded it as a medium of instruction. At its best the English novel is much closer to being a work of art, for its purpose is simply to give delight. The French novel, for all that it has the gravity of a work of art, rarely has its detached and luminous quality. This is something that goes back to the early French moralists—or, as we should call them, psychologists—and, accordingly, it is not surprising that where English novels tend to deal with courtship and marriage, French ones more often deal with irregular relationships. The one is a field for imagination, the other for observation. (Of course, there are other reasons as well: for instance, the marriage customs of the two countries, for though the English bride and groom are theoretically free agents, the French ones are not; and when we come to deal with the Russian novel, we find, as Tolstoy points out, a situation that is neither theoretically free nor determined.) For the same reason, French novels, unlike English ones, abound in generalizations; Stendhal, Balzac, and Proust delight in laying down the laws of human behavior.

But even for a Frenchman, Balzac is prodigal of generalizations. On an average, they occur at the rate of half a dozen to the page. "Perhaps it is part of human nature to pile burdens on those who make no protest. . . ." "She was like many people who are on their guard against those nearest them and blindly confide in the first stranger who comes along. . . ." "Like all narrow-minded persons, Madame Vauquer was unaccustomed to consider why events happen. . . ." "Though the human heart may pause to rest when climbing the heights of affection, it rarely stops on the slippery slopes of hatred. . . ." "Empty-headed people are all indiscreet because they have no thoughts worth keeping to themselves."

Whether or not one enjoys generalizations, one always feels with Balzac that one is getting value for money. Why, after all, trouble to describe human behavior if one learns nothing from it?

This mania for generalization is not confined to conduct, but includes every aspect of human appearance as well, from the line of a mouth to the cock of a hat. "Dark and stern features, full of lines as nearly all judicial features are . . ." "Such a nose expresses . . . a congenital disposition to the sort of attachment to great causes which so often degenerates into gullibility. . . ." Worst of all, "His thin lips were not wanting in charm, but his pointed nose and slightly projecting forehead showed defects of race; and his hair, of a tint like hair that has been dyed black, indicated a mongrel descent, through which he derived his mental qualities from some libertine lord, his low instincts from a seduced peasant girl, his knowledge from an incomplete education, and his vices from his deserted and abandoned condition."

One may say without malice that no other novelist ever claimed to know so much as Honoré de Balzac, and this is where one really sees the difference between him and an English writer. It would be hard to deduce from the work of Dickens and Thackeray what educated people of their generation really knew of any aspect of contemporary science, but if all the scientific books of the period were destroyed in some universal cataclysm, Balzac's works would still enable us to make a pretty shrewd guess at their contents. Already in *The Shagreen Skin* of 1831 we find the crisis that becomes apparent in English fiction only toward the end of the century, and then in a sufficiently attenuated form: the realization of the immense age of the earth and of man's insignificant place in its history. Science was Balzac's real inspiration; it adds a new dimension to his work as the New Learning adds a new dimension to the work of Marlowe and the early Shakespeare.

It also was responsible for his principal achievement; the organization of his fiction in the form of a study of society. "The idea," says one of his critics, "emerged from a comparison between humanity and the animal world created according to unity of composition. This idea, erected into a principle, had occupied the minds of scientists and theosophists. Balzac, believing that he was both one and the other, became interested in the question;

he had followed the discussions on it in which Cuvier and Geoffroy Saint-Hilaire had quarreled; had studied Swedenborg, Saint-Martin, Baader on the subject. Whatever its value, this principle, with the bringing into practise of the systems of Gall and Lavater, brought the novelist immense resources for the development of his characters, according to the law of species conforming to the circumstances in which they evolve." *

2.

But Balzac, like Marlowe, "still climbing after knowledge infinite," found his progress continually halted, and our scientific student reconstructing the knowledge of the early nineteenth century would be in considerable danger of reconstructing a certain amount of science which did not happen to exist at all, which, in fact, still does not exist. The conjunction in the passage I have quoted of men of science and theosophists, of Cuvier and Swedenborg, might indicate as much. It may be that "the concatenation of causes" implies that every single object is the result of all the forces that have shaped it, and its entire history ready to be read by the wise man. It may even be that, "since God has stamped each person's destiny in such a way that it can be read by the eyes of the seer upon his physiognomy," the human hand, "which is the instrument and sole mode of manifestation of the entirety of human action, might well serve as physiognomy's most concise

---

* Philippe Bertault: *Balzac, l'homme et l'œuvre.*

representation." One can only say that such seers are still lacking.

But Balzac was not impressed by the difficulties in his way.

Everything in human life, like everything in the life of our planet, is predestined—including the slightest and most trivial accidents. It follows that great matters, great designs and great thoughts are necessarily reflected in the smallest actions—so faithfully that if some conspirator shuffles and cuts a pack of cards in the presence of one of those seers known as gipsies, fortune tellers, charlatans and the like, he will at once betray his secret. As soon as one admits the truth of predestination— that is to say of the concatenation of causes—judiciary astrology resumes its ancient role as a mighty science: a science that calls for that power of deduction which was so greatly developed by Cuvier, but is at the same time spontaneous, and not—as it was in the case of that great genius—the product of long nights of toilsome study.

We begin to perceive that though science adds a new dimension to Balzac's work, as to Marlowe's, it does so in the way of Marlowe, by turning the New Science into the old magic. This is one way in which he separates himself from Stendhal and Jane Austen and comes closer to Dickens. There was another in that, like Dickens, he no longer wrote for elegant, educated people in drawing-rooms, but for a vast new public passionately interested in new ideas, but in clinging to the former we shall not go too far wrong. For though in origin at least the method is sci-entific, and though the object may seem to be scientific, the laws that govern the relation of things to people, the cut of a hat or the line of a mouth, either do not exist at all, or if they do, are far beyond our present range of knowledge. When he invents these laws Balzac at once separates himself from his rationalist forerunners and becomes a mystic. Mystic sounds better than salesman, though perhaps, like science and astrology, they may be linked. The element of charlatanism in Dickens's contemporaries is an extraordinary and baffling study.

It begins in Balzac with his very earliest works. He was deeply influenced by the romantic novels that influenced Jane Austen, and his own first efforts were in that manner, but whereas Jane Austen eliminated the romantic stuff from her own work by the most rigorous self-analysis, Balzac clung to it up to the end. Though he abandoned the writing of blood-and-thunder tales to write books like *Cousin Pons* and *Cousin Bette*, he never for an instant abandoned the principles of romantic literature. With him science and fancy both had to illustrate the same eternal laws, and if they failed to do so, he was quite prepared to take them in hand and show them where they were wrong.

It is his principal characteristic and the best clue to his work. Because of some psychological quirk, he refused to distinguish between fancy and fact, imagination and reality, intuition and judgment. In France the argument as to whether he should be regarded as a realist or fantasist has raged for generations. In fact, he is neither—or, rather, both—because, like Dickens, he insists on having the best of both worlds. *Ursule Mirout*, for instance, which begins as a powerfully contrived legal struggle over an old man's wealth, ends with the old gentleman's return from the dead in a dream to reveal the secret of a relative's crime. And this is not mere clumsiness or haste. It is conviction, for Balzac expounds the science of dreams as he expounds all the other imaginary sciences. How should we regard such a book, as novel or romance? Heine hit off his friend neatly when he said that Balzac's ideal government would be a republic run by monarchists.

And this was not, as it so often was with Dickens, entirely the result of writing for a new sort of public, half-educated, and with hankerings after the horrors of the past. Even Balzac's extraordinary marriage is proof of the curious duality in his nature. In *The Shagreen Skin* he had made his hero say that he could never conceive of love and poverty together, and here he was speaking for his author. But if Balzac was determined on marrying a rich wife, he also demanded a romantic one, and his acquaintance with Mme Hanska originated in a correspondence begun by her anonymously and facetiously. Balzac's share in it was not facetious, nor was it the first correspondence of its kind he had indulged in, and when he treated the subject in *Modeste Mignon*, he threw a revealing light on his own motives when he wrote: "Ernest was fascinated by the abyss of the unknown. The unknown is dark infinity, and nothing is more enthralling." He has his principles, this fat, jolly man who puffs upstairs to a Paris fortune-teller to discover if he will sleep with a duchess or make a packet on his latest investment, but they are not, strictly speaking, scientific.

He reconciles their contradictions by means of his peculiar religious belief, which may best be described as theosophical. Theosophy, like Christian Science and the idealistic philosophies, makes no clear distinction between subject and object. According to this creed, matter is to be regarded as a form of thought, while thought itself is regarded as a material agent, a sort of electricity or magnetic fluid that penetrates outside bodies and influences their behavior. To be frank, the former proposition did not greatly interest Balzac; he was more concerned with the latter, which offered a clue to the successful conduct of life with both duchesses and stockbrokers. Electricity was what they needed.

Unquestionably [Balzac loves words like "unquestionably"] ideas are projected with a force in direct proportion to the force with which they are conceived, and fly straight to the mark at which the brain aims them by a mathematical law as exact as that which directs the course of shells projected from a mortar. The effects produced are various. There are tender natures in which they lodge with devastating results, and there are strongly-fortified natures, brazen-fronted skulls, against which the wills of others flatten themselves and fall like bullets against a wall; then there are doughy, yielding brains in which other men's ideas are spent as shot is killed in the soft earth of redoubts.

Emotions have a similar effect, and indeed Balzac never distinguishes clearly among ideas, emotions, and will. All are simply a form of hypnotic suggestion, and the energy generated is similar to, if not identical with, electricity. Napoleon is a true electrician; Christ is a super-electrician, as we see from the number of his so-called miracles, though only a very unscientific person would find anything miraculous about them.

Now, undoubtedly (to use the firm language of Balzac

himself) "magnetism," as he usually calls this power, is an influence devoutly believed in by every small boy who, like Balzac himself, is unhappy at school or home. Usually he calls it "magic," and he "wills" people to do or say something, more particularly when he suspects they are about to do or say it anyhow. Only stern necessity moves him to "will" people to do something he suspects they are not going to do, and frequent contact with such "strongly-fortified natures, brazen-fronted skulls against which the wills of others flatten themselves and fall like bullets against a wall" is the most certain way to the dissolution of the myth of material thought.

Like the schoolboy, Balzac attributes importance to only one aspect of thought, and that is the exercise of the will. This is what finally makes him such a wretched psychologist; why Turgenev says of his characters that "not one of them has lived or ever could have lived." For most of us, there is a clear distinction between a thought and an event. We may desire to injure someone who has injured us; we may forgive him; we may make a friend of him; we may completely ignore him. Like Racine's heroine, we may respond with a *"Qui te l'a dit?"* when someone interprets our deepest wishes. Stendhal, like Balzac, had been deeply influenced by the example of Napoleon, which had made young men of the generation succeeding him attribute almost limitless power to the human will; yet when Stendhal describes Julien entering Mme de Renal's bedroom with the intention of seducing her, he knows that, for all Julien's willpower, he will then burst into tears and fall at her feet. Contradictory desires are the basis of all character-drawing. Balzac accepts in the most literal sense Christ's remark that a man who looks after a woman with lust has already committed adultery with her. The thought itself is an event and immediately links itself to the succeeding action.

But only an out-and-out idealist can accept this as psychology, for it makes it almost impossible for a character to have conflicting desires, and such a character is not really a human being but a monster as theatrical as Dickens's Mr. Tulkinghorn. A similar cult of the will in Renaissance times produced a similar crop of monsters: Tamburlaine, the Jew of Malta, Richard III. Old Goriot thinking of his daughters and old Grandet thinking of his gold are both monomaniacs. Balzac tells us that the only thing in the world that Grandet loved, apart from his money, was his daughter (and this may actually mean that he was thinking at least of Shakespeare's Jew, if not of Marlowe's), but as the novel progresses it is quite clear that this represents a conflict of desires far too complicated for a philosophy of thought as event, and the injured father, instead of lamenting his ducats *and* his daughter, confines himself strictly to the former. "The best brought-up girls may go wrong and give away you know what, as everyone knows is the case with girls of very good family, as well as among the middle classes and others, but to give away gold—!"

And it is not only the major characters in Balzac who are monolithic. Every single character in *Eugénie Grandet* is described as an aspect of a single, simple law. With Nanon, the maid, it is that her "simple heart and simple mind had room for only one feeling and one idea"—gratitude. With Mme Grandet, "this foolish secret pride, this high-minded generosity of sentiment, constantly misunderstood and wounded by M. Grandet, influenced the poor woman on all occasions." Eugénie herself has seen her cousin, Charles, for only one evening when she dedicates her whole life to him; after this, he becomes her monomania, as money is her father's, and she guards his property with the same ferocity as her father grabs it.

And this is how Balzac always sees his characters. "The eccentrics of London," he tells us, "always end by wearying of their passions, as they weary of life itself. In Paris, on the contrary, the monomaniacs live with their fancies, in a blissful state of spiritual concubinage." That is how he lives with his own creations, half demons, half men, and though his judgment continued to grow, and his passion for scientific classification enabled him to sweep more and more characters into his net and to extend his knowledge of them and their backgrounds, the characters themselves tend to remain in the fantasy world of Mrs. Radcliffe and Mary Shelley. They are the external expression of his own curious inner world, and that is why he can be inspired by them as Dickens is inspired by his own fabulous creations. The scene in which old Grandet, having to break bad news to his nephew, "did not feel embarrassed at having to inform him of his father's death, but could not refrain from something like a feeling of compassion when he knew him to be without a halfpenny," may be oversimplified, but it is oversimplified in the way of Elizabethan drama. Balzac's death scenes, like the death scenes in Renaissance plays,

are tremendous, for his monomaniacs, like theirs, spit
defiance in the face of death and die in their dreams. So we
have Grandet's last grab at the gilt crucifix; Goriot's
clutching at the hair of the two young men he imagines to
be his heartless daughters; poor old Pons's "Nothing here
will be stolen." "Ha, ha, my boy," the wonderful old
salesman says, rubbing his hands gleefully, "those were
men for you!"

It is not that he lacked the power to describe people who
do let things stand in their way, like Caesar Birotteau, an
honest man who feels bankruptcy as a personal dishonor,
or that he does not treat him with understanding and
respect. There is, after all, a touch of monomania [in
honesty of that sort. But he is not inspired by such mealy-
mouthed creatures, afflicted by memories of the past and
fears of the future, "unlike Nature, which recognizes no
past, which all the time begins again on the mysteries of
her inexhaustible childbirths," and his romantic vision
strays past them to linger lovingly on M. Molineux on
the sixth floor.

This annoying old man had neither wife, child, nephew nor
niece. He bullied his maid of all work too much to make her a
victim; for she escaped all contact with her master by doing her
work and keeping out of his way. His appetite for tyranny was
thus balked; and to satisfy it in some way, he patiently studied
the laws relating to rentals and party walls; he fathomed the
jurisprudence which regulates the dwellings of Paris in an infinite number of petty questions as to tenants, abutters, lia-
bilities, taxes, repairs, sweepings, decorations for the Fête-
Dieu, waste-pipes, lighting, projections over the public way,
and the neighbourhood of unhealthy buildings. His means, his

strength, in fact, his whole mind, was spent in keeping his proprietary rights on a complete war footing. He had made it an amusement, and the amusement had become a monomania.

And once more he sells us on the character. It is all very well for Turgenev to tell us that he never lived and could never have lived and that he does not possess one particle of the truth that makes the characters of Tolstoy's *Cossacks* so marvelously alive. I yield Turgenev's point without question. His generation had to find that truth, as Jane Austen's generation had to find it. But we cannot dismiss the generation of Dickens and Balzac so lightly. There is also a truth in them which is not that truth regarding the human heart of which Turgenev is speaking. It is a truth regarding society, regarding their century, which Turgenev himself, which Jane Austen, which even Tolstoy was incapable of expressing, and which ultimately could have been expressed only in the way in which they have expressed it.

For here, in these novels of Balzac, we see the modern world for the first time. It is true that the railway has not yet come, but the stagecoach does well enough for the fat commercial traveler Gaudissart, who is breaking down a rural and provincial economic system that has lasted since the early Middle Ages. With him come the daily newspapers and the first advertisement of goods "Approved by the Institute" (for he never neglects the blessing of science, as the medieval palmer never neglected the blessing of the Church). In the cities, as the stagecoach passes, we see the workers in their vile factories, manufacturing the products he sells, forming the Communist cells that will cause such heart-searchings to their great-great-grandchildren, turning away from the worker-priests who follow them, and who themselves are plagued by the great ecclesiastical leeches who feed on their blood.

If Balzac had been a more conscientious artist, he would have been a lesser man. It is precisely the fact that his imagination is always running wild which enables him to fire this mass of sordid material as though it were in fact what he believed it to be, a form of electricity shattering the mass from within.

chapter 7

Gogol's Shoe

If Gogol is less important in the history of the nine-teenth-century novel than Dickens, Balzac, or Thackeray, it is because until late in the century nobody even knew there was such a thing as a Russian novel. Vladimir Nabokov points out the astounding fact that in 1854, twelve years after publication, Gogol's most famous work appeared in London as an original work, the publishers reserving the rights of translation. By the end of the century, young people like my friend the Celtic scholar could say: "For me literature means three names—all of them Russian." Educated people had become aware, with a venge-ance, of the existence of the Russian novel.

The reason is, of course, that it had added an entirely new element to fiction. What that element is is not quite such an easy matter to define. "Compassion" was a great word among critics in my youth, though neither Dickens nor Balzac was exactly devoid of that. At the same time, it is true that there is in Russian literature a great sense of pity which is not present to anything like the same degree in the novels of other European countries. It is only when one asks oneself where this sense of pity comes from that one begins to realize that it is not quite the right word. I can define it to myself only as a new gravity in the approach to human beings considered as part of a larger social group.

The only novelist we have so far considered who approaches the Russians in gravity is Jane Austen. She is aware of people as objects in a way that cannot be compared with the awareness of any novelist before her or of more than a few after her. So aware is she of people that she can almost transfer entirely the narrative responsibility from events to character. She can make the character produce the events that she needs to sustain interest. But we have seen, too, that she does this by a rigorous isolation of her work to the sort of character and incident she felt she could completely comprehend. Even in middle-class homes we soon become aware that Teresa, Bessie, and Smith, who serve the drinks and cook the dinner, are real personalities with pleasures and griefs resembling ours. It is highly improbable that Jane Austen as housekeeper refrained from inquiring into their personal lives, yet nowhere does she ever let us see such a servant. It may be, of course, that she thought it low; other English novelists thought likewise and introduced the domestic staff as light relief. We cannot question her on her reasons. But we may be permitted to believe that it was part of the discipline she imposed on herself in order to arrive at her own truth.

Now, maid, nurse, or butler in a Russian novel may at any moment intervene and exist in his or her own right, a human being as much as the hero or heroine. This shows us at once how much a middle-class art the novel is, for the shock of reading a Russian novel is the shock of seeing a feudal society in action.

This explains much. It explains how Russian novelists pass easily from one class to another without, like Balzac, having to invent a new code for each. It does not explain the why. There were feudal countries nearer to France and England than Russia was—Poland is a good example —but they produced no great novelists. Is it that Russia was Orthodox and Poland Catholic? This, too, may have something to do with it, but it still leaves too much unexplained. What remains cannot perhaps be explained; it can only be described. Russia, nearer the Orient than Poland, was more backward than Poland, and somewhere in the feeling of inadequacy which assailed educated Russians there was set up a profound conflict that made them self-conscious as the Poles were not, as the Spaniards and Italians were not. Removed from the centers of European thought, their lives dictated for them by a stupid autocracy, educated Russians turned toward the West with something like anguish or away from it with a mystical fervor, and the ideals of feudalism and of democracy mingled in something like a new conception of life and destiny. Only this can account for the greatest quality of the Russian novelists, as it accounts for their greatest weakness, their mania for explaining, denouncing, apologizing for themselves and their race. It may be that Jane Austen's maids were never allowed to intervene in discussion, while Turgenev's were. At the same time, only once, to my knowledge, and then almost timidly does Jane Austen ever use the word "English" to explain a character.

2.

Gogol, then, is not very important in the history of the nineteenth-century novel. He is very important indeed in the history of the Russian novel because, in fact, he invented it. "We all came out from under Gogol's *Cloak*," said Turgenev. At the same time, even in the short history of Russian literature he fits into the pattern of his contemporaries, Dickens and Balzac. After *Pride and Prejudice*, *David Copperfield*, and then *The Warden*. After *The Princesse de Clèves*, *Eugénie Grandet* and then *Madame Bovary*. After Pushkin's *Queen of Spades*, *Dead Souls* and then Turgenev's *Rudin*. Each phase is essentially a reaction against the preceding one; a case of "We must always kill Father." Even Turgenev, for all that he had come out from under *The Cloak*, soon began to look on Gogol as Trollope looked on Dickens, Flaubert on Balzac. "I am feeling more and more where Gogol's shoe pinches," he wrote. "The striving after impartiality and integral truth is one of the few good qualities for which I am grateful to Nature." It may have been Nature; it may also have been the Time Spirit.

For Gogol, like Dickens and Balzac, is essentially a fantasist. He was born in 1809. In 1829 he ran away from his employment at St. Petersburg and made for North Germany, carrying with him some money with which his mother had entrusted him for other purposes. He wrote to her a most memorable and edifying letter, justifying his flight and theft on the most exalted motives. He could not, it seemed, bear the atmosphere of St. Petersburg, with its civil servants who "leave the remote provinces where they own land and where they might have become excellent farmers instead of the useless people they are. Why, if a person of gentle birth must

serve the state, let him serve it in his own manor; but
what he does is to dilly-dally in the capital, where not
only does he not find an office, but squanders an incredible
amount of money which he gets from home." This passage
seems to me extraordinarily significant for an understanding of Gogol, as does the passage in which he offers
amends to his mother by giving her power of attorney to
dispose of his own land in whatever way she thinks fit.
In reading Gogol and in studying books about him, I am
always struck by his extraordinary resemblance to Goldsmith. Nobody ever loved more the atmosphere of home,
and nobody ever kept farther away from it.

Back in St. Petersburg, Gogol made a reputation with
his retelling of Ukrainian folk stories and some wildly
Germanic fantasies. At the same time there is in his work
a growing tendency to realism. He made his first great
hit with a play, *The Government Inspector*, in 1836. This
deals with a corrupt administration expecting the arrival
of an inspector and identifying him in the person of a
junior clerk of considerable imaginative gifts. When the
row broke about this, Gogol left Russia and, except for
short visits, remained away from it for the rest of his
life, traveling about Europe. He was equally successful
with the first part of *Dead Souls*, which appeared in 1842,
but he dallied over the remaining parts, though the second
part, at least, was completed when he died. By this time
he was suffering from religious mania. A couple of weeks
before his death, he destroyed the manuscript of his novel.

Dead Souls is a picaresque novel that critics have repeatedly compared with *Don Quixote* and with *Pickwick*

Papers. It is Russian in the sense that its subject could not have been duplicated in any country except the southern half of the United States, for it describes a plausible rogue called Chichikov who sets out to acquire the title to dead slaves whose names still appear upon the census because, though they are really dead, they are legally alive and can be used as security for a substantial loan. Objective-minded critics assure us that this would not have been possible, as Russian law did not permit the break-up of slave families if they were to be transported to other regions and Chichikov would have been compelled to take living wives and children with his purchases, but we may take this as no more than proof that a great part of humanity still clings obstinately to the theory that the novel should be written within the limits of probability.

Only the first part of the book was published. The fragments of the second part which we possess are in a different vein, didactic rather than picaresque, and we know that Gogol gave his friends to understand that he had planned it as a sort of *Divine Comedy*, and that the third part would describe the redemption of Chichikov. But by this time he was a mentally sick man addressing sermons in letter form to his friends in Russia, haunted by hellfire, and giving over the direction of his soul to an illiterate priest called Father Matthew. Degeneration would scarcely be too strong a word for what critics feel about the second half.

Now, decline in a writer is a subject that needs to be tackled with considerable reserve, particularly in one like

Gogol, who usually made at least eight drafts of anything he wrote. We know that he burned a complete
draft of the second part, and we know that people who
heard him read it saw no decline in it. In fact, we have
no indication that the published chapters are anything
but early drafts. All we have to go on is his own admission
that in the last years of his life he was finding it harder
and harder to write.

The question is of importance because before we can
judge the book we should have some notion what the
author was getting at. Now, the didacticism of the second
part is not exactly a new thing in Gogol's work, though
the degree in which it is present may surprise us. After
The Government Inspector appeared and was attacked, he
wrote a didactic interpretation of it in which he explained
that the real Government Inspector was the Conscience
of Man and the other characters the passions. Mr. Nabokov, whom I have already quoted, takes this as evidence
that Gogol misunderstood and distorted the sense of his
own work. That may be so; yet I find it hard to think of
any work of art, however great, as an absolute or to
believe that its author, however foolish, can be completely
incapable of understanding it. There is, it seems to me, a
reasonable possibility that Gogol knew what he was
talking about, and that, however foolish his explanations
may be, they are worth listening to patiently.

The truth is that Gogol was and remained an intensely
subjective writer. Though he gradually gained control
over his own fantasy in the same way as Balzac did, it
always remained there, intact and unmodified by observa-

tion and analysis. Like Goldsmith, he always writes of himself. "Having taken some bad feature or other of my own, I persecuted it under a different name and in a different character, endeavouring to make it appear before my eyes as my deadly enemy—an enemy who had inflicted a terrible injury on me; I persecuted it with malice, with irony, with anything I could get hold of. Had anyone seen those monsters which came from my pen at the beginning, he would have shivered with fear."

It is this which makes him such a wonderful chronicler of Tsarist Russia. Fantasy is the folk art of every autocracy. Where decisions are arbitrary and the secret manipulations of a single official can bring about the downfall of any individual, people live in fear of the unknown. In such an atmosphere anything is possible. Gogol's clerk Khlestyakov can paralyze the administration of a whole area with fear. So, in *Dead Souls*, when the problem arises as to who Chichikov is, it is suggested that he may be a shadowy captain who lost an arm and leg in the Napoleonic wars, and when someone points out that Chichikov has two of both, the postmaster explains that "mechanical devices had been much perfected in England." He may even be Napoleon. Three years before, a prophet had appeared, "wearing bast shoes and an unlined sheepskin coat, and smelling terribly of stale fish; and he had announced that Napoleon was Antichrist and was kept on a stone chain behind six walls and seven seas, but that afterwards he would break his chains and master the whole world. The prophet was very properly jailed for this prediction, but nevertheless he had done his job and set the merchants in a flutter."

Under such a rule, authority itself takes on the quality of fantasy. Of the local administrators, Gogol says: "They all felt suddenly guilty of sins they had not even committed," comments shrewdly on the absence among them of "that essential thing which the run of folk call common sense," and concludes that "for some reason, we Russians have not been created for representative institutions."

But what are we really dealing with in these brilliant scenes? Is it autocracy or a psychological state? For all this time Gogol himself is driven on by a sense of undistributed guilt which sends him flying from place to place in the attempt to escape it. There is no doubt in my mind but that Janko Lavrin is right when he says that Gogol never broke free from his childlike mother, and that the sense of guilt originates in the self-abuse to which he was condemned by his failure to make contact with another woman. But between Gogol's Tsar and Gogol's God there is very little difference; if anything, the heavenly Tsar is a little more capricious than the earthly one. He was able to master the personal fantasy by turning it into literature, but even the literary exercise is never with him more than a temporary expedient, nor is it ever free of the pangs of conscience in which it originated.

Our problem, then, is to decide whether Chichikov is no more than the amusing rogue of picaresque comedy (in which case the idea of his redemption is pretentious and absurd and Gogol was really insane when he attempted it) or whether he is something different, something out of the nineteenth century, a modern Everyman in whom we are expected to see an aspect of ourselves. The former view turns Chichikov into a flat character and makes the significance of the book depend upon the wonderful caricatures of men and women whom he meets on his travels; a series of disjointed episodes, disconnected not only from their sequel, but also from one another.

The second view is, I am quite sure, the correct one. It is the meaning behind the repeated statements that Chichikov was neither too young nor too old; too handsome nor too ugly; too stout nor too thin; too distinguished nor too humble. He is, in fact, the average sensual man, and before the first part of the novel was complete, Gogol no longer attempted to conceal this meaning from himself or his readers. "And if any one of you is full of Christian humility in the solitude of his heart rather than for all the world to hear, in moments of communion with himself he will ponder this weighty question in the depths of his soul: 'Is there not a trace of Chichikov in me too?' "

Chichikov is not really a rogue. He is merely Everyman playing his eternal part. His vision is consistently a snug middle-class one of wife and children, and he is particularly devoted to the children, whom—like Gogol himself —he has failed to beget. His life is really a distressful one, for though he is a clever man and even a conscientious one in a world of thieves and liars, his own little theft, his own little falsehood is forever being exposed. When we meet him, he has already lost two tidy little fortunes —one acquired in the Treasury, another in the Customs. He will also lose the fortune he acquires through his brilliant deal in dead souls. It is a foregone conclusion because essentially he is a decent man, a man whose heart can rise to the inspiration of a good landowner or a saintly merchant. Yet he cannot save himself from falling into petty acts of knavery which the real knaves exploit against him. Nothing, in fact, can settle Chichikov's problem but salvation. Hence, in principle and in spite of the critics, Gogol is right.

It is only by realizing this that we can realize the difference between Gogol's caricatures and those of Dickens and Balzac. In all of them the caricatures are produced by the addition to the realistic imagination of Jane Austen and Stendhal of the romantic imagination of Mrs. Radcliffe and Monk Lewis. All of them tend to let their characters turn into monsters. But whereas the monsters of Dickens and Balzac represent little more than passions run wild, Gogol's represent, as well as a fantasist could see it, life itself, his own life, above all, Russian life. For no more than Turgenev can Gogol resist identifying himself with his native land.

It is this which gives his caricatures such extraordinary richness compared with the puppets of Dickens and the monsters of Balzac. Gogol has an amazing power of generalizing from slight aspects of his own character in order to form the impression of a type, almost of a community. We have seen how Balzac generalizes in the attempt at creating a universal law. Gogol generalizes in

order to explain Russia to his reader. Chichikov adopts an offhand tone to the old woman Korobochka, and at once we get:

It is appropriate to say here that if in Russia we have not quite caught up with foreigners in some respects, we have far outstripped them in behaviour. It is impossible to enumerate all the shades and refinements of our intercourse. A Frenchman or a German . . . would be inclined to address a millionaire or small tobacconist in much the same terms, although in his soul he would of course be fawning on the former. With us it is quite different: we have experts in sophistry who will sing quite a different tune in front of a landowner with two hundred souls and one with three hundred; quite differently again in front of one having three hundred souls and another possessing five hundred . . . in short, were you to count up to a million there would be no lack of shades.

Nor could we imagine that at the end of a picaresque story in which an amiable rogue had been discovered in a fraud, Dickens would burst into a great pæan to England like the pæan to Russia which closes the first part of *Dead Souls.*

Russia, where are you flying? Answer me! There is no answer. The bells are tinkling and filling the air with their wonderful pealing; the air is torn and thundering as it turns to wind; everything on earth comes flying past and, looking askance at her, other peoples and states move aside and make way.

Redemption is surely the least we can demand for such a hero as passes to this great music. But here we come to the real difficulty of the fragments of the second part which have come down to us. Without admitting that they are more than early drafts, we are still compelled to ask whether the completed version that Gogol read to his friends was really quite so good as they thought. Because, as Janko Lavrin astutely points out, this is the real difficulty of the subjective writer like Gogol. To save Chichikov's soul, he has first to save his own, and nothing in Gogol's later life suggests that he had the intellectual wherewithal. In fact, with him, as with Dostoevsky and even with Tolstoy, we are face to face with the peculiar fact that the Russian tends to associate redemption with the idea of surrender and ultimately with the instincts. Now, Gogol's judgment had grown enormously in the discipline of his art, but his instincts had remained almost atrophied, childlike, no more ripe for redemption than for marriage. We can see that for ourselves if we compare the crazy letter he wrote to his mother at the age of twenty when he had stolen her money and fled from Petersburg with the later correspondence that Byelinsky so savagely denounced. It is all to the same tune, "serving the state in one's own manor" instead of dilly-dallying in the capital.

Pursued by guilt like Goldsmith, Gogol was haunted by some vision of childhood and home which, in the final analysis, was a vision of his mother and an Eden to which he could never return. "And as the hare whom hounds and horn pursue pants to the place from which at first he flew," when he felt the necessity for representing the redemption of Chichikov, it was to this vision of childhood innocence he returned, only to flounder in ill-digested chauvinism and religiosity. He had turned his magnificent

intelligence on the passions in himself; he had not turned
it on his own ideals; and when he tries to represent these,
they turn out to be a life without French, without pianos,
dancing or fashionable clothes—"a simple and sober
life," as one of the characters describes it. Gogol's intelligence is purely negative; when he turns it on the enemies
of his ideal, like the mad Colonel Koshkaryov, who has
learned organization and method abroad, the fun is as
good as ever; it is only when he has to depict the alternative to Koshkaryov that Gogol collapses into his chaos
of negations; no lawns, no factories, no busts of Shakespeare, no porticoes, no back scratchers, no tea, no views,
no . . . no . . . no . . .

Perhaps, after all, the man who sobbed after the destruction of his masterpiece was not haunted so much by
the fear of hell as by the fear of his own negations.

chapter 8

Thackeray: Vanity Fair

Whether Thackeray was attracted to Maginn and Sylvester Mahoney because of circumstances or for some deeper reason is hard to discover, but he is certainly easier to understand when you relate him to this pair and to their eighteenth-century journalism. That style of journalism was not, of course, confined to Ireland, nor did it originate there, but it made its home there and can be studied by anyone with the necessary lack of fastidiousness, in the proceedings of the Irish Houses of Parliament and in the literary products of its healthiest surviving descendant, the Irish Catholic style of controversy in the United States.

It is not improperly associated with a subject country because there is in it a sort of dictatorship of the mind. It is not concerned with truth. It does not aim at disproving a man's contention or at persuading him of his error, but at using words like a shillelagh and knocking him unconscious. It is witty, but with a wit that delights to humiliate and wound. It rarely produces works of originality, but it always knows how to ridicule them. It derides everything, even itself—mostly, perhaps, itself—and perhaps nothing one could say of Thackeray is more characteristic than the fact that he wrote an inflated "Ode" on the Crystal Palace Exhibition for *The Times* and a skit on the same subject for *Punch*, thus canceling out with the greatest neatness the two poles of his thought which Carlyle described as sentimentalism and play-acting.

Thackeray had gone through this phase in his youth, but he never entirely lost his taste for it, and it marked everything he did and wrote. Because of it, he is unique among Victorian novelists in having no romanticism in him. He and Balzac share the honors for the best descriptions of the money mania that swept Europe during the Industrial Revolution, but whereas Balzac's financiers turn, as we have seen, into magicians of the romantic revival, Thackeray's are life-size figures, as gullible and as gulled as anybody else by the appearance of things. He does not stand gaping as Balzac does at the display of magnificence in the European royal houses. He tears aside the hangings and shows us the English court or some petty German court motivated by the same vanity and greed that motivate his flunkeys and lodging-house keepers.

As a result, he does not share at all in the Victorian inflation of values. When we read of Dickens talking complacently to Emerson about the necessity for his son's enjoying sexual intercourse, we know at once, as I have said, that the old lady in the manor house has left the gentlemen to their wine. Thackeray, a much more moral man than Dickens, does not wait for his patron to leave before letting the table know that she is a humbug.

The times are such that one scarcely dares to allude to that kind of company which thousands of our young men in Vanity Fair are frequenting every day, which nightly fills casinos and dancing rooms, which is known to exist as well as the Ring in Hyde Park or the Congregation at St. James's, but which the most squeamish if not the most moral of societies is determined to ignore.

So clearly is Thackeray distinguished from his contemporaries that he might almost be found in the camp of the succeeding generation, the Trollopes, Turgenevs, and Tolstoys who repudiated the romanticism of their literary forefathers and searched for what Turgenev called "integral truth." Yet, though nearer to them than to Dickens or Balzac, he is not really of their number either. What enabled him to see the real man under the all-powerful prince or banker was not the respect for "integral truth," but a profound, melancholy realization of historical truth, a brooding awareness of the ultimate futility of all human endeavor: "Vanity Fair." His novels are chock-full of epitaphs and inscriptions, mostly false, from the Pendennis monument to the Osborne one; old dance cards, old invitations, faded, illiterate love-letters that sum up the miserable achievement of rogue and true man before both are transferred to the charnel house of history. He shares with Turgenev a predilection for turning his stories into reminiscences—usually of an old and tired man; with a faint flavor of old romances and of passions long dwindled into senility and dust. And, as with Turgenev—far more than with Turgenev, who has not the historical imagination—though it sometimes gives his work a certain unity of tone and a gentle nostalgic coloring, it also weakens it, for the sentimentality of retrospection robs characters of their sharpness and incidents of their importance. "It'll all be the same in a hundred years"—or, as a little girl in an Irish village once expressed it to me, "The flowers is fading and we'll soon be fading ourselves"—though a sentiment of unimpeachable classical provenance, is dangerous to a writer who must show us in the light of eternity the importance of a missing check for twenty pounds. The device of the puppet show in *Vanity Fair* is merely another method of indicating that it does not really much matter whether the characters are good or bad, noble or ignoble; they must die just the same.

> *"Dust and ashes," so you creak it, and I lack the heart to scold.*
> *Dear dead women, with such hair too, what's become of all the gold*
> *Used to fall and brush their bosoms? I feel chilly and grown old.*

2.

Even when one has studied Thackeray's life, it is hard to see why this perverse and gloomy strain should exist in his work. His life does not seem to have been particularly tragic, and what sufferings it brought he faced in a manly, uncomplaining way. He was born in India in 1811. His father died when he was four, and after two years more with his beloved mother, he returned to England and she married again. He seems to have welcomed the marriage as providing a possible reason for her returning to England also.

In his good-natured, easygoing way he ran through a fortune, and with real courage and industry made himself another from literature. He married an Irishwoman, and after the birth of his two daughters, his wife became incurably insane and had to be removed. He had sentimental relations with other women, particularly the wife of a friend named Brookfield, but they seem to have gone no further. In life he appears as a man who was both courageous and kindly.

But his novels are not courageous, nor are they in the least kindly. *Vanity Fair* is no mere random choice of a title; it expresses the whole meaning of the book. It is a wonderful novel, and a highly original one. Among English novels it comes closest to the Russian ideal of organic form, of a story that tells itself without recourse to invention by virtue of a certain unity of viewpoint and tone. The viewpoint, however, is an exceedingly disillusioned one. The mainspring of all human actions, if we are to believe the author, is self-interest. From the servant girl up to the Princess, the only motive to be distinguished is that of getting something for oneself. Intelligent people recognize this and act accordingly, and those who do not, behave as they do because their self-interest is of a different sort or because they are too stupid to do anything else. "To part with money is a sacrifice beyond almost all men endowed with a sense of order. There is scarcely any man alive who does not think himself meritorious for giving his neighbour five pounds. Thriftless gives, not from a beneficent pleasure in giving, but from a lazy delight in spending." Virtue, in Thackeray's eyes, is always weak or stupid. "She was a very good woman," he says of Lady Grizzel, "good to the poor, stupid, blameless, unsuspicious." If she had been an out-and-out criminal, he could not have blasted her more effectively.

This means that the contrast Thackeray sets up between instinct and judgment differs widely from that of all other novelists I know of. In Jane Austen the instinct represents the imaginative life, while the judgment represents morality. In Stendhal the instinct is also an aspect of the imagination, though the judgment usually represents irony. In Thackeray it would almost seem as if the instinct always represented some form of weakness, while the judgment represented selfishness. At any rate, it is he who links the two in describing Osborne's behavior after his son, George, is killed at Waterloo.

> Which of us is there can tell how much vanity lurks in our warmest regard for others and how selfish our love is? Old Osborne did not speculate much on the mingled nature of his feelings, and how his instinct and selfishness were combating together.

The thinking here is childish, as Thackeray's thinking so often is; it is the price one has to pay for so disillusioned a viewpoint; and, for what it is worth, the point he is making had been dealt with pretty effectively by Christ in the parable of the Good Samaritan. But it is clear from this, as from many other passages, that he regards instinct as weakness; selfishness, for all that he affects to denounce it, as strength. It was his preoccupation with selfishness which made him so much better a historian of his period than Dickens.

It is also characteristic of the novel that its real heroine, Becky Sharp, is an adventuress and the personification of human selfishness. She is also, by the same token, a prostitute and a murderess, though Thackeray deals gingerly with those aspects of her character while grumbling at the necessity for doing so. At the same time, what makes the book so remarkable is that, whether Thackeray likes it or not, he turns her into the heroine and even, in his shallow way, tries to defend her. "And who knows but Rebecca was right in her speculations, and that it was only a question of money and fortune which made the difference between her and an honest woman?"

Who *does* know? The answer quite obviously is "Thackeray and no one but Thackeray." The mere fact that the question can be asked at all shows that Becky Sharp is something more than a character in a novel. If one wishes to prove it, one need only turn to Trollope's picture of Lady Eustace in *The Eustace Diamonds*. As Trollope himself knew, Lady Eustace is Becky Sharp's sister, but such a question would be absurd as applied to Lady Eustace. Trollope's character has not become, like Thackeray's, a household word, but perhaps for that very reason she is a consistent, unshakable portrait of an adventuress. Three sentences are sufficient to show how Trollope understands her.

In the ordinary scenes of ordinary life, such as befell her during her visit to Fawn Court, she could not acquit herself well. There was no reality about her, and the want of it was strangely plain to most unobservant eyes. But give her a part to play that required exaggerated strong action, and she hardly ever failed.

But Becky's appeal is deeper than Lady Eustace's, and

it is deeper because, though she is to a certain extent a character, she is also a point of view, and that point of view is very close to Thackeray's own, at least to that part of it which he would have attributed to his judgment. Becky lives by discovering the weak points of others and flattering their vanity or stimulating their lusts while herself remaining quite cold and, indeed, good-humored about it all. Becky is "bad," but she is also clever.

Now Amelia, her protagonist, is of course "good," but she is also intolerably stupid. And here we come to the most interesting point in Thackeray's moral dilemma. Amelia is also a mother in a sense in which Becky is not a mother at all. There was something about maternity that fascinated Thackeray, apparently because it broke down the crust of egotism and selfishness in a woman and left her vulnerable to circumstances. In an admirable passage of analysis, Lord David Cecil has pointed out the inconsistency of Becky Sharp's boxing her child's ears when she finds him listening to her singing, and argues quite correctly that "people of her temperament neglect their children, but their very selfishness makes them good-natured to them." At the same time, this is not slipshod writing on Thackeray's part, as Cecil believes. It is quite deliberate and considered, and the same attitude is repeated again and again in the latter part of the book. Becky, as one of her lovers informs us, cannot like children "any more than the Devil can like holy water," and again and again we are told flatly that "gentle thoughts and simple pleasures were odious to Mrs. Becky; they discorded with her; she hated people for liking them; she spurned children and children-lovers." This is not carelessness, but a contradiction in Becky's character required by the fact that she is something other than a character, by the fact that she represents a point of view.

Becky is part of the antithesis that racks Thackeray more than any other novelist I know of. Every great writer, of course, has such antitheses; no matter how much of his material he draws from real life, his characters and situations necessarily form masses and contradict one another in ways that ultimately reveal the whole bent of his nature, but few writers are trying to balance such an unstable antithesis as Thackeray. Becky *cannot* like children because she is antithetical to Amelia, who can like nothing else. This was one of the ways his instinct operated, and if he had to have good women, he preferred them as mothers. When dealing with them he sometimes becomes unendurably mawkish, almost obscene.

As his eyes opened and his mind expanded, under the influence of the outward nature round about him, she taught the child, to the best of her humble power, to acknowledge the Maker of All; and every night and every morning he and she—(in that awful and touching communion which I think must bring a thrill to the heart of every man who witnesses or who remembers it)—the mother and the little boy—prayed to Our Father together, the mother pleading with all her gentle heart, the child lisping after her as she spoke. And each time they prayed God to bless dear papa, as if he were alive and in the room with them.

It is scarcely possible to believe that this was not writ-

ten with the shadow of a sneer, and, indeed, remembering
the Crystal Palace ode and the skit on the same subject
that accompanied it, I wonder if Thackeray could ever be
unselfconsciously emotional. But this was as earnest as
he could be, because Amelia—as he, Mrs. Brookfield,
and her husband all agreed—was inspired by Mrs. Brookfield. He had not concealed the Brookfield relationship
from his mother, and she had done her best to console him.
This is how he described her to Mrs. Brookfield at the
time.

I look at her character and go down on my knees as it were
with wonder and pity. It is Mater Dolorosa, with a heart bleeding with love. Is not that a pretty phrase? I wrote it yesterday
in a book, whilst I was thinking about her—and have no shame
somehow now in writing thus sentimentally to all the public;
though there are very few people in the world to whom I
would have the face to talk in this way tete-a-tete.

There is little question but that there was in Thackeray
a childish strain that attracted him to women who resembled his mother, women who were soft, stupid, and
indulgent. And there is no question but that the mature
man in him was attracted to women of a very different
type—cold, sensual, calculating women like Becky Sharp,
Blanche Amory, and Beatrix Esmond. That is why
Vanity Fair has the eternal appeal of its originality. It is
the only novel written by a man of mature mind which
makes a cold-hearted scheming adventuress into a heroine,
and does it so successfully that, in spite of ourselves, we
are charmed into accepting her point of view.

3.

It is the same conflict that gives us one of the most remarkable novels in English. Trollope, a discerning man, once told Thackeray that *Esmond* was not only his best work, but so much his best that there was none second to it. It is a historical novel, but Thackeray did not make it so merely for the sake of romantic effect. He did so because, as I have said, his was a historical imagination and he liked in history to see the representation of his own feelings on the vanity of earthly things. Here everything turns into one of the memorials he loved. Another advantage of history was that it enabled him to see things in antithesis, like those characters in *Finnegans Wake* whose names and natures change, but whose attitude persists. This, too, is characteristic of the historical imagination, wryly and wistfully fascinated by the extremes to which poor simple mortals extend their fantasies. We can see it already in *Vanity Fair* in the scene in which Lord Steyne eggs on his sons' tutor, the parson, and his wife's chaplain, the Catholic priest, with "Bravo, Latimer!" and "Well said, Loyola!" alternately, the historical echoes deepening the mockery. *Esmond* is full of such antitheses: Catholic and Protestant, Tory and Whig, Webb and Marlborough, Old World and New World, France and England—the whole overshadowed by the real antithesis of mother and daughter, Amelia Sedley and Becky Sharp.

Besides, for him who loved to pull off the romantic masks, history provided the perfect field of observation and mockery. How else could he have drawn such a character as Marlborough, the greatest general of his age and the most venal of men, or, on the Jacobite side, the Pretender, "content to lay the dignity of his birth and grief at the wooden shoes of a French chambermaid and to repent . . . in ashes taken from the dust-pan"? There is Harley, Marlborough's rival, who "disdained no more than the great fallen competitor of his the meanest arts, flatteries, intimidations that would secure his power," and St. John, "whose talk was always of liberty," but who "no more shrank from using persecution and the pillory against his opponents than if he had been at Lisbon and Grand Inquisitor." It is not only that in history one can see all those things which are hidden from us by the conventions and pretenses of contemporary life, but that one can see them without pain, the charity (or contempt) of indifference and forgetfulness descending upon all alike. Vanity Fair! Vanity Fair!

Yet even in history Thackeray is stopped dead by certain types—Swift, for instance. Though the antithetical portraits of Steele and Addison are a joy, Swift's one brief appearance is in the form of a gross and brutal caricature. What was it in Swift that Thackeray always resented so deeply? Perhaps it was that there was more than a bit of the vulgarian in Thackeray's make-up, and that Swift's lofty scorn saved him, even among the dead, from being patronized by a bounder.

But the most important thing in *Esmond*, the thing that makes it a masterpiece, is the solution of the personal conflict that rages in *Vanity Fair*. The truth is, as I have said, that though Thackeray was attracted to Amelia Sedley, he was really in love with Becky Sharp, and in *Esmond* he can express that love, but express it side by side with the contradictory love that stemmed from his mother. That this is not a mere accident is shown by the peculiar and elaborate construction that makes it possible for Esmond to regard Lady Castlewood as a mother. The antithesis is the same as in other books; Beatrix is as worldly as her mother is unworldly, but this time worldliness and unworldliness are elevated onto one plane. The reader should notice in particular the very peculiar lighting in the scenes that describe the two women and Esmond, for again and again we get their heads set against the light, so that the gleam about them suggests a halo. This is not at all a simple mechanical trick, for whenever it occurs it produces in the reader a curious romantic shock. "I knew you would come, my dear, and saw the gold sunshine round your head." But the whole book is full of light-metaphors that produce an extraordinary brilliance of effect, as in that wonderful entrance of Beatrix with the candle in her hand, which makes the reader sigh with the author: "As he thinks of her, he who writes feels young again, and remembers a paragon."

In these two women Thackeray was at last able to fuse the two sides of his character, that which hankered after his mother and that which hankered after cold, sensual, worldly women, and to unite them in one family, so that when Esmond marries the mother he establishes a new and intimate relationship with the daughter. It is not too much to say that *Esmond* succeeds because it is the perfect solution of an Œdipal situation that underlies all Thackeray's work. That sort of situation is not at all unusual, for Stendhal analyzed it very acutely in himself, nor is it in the least abnormal; it is the way in which life resolves an inescapable conflict between a boy's love of his mother and of the woman who will be his children's mother. It is, perhaps, more important in Thackeray because it requires something of the kind to account for a quality that every critic perceives in him. For Cecil, in his excellent essay, it is "a false note." For me it is a despondency more deeply rooted than Hardy's, a truly Nordic gloom. I do not think it farfetched to suggest that this gloom originated in the years when Thackeray, a boy of six, welcomed his mother's remarriage in the hope that it would hasten her return to him.

In most writers there is an adolescent element that never grows up, no matter how phenomenal their development in other directions may be. In Thackeray it is childish rather than adolescent, and if Harry Esmond is the perfect hero of the perfect children's book, it is because in effect he carries out the small boy's daydream of marrying his own mother.

The Quest for Integral Truth

chapter 9

Turgenev and the Cult of the Will

By 1850 the sort of story-telling practiced by Dickens, Balzac, and Gogol was already old-fashioned. In France, Flaubert was denouncing the brutal materialism of Balzac; in England, Trollope was saying that none of Dickens's characters were human beings at all: "It has been the peculiarity and the marvel of this man's power that he has invested his puppets with a charm that enabled him to dispense with human nature." Exactly the same sort of thing was being said by Turgenev about Balzac. "All his characters are so marvelously typical, they are so exquisitely worked out and finished to the last detail—and yet not one of them has lived or ever could have lived, and not one of them possesses even one particle of the truth which makes the characters of Tolstoy's *Cossacks*, for instance, so marvelously alive." Even Gogol, for whose memory Turgenev had suffered exile, failed to satisfy him. "I am feeling more and more where Gogol's shoe pinches. The striving after impartiality and integral truth is one of the few good qualities for which I am grateful to Nature." In fact, all over Europe, novelists were reverting to the standard and practice of Jane Austen and Stendhal.

In this new phase the Russian novelists were the luckiest, for not only were they dealing with entirely new material, but they were also writing for and about a people that still lived spiritually in the eighteenth century. Members of the Russian aristocracy took up this peculiarly middle-class form and wrote novels and stories that use the whole of society for their material, whereas in other countries—particularly in England, where social stratification was well defined—characters tend to be falsified whenever they move outside the author's own class. Contemporary snobbery affected to prefer Thackeray to Dickens because Thackeray knew how to describe gentlemen while Dickens did not, and this is also Mme de Villeparisis's complaint of Balzac, as recorded by Proust. That peculiar unity of tone which Jane Austen achieved by artificially limiting her material occurs quite naturally in the work of Turgenev and Tolstoy.

Not only this, but the fact that the whole of Russian society had one foot in the eighteenth century means also that the ideas of order proper to that age are reintroduced into the novel. Turgenev and Tolstoy are orderly writers as Stendhal and Jane Austen are orderly writers. Though they use local color in the same way as Dickens and Balzac, they use it with economy and grace.

In Turgenev's *Sportsman's Sketches*, which were being published throughout the forties, we find this new, artistic story-telling, and with it a new technical device that was to be very important in the history of Russian literature, above all in the short story, though in a different way it also influenced the novel. If we compare a detective story with a novel of Trollope's, for instance, we see that Trollope has to tell his story in precisely the same way as the detective-story writer, rousing the reader's curiosity and burning up a certain amount of interest in the satisfaction of it. Every novel that rouses curiosity loses something in the rereading; a novel that rouses *only* curiosity can scarcely be reread. The narrative line of a story is a horizontal one, a line through time, but the true story-teller simultaneously creates a vertical, spatial movement about it without interrupting it. Every development in the art of story-telling from Scott's use of local color to Joyce's dissociated metaphor has this end in view.

What Turgenev did in *A Sportsman's Sketches* was to graft on to the dynamic narrative line the formal static quality of an essay or a poem. Actually, it would seem as if the modern short story derives from the sort of travel book which flourished during the Enlightenment and afterward, and which had titles like *Manners and Customs of the Scottish Highlanders* and *Traits and Stories of the Irish Peasantry. A Sportsman's Sketches* is the sublimation of such a book, for it has a vague general subject that enables the writer to take the when, where, and how of the novelist and tale-teller for granted. At a pinch, one can say that the stories illustrate the life of a huntsman or the lives of peasants in a particular area of Russia in the beginning of the nineteenth century. The stories require no particular formal structure; they are assimilated to the essay form. Of all story-tellers before Turgenev one may say that their work is an imaginative rearrangement of historic material. There seems to be no *a priori* reason why one should assume that Turgenev's work is anything but historic material, and it is clear that this is the meaning he attributes to "integral truth."

If we take the most beautiful of these stories, written in 1851, *Byezhin Meadow*, we find that it contains only a shadow of narrative line. Mainly, it is a lengthy description of the narrator alone with a group of small boys who are herding the family horses on the prairie during the summer nights, and who pass the long hours telling ghost stories. They scare themselves with these, and when one of the boys, Paul, goes to the river for water, he fancies he hears the voice of a drowned comrade calling him. Even this dramatic episode is deliberately written in a low key.

"Well, boys," he began after a silence, "there's something bad."

"What?" asked Kostya hurriedly.

"I heard Vassily's voice."

Everyone shuddered.

"What's that you say?" whispered Kostya.

"So help me God. I'd just begun to bend down to the water and suddenly I heard my name being called in Vassily's voice, as if it was from under the water. 'Pavel, Pavel, come here!' I went away. I got the water, though."

"Good Lord!" said the boys, crossing themselves.

"That was a water-goblin calling you, Pavel," added Fedya. "And we were just talking about Vassily."

"Oh, that's a bad sign," said Ilyusha with deliberation.

"Well, never mind, forget about it," said Pavel resolutely, and sat down again. "You can't escape your fate."

One cannot help noticing how all through the key is deliberately lowered, effect after effect is thrown away, and how even the slight surprise of the climax is passed over with studied nonchalance. "I am sorry to say that Pavel died before the year was out. He was not drowned, but killed by a fall from a horse. A pity, he was a splendid lad." Turgenev almost gives away his method in a single sentence: "He was not drowned, but killed by a fall from a horse." Here we can see him discounting the narrative shock to prevent the reader's attention straying from the real effect he is trying to make. This is eerie, too, but of a different order of eeriness from that of the corpse on the stair or the ghost in the cellar. His theme is the mystery of human existence, of humanity faced with the spectacle of infinity. *Le silence éternal de ces espaces infinis m'effraie.*

All the Russians did not adopt this technique—Leskov, for instance, continued to write the old-fashioned tale with great originality and beauty—but those, like Chekhov, who did adopt it have an artistry that is lacking in other nineteenth-century story-tellers, and compose stories with the very minimum of episodic interest. "To do something with the least possible number of movements is the definition of grace," according to Chekhov. It isn't, but it is the definition of the peculiar grace we find in the stories of Turgenev and himself.

2.

In his novels Turgenev attempted to do what he had already done with the short story. He invented a new form for them. Their form is organic, not imposed. There is no such thing in them as a real intrigue, and the reader's curiosity is only mildly roused. People meet, talk in a civilized way about subjects of civilized interest, fall in love, and either marry or separate. They do not commit murder or suicide. The emotions evoked by them are reflective and philosophical rather than dramatic or violent.

The novels have a grace that has—mistakenly, I think —been called "classical." We do not have to study characters walking a tightrope of narrative, but see them, more or less as they are, in everyday life, so far as artistic form permits it. The disadvantage of intrigue is that we do not see characters in normal circumstances, and tend to lose interest in them when we find that they are not going to fall off the rope—still more when we know that they are. Tolstoy, who followed Turgenev's example in the use of organic form, argued that in the novel of intrigue "the interest in events predominates over the interest in details of feeling," which is true. But in this there is a fundamental difference between the short story and the novel. Intrigue has the great advantage of enabling a novelist to make his characters show their paces, to submit them to a variety of tests and develop them in unexpected ways. Without the missing check in *The Last Chronicle of Barset* we should never have been able to plumb the full depth of Crawley's misanthropy.

But, above all, intrigue imposes a standard of mere relevance, and saves the English novel from the atmosphere of utter irrelevance we so often find in Russian novels —in *Anna Karenina*, for instance, where anyone who believes in the relevance of the title to what he is reading is liable to go clean off his head. And, for all Turgenev's grace and precision, he seems to me to make mistakes that would be quite impossible in a novel of intrigue.

A House of Gentlefolk provides an excellent example. Turgenev begins in his usual way with a number of charming chapters that describe everyday life in the Kalitin household. It is only in the seventh chapter that the principal character, Lavretsky, appears; and in the eighth chapter begins a flashback of nine consecutive chapters that describe his background and upbringing, youth and marriage. To me these chapters are an inexcusable error in construction. Turgenev has begun at the wrong point.

But there are far more serious weaknesses in Turgenev than those of form. He was a man of extraordinary intelligence with a passion for social justice as sincere as that of any of his revolutionary contemporaries and considerably more mature. Believing that Russia was a bad case of arrested development, he insisted that her only salvation lay in the adoption of Western methods and institutions. He had no patience with the Slavophile group who believed in a special Russian mission to save the world. Even nationalism exasperated him. "For a man with a heart," he wrote, "there is only one fatherland—democracy—and if the Russians are victorious, this will receive its death-blow."

These are typical liberal sentiments, and they brought him under fire from two opposing groups, the Slavophiles, who may be described as rudimentary fascists, and the radicals, who believed that literature existed merely to subserve social ends. Like Chekhov at the end of the century, he was batted about by the two parties. It was not that he did not see that the radical criticism was as meaningless as the Slavophile. He had himself a superb critical intelligence, and knew and repeated that literature has a value in itself apart from and superior to its views and tendencies, and that "to a man of letters, politics is poison." But *A Sportsman's Sketches* had been given credit for influencing opinion in the emancipation of the serfs, and for the rest of his days Turgenev tended to translate everything into political terms. It seems an extraordinary thing to say of this exquisite artist, but he scarcely wrote a significant story that is not political. Even in later years, when he had begun to suspect the "Art for Art's sake" creed of Flaubert and his French friends and wished to describe his own disillusionment, he planned to describe it in the form of a novel dealing with the difference between French and Russian socialists.

It is part of the price that Russian writers had to pay for the political backwardness of their country. For even when the Russian novel seems to be at its most European, most classical, most eighteenth-century, it suddenly reveals an extraordinary self-consciousness; the sort of rambling, self-critical, self-centered clumsiness one associates with a provincial capital.

And this is where we touch on Turgenev's real weakness as a novelist. The liberal views he expressed in opposition to the paralysis of Russian traditional life ran counter to something very deep in himself. His own will had been damaged by a wretched childhood. His half-crazy mother, an unconscious Lesbian, was a neurotic who expressed her masculine protest in the flogging of her male slaves and of her sons. Everything in her was dictated by this hatred of masculinity, and she wrote to Turgenev as though he were a girl, addressing him as *"ma chère fille, ma Jeanette"* and telling him that "she alone had conceived him." Hence the gossip about his effeminacy, about his protests against his valet's bullying —"You're clever and I'm a fool, but I know enough to know when I'm cold"—and the obvious masochism—an inheritance from a sadistic mother—that led to the lifelong frustration of his affair with Pauline Viardot and his admission that he was happy only when some woman put her foot on his neck and ground his nose into the dirt. There were minor contributory factors linked with this: his Hegelianism and Byronism and early love of poetry, which finally led to his guying philosophy and developing a distrust for poetry second only to Jane Austen's.

The tragedy of his allowing himself to slant his novels politically was that he was doing something for which he was totally unequipped by nature. He translated his own personal problems into political terms, and so produced something that is neither a real personal revelation, like the novels of Jane Austen, which his in so many ways resemble, nor a serious objective study like his own *Sportsman's Sketches*. Nobody can reread these novels over a period of thirty years, as I have done, without being driven frantic by the feeling that their political superstructure has little or nothing to do with the substructure and consists largely of rationalizations and symbols. The substructure resembles the substructure in the novels of Jane Austen and Stendhal; it is a straightforward personal conflict between the instincts and the judgment. But in the superstructure this conflict is being transformed into one between the old Russia, with its witchcraft and brutality, and the new Russia, which Turgenev anticipated rather than saw, and to which he attributed the virtues he believed he saw in Europe. And in this process, which I can describe only as misplaced generalization, the whole conflict is being utterly distorted and real reconciliation made impossible because the real problems of Russia, on the one hand, are being ignored in favor of the imaginary problems of Turgenev, while the real problems of Turgenev are distorted into the imaginary problems of Russia. The denunciations of Russia for idleness, laziness, and lack of willpower turn out to be denunciations of Turgenev himself. He is his own Russia, the giant with the paralyzed will. And this is not genuine personal self-criticism like Stendhal's, but an arbitrary despondent attitude like Thackeray's.

Even his criticism tells us only about himself. *Hamlet and Don Quixote* describes the contradiction in different terms, but it is precisely the same contradiction. He is Hamlet, dreamy, cynical, and ineffectual, while the work of the world is done by the Quixotes, even if they are only tilting at windmills. And even suppose we say that Quixote is mad, "Who," Turgenev asks, "knows exactly where reality ceases and fantasy begins?"

3.

One can see all this in *On the Eve*, which, though it is not his best novel, illustrates both his strength and weakness as a novelist. The idea of the book came to him, we are told, in the form of the character of Yelena, the heroine, but "a hero was lacking, a person of such character that Yelena, with her powerful though still vague yearning for freedom, could abandon herself to him."

This character appeared when a friend showed Turgenev a manuscript account of his own early love for a young woman he had met in Moscow. Later this girl got to know a Bulgarian named Katranov, "fell in love with him and went away with him to Bulgaria, where he soon died." When he read through his friend Karatyeev's notebook, Turgenev says he cried involuntarily: "That's the hero I've been looking for."

"In sharp contrast to the hero of the novel," says Turgenev's excellent translator, Mr. Gardiner, "who was without artistic sensibility, Katranov was a poet and had had both original work and translations published."

This is perceptive, but not quite accurate, and overlooks the typical dilemma of Turgenev whenever he has to deal with poetry. Turgenev certainly intended that, unlike Katranov, his hero, Insarov, should have no feeling for poetry, but he made a singularly bad mess of the operation, for when we first meet Insarov, he is translating Bulgarian songs and chronicles. We are not required to believe that these are necessarily good translations because when he reads them to Bersenyev, the latter "thought the translations were accurate, but not sufficiently lively." Then a few pages later Shubin describes Insarov as having "talent, none, poetry a blank," which is clearly Turgenev's intention regarding him. Yet a little farther on, Insarov himself says to Yelena: "We have such wonderful songs. As good as the Serbian. But just wait, I'll translate one of them for you." This may be the language of a man who is not himself a poet, but emphatically it is not the language of a man with no taste for poetry. And yet, twenty pages later we find Yelena saying: "We two have tastes in common; and neither of us cares for poetry or understands art."

In those very contradictory impressions we catch a glimpse of the conflict in Turgenev himself, a conflict that distinctly resembles the conflict in Jane Austen. She distrusts poetry (by which she is obviously deeply attracted), seeing it as a way of weakening the judgment; Turgenev distrusts it as a way of weakening the will. He found it difficult to make a hero of a man who did not love poetry, but impossible to believe that a man who loved poetry as he did could be a hero. Poetry belongs to the Hamlets, not to the Quixotes, who do the world's work. Turgenev was a man saturated in poetry who attributed all the weaknesses of his character to an overindulgence in it, and his only conception of a hero was a man so compact of will that he would have no time for such dissipation of energy.

Insarov, then, is the Quixote principle as opposed to the Hamlet principle of Shubin. Turgenev's complaint is that there are no such people in Russia, only Hamlets, dreamers, gasbags. One may love such people, but one cannot possibly respect them; they are, to quote his own phrase, "superfluous men." He has only one notion of a hero: someone who never reverses a decision, as he never fails to carry out a promise. Insarov, unlike the dreamy Russians with whom he is contrasted, chucks a drunken German in the water. "He doesn't only talk—he's done things and is going to do things." "He is a man of iron" we are told elsewhere. Trollope, with his conviction that firmness of purpose was merely another name for hardness of heart, would scarcely have approved.

But it is Insarov, and not Shubin or Bersenyev, for all their tenderness and charm, who gets away with the girl Yelena. As the superfluous men represent the physical body of Russia, the typical Turgenev heroines represent its soul, and she gives herself without question to the first man of action who crosses her path. Chekhov, an exceedingly masculine man, detested Turgenev's heroines, and small wonder, for it is to them that Turgenev grants the willpower that he felt was lacking in himself. For all his supposed masculinity, it is not Insarov who makes the pace, but Yelena. "You want to force me to say that I love you," she says. "There—I've said it." So, too, Rudin in the novel of that name says admiringly of Natalie: "What strength of will!" A man who could be happy only with a woman's foot on his neck could scarcely have denied his heroines initiative.

In *Fathers and Sons* Turgenev does what Jane Austen did in *Mansfield Park*, and produces what could almost be described as a caricature of his own method. Insarov may have been permitted a mild interest in folk poetry, but Bazarov dissects frogs. He is contrasted with the family of his adoring young disciple, Arkady—gentle, vague, and, above all, poetic. "A good chemist is more useful than a score of poets" is one of the remarks by which he shatters the Old World complacency of the Kirsanovs. Arkady's father, Nikolai, is in a really bad way.

"A couple of days ago I caught him reading Pushkin," Bazarov went on meanwhile. "Will you please explain to him that this won't do? He's no youth, it's time he gave up such nonsense. Where's the sense in being a romantic nowadays? Give him something practical to read."

As in *Sense and Sensibility*, love of landscape beauty is another intolerable affectation to Bazarov, though where Edward admires scenery that "combines beauty with utility," Bazarov declares that "Nature is merely a workshop and man the craftsman." It is all too much for old Kirsanov, who goes about muttering: "But to reject poetry? To lack all feeling for art, for Nature . . ." It is all beautifully done, but one would be so much happier if only one felt that Turgenev were doing it with his tongue in his cheek. It is one of those occasions when I feel that we cannot be too grateful for the English novel with its inherent sense of proportion. When Bazarov talks of old Kirsanov reading Pushkin, I am irresistibly reminded of Marianne Dashwood's view that "a woman of seven and twenty can never hope to feel or inspire affection again; and if her home be uncomfortable or her fortune small, I can suppose that she might bring herself to submit to the offices of a nurse, for the sake of the provision and security of a wife," but I wish I could feel that Turgenev were laughing with me instead of generalizing Bazarov's half-baked views into an attitude to life, and, worse, an attitude to life which Turgenev himself respects. This, of course, is only one aspect of the book, which mounts to a tragic climax impressive even in Turgenev, but it is not one an admirer can afford to ignore.

And it is apparent even in novels in which there is no man of action, novels like *Smoke*, in which Turgenev projects his own tragic obsession with Pauline Viardot, the snake-woman who appears in so many of his stories and wreaks havoc on men's lives. For even here the little drama of betrayal and disillusionment is played out against a background of chattering Russians, radical and aristocratic, and somehow all the time it is as though Turgenev is trying to persuade us that Gregory Litvinov betrays Tatiana because he is a Russian like them, because to the Russian everything is "smoke," a passion for chemistry which sends a hundred Russian students to Heidelberg one year and next year produces only thirteen. But in fact the two things have absolutely nothing to do with each other, and the personal drama is being robbed of most of its intensity by the political drama that it seems to evoke. It is as though Turgenev, endlessly brooding over his own weakness with regard to his mother, his weakness with regard to Pauline Viardot's promiscuity, rationalizes it all in political or racial terms. "The Russians are this, the Russians are that. It's the fault of history, of tradition, of philosophy or poetry or something else." The cloud of rationalization comes between him and the object till he can no longer see it clearly.

Yet the fact is that he could, on occasion, see clearly.

There is only one of the novels which seems to me to be first-rate. That is the comparatively little-known *Torrents of Spring*. In form it is almost identical with *Smoke*. Like *Smoke*, it has a German setting. A young man, Sanine, falls in love with and becomes engaged to a pretty Italian-German girl, and then allows himself to be seduced by a wealthy married woman, one of the usual snake-women Turgenev describes. The whole book is a triumph of organic form. No character in it exceeds the dimensions of everyday life, and even the duel scene is leveled out to a mood of semi-comedy. And nowhere does Turgenev try to explain to us why Sanine is a young man of weak character; nor is it necessary for him to do so. The absence of the cloud of rationalization makes this particular novel a joy in the clarity and purity of its atmosphere.

Even so, it does not seem to me to represent Turgenev at his greatest, and at his greatest he was a magnificent writer. I find it hard to follow Edward Garnett and George Moore in their rhapsodies about him. I find it even harder to follow people like Maurice Baring when he says: "If Pushkin is the Mozart of Russian literature, Turgenev is the Schumann; not among the very greatest, but still a poet, full of inspired lyrical feelings, and a great, a classic artist, the prose Virgil of Russian literature." My difficulty may come of the fact that both his admirers and his traducers think of him as "classic." "Classic" is about the last thing I think Turgenev is. To me he is a major writer with colossal faults. Apart from *A Sportsman's Sketches* and *Torrents of Spring*, his most significant works are his long stories or short novels, which are so rarely referred to. In these one can see the conflict in him correctly stated, and the real conflict in Turgenev is not that between contemplation and action, but that between barbarism and civilization. The trouble with Turgenev is that, in the words of the Irish poet, "his back is still aching for the lash." Superficially one can see this even in the novels—for example, the curious caricatures of the old people in *Virgin Soil*, the portraits of Bazarov's parents in *Fathers and Sons*, and the portrait of Arina Vlassyevna in the same book.

Arina Vlassyevna was a genuine Russian gentlewoman of the old school; she might have lived some two centuries back, in the old days of Muscovy. Very devout and impressionable, she believed in all sorts of omens, fortune-telling, charms and dreams; she believed in the visions of mad prophets, in spirits, in wood-sprites, in the evil eye, in spells, in folk remedies, in "Thursday salt," and in the imminent end of the world; she believed that if the candles failed to go out at Vespers on Easter Sunday a good crop of buckwheat would result, and that mushrooms stopped growing when seen by the human eye; she believed that water was the devil's haunt, and that every Jew had a bloody mark on his breast. She was afraid of mice, adders, frogs, sparrows, leeches, thunder, cold water, draughts, horses, goats, ginger-haired people and black cats, and deemed crickets and dogs unclean creatures; she ate no veal or pigeon, crayfish or cheese, asparagus or Jerusalem artichokes, hare, or, finally, watermelon, because a sliced watermelon reminded her of John the Baptist's head.

There are two stories of Turgenev's I should choose to demonstrate both the sort of man he was and the real nature of the conflict in him. Both are marvels of story-telling. *Punin and Baburin* describes his life as a boy on the estate of his terrible mother, the grandmother of the story. In later life he used to point out the window where she sat to survey the wretched peasants she had condemned to exile or the army, and this incident too is resurrected. The story describes two old freaks: Baburin, the illegitimate son of a good family, goes through life nursing his grievance and rescuing lame ducks like Punin, the half-witted old poetaster who shares his room and board. It is the Quixote-and-Hamlet grouping again. Baburin, after being employed by the narrator's grandmother, quarrels with her when she sends one of her peasants into exile, and leaves in disgrace. When the narrator meets him again after seven years, he has picked up another lame duck, an orphan girl also of good blood whom he wishes to marry. But she is carrying on an affair with a friend of the narrator. Twelve years later the two meet again. This time Punin has died, and Musa, having been abandoned by her aristocratic lover, has again been rescued by Baburin, who has married her. By this time, too, he is involved in revolutionary politics, and is finally arrested and sent to Siberia, where she follows him. When he dies there, she, a dedicated soul with something broken in her, remains to continue his work.

In essence this is the material for a Turgenev novel, but the treatment is entirely different. As in *Torrents of Spring*, the cloud of rationalization has disappeared. But unlike *Torrents of Spring*, this story is marred by no generalization of the characters. Musa is no dream-woman. When we meet her first, she is a little cat, a "spitfire," as the narrator calls her, with a woman's love for walking on precipices. Baburin is drawn objectively, and though he commands our respect, it is given against our will. In this story Turgenev has found the real embodiment of his dreams, and it turns out to be something different, sterner, coarser than the embodiment in the novels.

Old Portraits, the second story I choose, is one of those masterpieces which elderly writers sometimes toss off with a mastery of technique that leaves criticism gasping. It is probably one of the three or four great short stories of the world, and is told in a gossipy offhand style that might easily belong to a letter of Mme de Sévigné. Its form is like that of *Torrents of Spring*, a sharp contrast between two ways of life or two attitudes to life. It describes an eighteenth-century couple who sum up all that was finest in their civilization, Alexey Sergeitch and his wife, Malania. Alexey likes talking about the old days and the Empress Catherine, but not too much. "Enough," he says. "Those were good times, but enough of them!" Malania is a complete chatterbox.

Alexey Sergeitch's death is one of the great things of nineteenth-century story-telling in its superb blend of nostalgic sentiment and precise and humorous observation. It is one of the few things in Turgenev that can truly be called "classic," and is as close as makes no difference to great poetry.

"No, no pain . . . but it's difficult . . . difficult to breathe." Then, after a brief silence, "Malania," he said, "so life has slipped by—and do you remember when we were married . . . what a couple we were?" "Yes, we were, my handsome, charming Alexis." The old man was silent again. "Malania, my dear, shall we meet again in the next world?" "I will pray God for it, Alexis," and the old woman burst into tears. "Come, don't cry, silly; maybe the Lord will make us young again then—and again we shall be a fine pair." "He will make us young, Alexis." "With the Lord all things are possible," observed Alexis Sergeitch. "He worketh great marvels—maybe he will make you sensible. . . . There, my love, I was joking; come, let me kiss your hand." "And I yours." And the two old people kissed each other's hands simultaneously.

Then, as if casually, Turgenev slips into a digression about a slave of Alexey Sergeitch, a coachman called Ivan who was "a great joker, a most comic fellow; he was great at all sorts of tricks—he used to fly kites, let off fireworks and rockets, to play all sorts of games, gallop standing up on the horse's back, fly higher than all the rest in the swing and could even make Chinese shadows." Ivan has been one of the family for so long that no one even suspects that he is really someone else's property. When the mistake is discovered and the slave's return demanded, Alexey Sergeitch tries to buy him, but finally has to send him back to the owner, a harsh man who will stand no nonsense. The comic little character threatens to kill his new master, but no one takes him seriously. He repeats his threat when he enters his master's house and is cruelly flogged. Then he appears to settle down, and even becomes friendly with his new master. But one frosty day he says: "I warned you, Ivan Petrovitch—you've only yourself to blame," chops off his master's head, and drives to the court with the body.

"They took Ivan, tried him, sentenced him to the knout, and then to hard labour. The light-hearted, bird-like dancer was sent to the mines and there passed out of sight for ever. . . .

Yes, one can but repeat, in another sense, Alexey Sergeitch's words: "They were good old times, but enough of them."

It is not often that Turgenev lets fly with the thunder-bolt, and when he does, one remembers it forever. But one realizes also that his heart was buried here, in this savage, colorful century, and that it was only his mind that followed Baburin, seeking justice for little Ivan and all the ruined lives it left in its wake.

chapter 10

Tolstoy and the Surrender of the Will

I have deliberately used the word "poetry" about Turgenev, but it is the last word I should use in discussing Tolstoy. Tolstoy's supreme quality as a story-teller is a superb narrative gift that enables him to see and describe with absolute fidelity what his characters are doing and thinking. In every way he is the opposite of Turgenev. If I were to parody a Turgenev novel, I should begin with something like "It was a cold night in late December when an old, white-bearded man of at least thirty-five years was warming his shrunken limbs by the fire while studying the portrait of a beautiful, full-bosomed woman which stood upon his mantelpiece." Turgenev, in other words, is too relaxed, too inclined for an emotional sprawl. Tolstoy, on the other hand, has electricity rather than blood in his veins; his old men have more vitality than Turgenev's young ones, and when I read him I find myself murmuring: "Steady now, old chap! Relax, for God's sake! Everything is going fine. Look out or you'll fall off that bicycle!"

But nothing ever halts Tolstoy. Those tiny, harsh, disjointed sentences ripple on with the whirr of a well-oiled mowing-machine and, wherever they pass, seem to sweep up every detail in their path. It is easy to under-estimate this gift and, as George Moore does, make fun of the way Tolstoy describes the bead of sweat on the maid's neck; but this is the very quality one misses in the German novelists, this plastic sense which makes it possible for him to catch up great masses of detail and give substance to his narrative without ever halting its onward rush. For anyone who wishes to learn the art of writing, he is the perfect model. The dreariest scene comes out as fresh as paint from the minute observations and contradictions of which it is composed. By comparison with Turgenev's narrative style, Tolstoy's has an extraordinarily braced, tonic quality, as though we were breathing the air of great heights. Look at this little passage from *Anna Karenina*.

"What is it?" asked Stepan Arkadyevitch, coming in and addressing his wife.

By the tone of his voice both Kitty and Anna knew that the reconciliation had taken place.

"I wanted to put Anna in here, but we should have to put up curtains. No one knows how to do it, so I must," said Dolly in reply to her husband's question.

"God knows if they have made it up," thought Anna as she noticed Dolly's cold and even tone.

"Don't, Dolly, don't make mountains out of molehills. If you like, I'll arrange everything."

"Yes," thought Anna, "it must have been settled."

"I know how you arrange things," said Dolly with a mocking smile. "You give Matve an order which he doesn't understand, and then you go off and he gets everything into a muddle."

"Complete, complete reconciliation, complete," thought Anna. "Thank God!"

As story-telling, this passage could not be bettered, and it is not exceptional, for it was selected at random, and one could select thousands of equally effective little scenes from Tolstoy's work. Literally, there is not in it a single word that does not carry the reader's attention forward, without recourse to trickery. And yet, as with Turgenev I find myself sometimes wishing for a brisker tone, so with Tolstoy I frequently find myself pining for a more relaxed and meditative one. The air of great heights is all very well, but it gives the reader palpitations. I sympathize with Tolstoy's views about organic form, and agree that in an English novel the intrigue makes the interest in events predominate over the interest in details of feeling, but when I read a passage like the following from *Two Hussars* (and this, too, is not exceptional but typical), I cannot help thinking that details of feeling obscure the feeling itself. He is describing a young officer who has embezzled government money, and this is how he does it:

"I have ruined my young life," he said to himself; not because he really thought he had ruined his young life—he was not, indeed, thinking about it at all—but the phrase happened to occur to his mind.

"What am I to do now?" he meditated. "Borrow from some one and go away." A lady walked along the pavement. "What a foolish-looking lady!" he thought inconsequently. "There's no one to borrow from. I've ruined my young life." He reached the shops. A merchant in a fox-lined cloak was standing at the door of his shop touting for customers. "If I hadn't taken up the eight, I should have made up what I'd lost." An old beggar-woman followed him, whimpering. "There's no one to borrow from." A gentleman in a bear-skinned cloak drove by; a watchman stood still. "What could one do out of the ordinary? Take a shot at these people. No, it's a bore. I've ruined my young life. Ah, these are nice bridles hanging there with ornaments on them. I should like to drive in a sledge now with three horses—ah, the darlings!"

It is a wonderful description of the squall of inconsequence which hits our minds in moments of crisis; the supernumeraries who, in Tolstoy's moments of crisis, always pass by to divert the character's attention; the contradictions that multiply; the repeated phrase "I've ruined my young life," which links the lesser inconsequences, yet is itself the most inconsequent of all. It is all brilliant, but something has been left out—the reader's tendency to palpitations!

2.

The distinction between Turgenev's style and Tolstoy's marks the profound difference between the two men. Turgenev was a democrat, a liberal, and a rationalist, whereas Tolstoy's views developed from a violent conservatism to a still more violent anarchism. Turgenev was gentle and weak-willed; Tolstoy was arrogant and imperious. "I stand in the doorway with a dagger or a sabre and I say 'As long as I live, no one shall enter here. That is what I call conviction.' " It is also what a great many people call exhibitionism.

Yet, different as the two men are, they are alike in one thing: for both of them the real problem is that of the will as judgment. Turgenev feels his own weakness of will almost as a disease, and in his finest work one sees in him the longing to retreat into a traditional intuitive life untroubled by the need for individual action; but though Tolstoy begins by challenging every accepted opinion, he ends by preaching a religion that involves a complete abnegation of the will. Russian literature in its three greatest novelists is haunted by a desire for the surrender of the will, and though this takes on forms familiar to us as Europeans, it is not a European thing at all. It is an Oriental thing, and it marks the real distinction between these great novelists and their English and French contemporaries.

What Tolstoy's friend Fet described as his "involuntary opposition to all accepted opinions" turns out, on examination, to resemble an inferiority complex that puts Stendhal's in the shade. On the face of it, it seems to be purely anarchic. Again we must notice the contrast between him and Turgenev. Turgenev, hampered by and suspicious of the instincts that he attributes to his brutal, domineering mother, is forever in search of a father figure and of any form of authority. When he cannot find one, he invents it, as in Insarov and Bazarov. Tolstoy, on the other hand, who seems to have lived in revolt against the very idea of a father, accepts no authority other than that of his own blind instincts. Or so it would seem, though it is not quite so simple as that.

He challenged all accepted views on literature, art, education, history, war, medicine, religion, and science. He realized—what everyone else who had written on music had failed to perceive—that Beethoven's "Kreutzer" Sonata was a most obscene work. When, in later life, he concluded that *Hamlet* and the Ninth Symphony were bad art, and that *Les Miserables*, *The Christmas Carol*, and *Uncle Tom's Cabin* were good art, he merely defined the sort of thing he had been saying all his life. The former works are bad because they are understood only by small groups of educated people; the latter are good because they appeal to great numbers of simple people to whom they teach moral lessons valuable in themselves. These ideas are neither so perverse nor so paradoxical as they appear, and the understanding of them is essential to any understanding of such novels as *Anna Karenina* and *War and Peace*, for without them the novels could never have been written. Through these ideas Tolstoy transfers to the unconscious mind or the intuitions of great masses of people certain decisions that the individual man tends to regard as his responsibility only.

It is the same with education. The educational authorities in Marseille inflicted on the children in their charge an atrocious curriculum that the citizens remedied as soon as they were old enough by reading *The Three Musketeers*— "an unconscious school undermining a compulsory school and making its contents almost worthless." He started a school himself to show how the job should be done, but the educational authorities in Russia were as blind as those in Marseille, and the children Tolstoy had educated were regarded as rather less bright than those educated in regular schools.

"Natural" art, "natural" education, "natural" religion —these were the things that Tolstoy sought, and they could be found only in the masses. His task was merely to interpret the wisdom of the masses. He had no difficulty in proving that, instead of the ten commandments of the Mosaic law, Christ had left only five: "Do not be angry; do not lust; do not swear oaths; resist not him that is evil; and love your enemies." Christ's own recorded view that no commandments were more important than the first two might safely be ignored: he probably did not understand or had been badly reported. At any rate, the Gospels were in such a shocking state that Tolstoy had to rewrite them himself. Like most people with a mother-directed mind, he was almost devoid of humor, and in real life must, I think, have been a most objectionable man.

He has all Balzac's knowingness with none of his balance and good humor. None of his major works is entirely free of his obsessive anarchism. When Kitty in *Anna Karenina* falls ill, it is merely an occasion for fulminating against doctors, though whether Tolstoy objected to doctors because of their ignorance or the liberty they enjoyed of seeing women naked is not clear. It is the same in *War and Peace* when Natasha falls ill.

They talked much in French, German, and Latin, blamed one another and prescribed a great variety of medicines for all the diseases known to them, but the simple idea never occurred to them that they could not know the disease Natasha was suffering from, as no disease suffered by a live man can be known, for every living person has his own peculiarities, and always has his own peculiar, novel, complicated disease unknown to medicine—not a disease of the lungs, liver, skin, heart, nerves, and so on mentioned in medical books, but a disease consisting of one of the innumerable combinations of the maladies of these organs. This simple thought . . .

The repetition of the word "simple" identifies Tolstoy, as it identifies Balzac, as a bit of a charlatan, for, whatever else this theory of medicine may be, it is certainly not "simple." And in this the doctors are no worse than the military men, for all the generals in the same book make their troop movements without the slightest notion of what the result will be, having failed to observe the "simple" fact that all the circumstances could not be known to them. Accordingly, Tolstoy has to write his enormous novel to correct the errors of the military historians, who not only had failed to observe the same "simple" fact that the generals had failed to observe, but had also failed to observe the "simple" fact that the details of such operations could not be accurately ascertained. To "natural" art, education, and religion, we are now compelled to add "natural" medicine, tactics, and history.

To these we may later add "natural" morality. It took Tolstoy the best part of his life to come to his final conclusions about society, but even then he failed to see why others did not reach them in five minutes. "He asked a very simple question: 'Why and by what right do some men imprison, torture, exile, flog, and kill other men, while they themselves are just like those they torture, flog and kill?' "

There is peculiar appositeness in the fact that, just as Turgenev portrays his ideal self in the form of strong-willed men, Tolstoy portrays his in the form of holy simpletons, Pierre and Levin, to whom are revealed the great truths hidden from the rationalists. Tolstoy was neither holy nor simple, and his portraits of himself are outrageously false, but in one thing he was correct—the significance he attached to the childlike candor he brought to the contemplation of life.

3.

This childlike candor is of very real importance to any artist: it is the hallmark of his originality; it proves that he has a personal vision of life to express. And Tolstoy was among the most original writers who ever lived.

At the same time, a writer of extreme originality like Tolstoy works best when he is dealing with a subject that enables him to express his originality fully. When he deals with doctors, as in the passage from *War and Peace* I have quoted, his originality tends to appear as perversity, and the same is true of the chapters in which he discusses generals and their plans. If *The Cossacks*, which was such a favorite with Turgenev, remains one of the most readable of his books, it is because Tolstoy was writing close to the real source of his inspiration: the wild, natural, instinctive life of those who live far from towns. Tolstoy was profoundly influenced by Rousseau, and he found inspiration in life lived in this particular way. "The people live as nature lives," he writes. "They die, are born, couple, and more are born—they fight, eat, and drink, rejoice and die, without any restrictions but those that nature imposes on sun and grass, on animal and tree."

"There is likewise a wind upon the heath." In a passage like this one can feel the influence of Rousseau, for the description of primitive life is too simplified; nobody really lives or dies like that, least of all a Tolstoy; but it is true that he was closer in spirit to the half-barbarous Cossacks than ever he was to his civilized friends and relatives in Moscow. To begin with, they did not exacerbate his vanity by the imposition of new authorities, and they had none of the conventional attitudes that always roused his anger. On the contrary, the conventional attitudes were now his, while theirs remained fresh and unspoiled. Olenin, who is Tolstoy himself, has such attitudes to love and self-sacrifice, but Lukashka and his sweetheart, Maryanka, have none of them. When Olenin nobly presents Lukashka with a valuable horse, Lukashka feels no conventional gratitude. On the contrary, his mind is filled with vague suspicions that the cadet is playing some clever trick on him and has evil intentions toward him. "What those intentions were he could not decide, but neither could he admit that a stranger would give him a horse worth forty roubles for nothing, just out of kindness." So, too, when Olenin falls in love with Maryanka, her reactions are entirely novel to him.

"Will you marry me?" he had asked.

"You'll deceive me and not have me," she replied cheerfully and calmly.

"But do you love me? Tell me, for God's sake!"

"Why shouldn't I love you? You don't squint."

If Tolstoy's quality as a story-teller is principally his amazing narrative gift, this is related to that secondary quality of giving the reader "no marble, no conventional phrase." It is all original and frequently astonishing.

But you cannot practice originality with impunity. To think conventionally is to think in masses, seeing the object as a painter sees it when he half closes his eyes. When a person we love dies, we usually think of our grief conventionally, suppressing certain details as contradictory and embarrassing. It is part of Tolstoy's genius

157

that he does not suppress these contradictions. It is also part of his weakness that he could not do so, he could not think in masses. In his major works, like *War and Peace* and *Anna Karenina*, there is a withdrawal of conventional attitudes, and the eye of the child, the eye of the barbarian, picks out a wealth of interesting or charming detail, but it picks the details out without sorting them, without suppressing them, without seeking for the significant groupings that the painter tries to discover by half shutting his eyes.

In *War and Peace* there are two passages, very close together, which show him at his worst and best. The former is the description of the opera in Book VIII, in which he plays the well-known eighteenth-century trick of describing a conventional spectacle as it would appear to an outsider unfamiliar with the convention by reducing it to its component details.

First, the man in the tight trousers sang alone, then she sang, then they both paused while the orchestra played and the man fingered the hand of the girl in white, obviously waiting the beat to start singing with her. They sang together and everyone in the theatre began clapping and shouting, while the man and woman on the stage—who represented lovers—began smiling, spreading out their arms, and bowing.

Now, anything Tolstoy ever disliked looked exactly like this to him. It broke up into tiny little pieces like a mosaic falling from a wall. Up to the time of his conversion he regarded religious services as beautiful in themselves, but in *Resurrection* the Mass goes the same way as the opera and *King Lear*.

The priest, robed in a very peculiar and very inconvenient garment made of cloth of gold, cut and arranged small pieces of bread in a saucer: these he put into a cup filled with wine, at the same time uttering various names and prayers.

But when we have studied the description of the opera, it is worth turning back a few pages to read the description of "Uncle's" singing to Natasha.

Uncle sang as peasants sing, with full and naïve conviction that the whole meaning of a song lies in the words, and that the tune comes of itself, and that apart from the words there is no tune, which exists only to give measure to the words. As a result of this, the unconsidered tune, like the song of a bird, was extraordinarily good.

It may be, of course, that Tolstoy is here merely paraphrasing the work of some nineteenth-century folklorist, but even if this were true, the description would still be excellent. I do not think he is quoting any authority; I believe he is writing out of his own unaided observation, and it is a most remarkable observation because this, in fact, is exactly how folk-singers perform all the world over, and this is the secret of their charm.

Now, there is obviously a great deal more to this than the fact that Tolstoy liked folk song and disliked opera. It means that everything he writes is based upon a theory that exaggerates the importance of "nature" and underrates the importance of "art." His mind was slanted toward the intuitive thing represented by folk song and away from the rational thing represented by opera; the freshness and purity of his observation come of the fact that his mind had never been allowed to grow abstract with general ideas or stale with conventions; but his intellectual limitations, which were many and serious, come from the same source. It is something of the same attitude, with something of the same limitations, that is familiar to us in D. H. Lawrence.

Those intellectual limitations are all over his masterpiece, *War and Peace*. It contains some of his greatest writing, and yet it is exceedingly hard to read. I do not think one is unduly put off by its length. Proust's novel is longer and I have rarely wished it less. *The Brothers Karamazov* is exceedingly long and digressive, but it holds my attention in a way that *War and Peace* has never done.

This may be due partly to the fact that Tolstoy used organic rather than imposed form. Organic form is excellent when the material itself is organic: when the book deals with one simple action and one simple group of people. When, as in *War and Peace* and *Anna Karenina*, it deals with a complex of actions and several groups of people, the relations between whom cannot be satisfactorily established, it tends to make the whole book amorphous. We are back to our old difficulty with the English novel. Here, perhaps, "the interest in events tends to dominate over the interest in details of feeling," but in *War and Peace* the interest in details of feeling certainly dominates over the interest in events, which is a peculiar thing to say of a book that professes to be history.

But that is not really the main weakness of the novel. That weakness is intellectual. Beside the story of a group of families which forms the substance of the book runs another novel that might have been called *Order and*

Anarchy. The villain of this interesting historical novel is Napoleon, who acts and thinks in an orderly way and believes that he is influencing events. The hero is the aged Kutuzov, who does not really try to influence anything, but eats chicken, says his prayers, reads a novel, or falls asleep at important moments, thus allowing events to dictate their own progression. Napoleon is opera, Kutuzov folk song; Napoleon is the educational authority of Marseille, Kutuzov is the Marseille public that educates itself by reading Dumas. In other words, Kutuzov merely represents the anonymous mass of the Russian people, and what he really does is to refer to their unconscious mind or intuition the responsibility for the decisions that arrogant, intellectual men believe themselves to have taken.

Now, this attitude overflows into the first novel, *War and Peace* proper, in several ways. It overflows into the complex of actions and the multiplicity of groups which give the book its amorphous air. It is not only that Tolstoy wished to describe such groups and actions. It is also that his peculiar attitude to the individual made it impossible for him to create a book organized about one strong central figure, for any such figure would, of necessity, have stolen the story in the way in which Napoleon has stolen the history books.

It also explains why it is so exceedingly hard to become familiar with any of the characters who are presented in such brilliant detail. Again, it is not only that Tolstoy would have considered it blasphemy to understand a character in the way in which Jane Austen or Trollope understood a character; it is also that he was incapable of doing so. His genius was for feeling rather than for understanding; he feels his characters very deeply, particularly the younger women, whose instinctive and almost animal perceptions were so very close to his own. Take the description of Natasha on her rampage through the house.

"What can I do? where can I go?" thought she, as she went slowly along the passage.

"Nastasya Ivanovna, what sort of children shall I have?" she asked the buffoon who was coming towards her in a woman's jacket.

"Why, fleas, crickets, grasshoppers," answered the buffoon.

"O Lord, O Lord, it's always the same! Oh, where am I to go? What am I to do with myself?" And, tapping with her heels, she ran quickly upstairs to see Vogel and his wife, who lived on the upper story.

Two governesses were sitting with the Vogels at a table on which were plates of raisins, walnuts, and almonds. The governesses were discussing whether it was cheaper to live in Moscow or Odessa. Natasha sat down, listened to their talk with a serious and thoughtful air, and then got up again.

"The island of Madagascar," she said. "Ma-da-gas-car," she repeated, articulating each syllable distinctly, and, not replying to Madame Schloss, who asked what she was saying, she went out of the room.

Her brother, Petya, was upstairs too. With the man in attendance on him, he was preparing fireworks to let off that night.

"Petya, Petya!" she called to him. "Carry me downstairs."

Petya ran up and offered her his back. She jumped on it, putting her arms round his neck and he pranced along with her.

"No, don't . . . the island of Madagascar," she said, and, jumping off his back, she went downstairs.

Nobody else had ever written quite like that. It is delightful in its spontaneity and vividness, but though feeling may do very well for a shorter story, it seems to me insufficient to sustain interest in a character over such an enormous span as *War and Peace* presents. I never grasp Natasha in the way I grasp Emma, whose author understands her both emotionally and intellectually, or the old prince as I grasp Mr. Crawley, who is understood even more than he is felt—and he is felt very deeply indeed.

Anna Karenina shows a very interesting development in Tolstoy's thought. In *War and Peace* he had taken the attitude he had advocated in *The Cossacks* and made it into something like a universal system that required great masses of people to express it fully. *Anna Karenina*, which, in my own view at least, is in some ways an even finer book, follows a similar plan. Its title is a hideous misnomer, as Anna is only one character in another complex of families, and the book concludes not with her tragic end, but with Levine's triumphant discovery of "natural" morality. It is really a study of several marriages and of considerable numbers of characters, and its title should obviously be something like *Love and Marriage*. That generalized approach leads, as in *War and Peace*, to a certain amorphousness that has often bogged me down in the rereading, as I fancy it has done with others.

But the discovery that Levine makes in the last chapters was to have important effects on Tolstoy's development as a writer. To begin with, it almost stopped him writing. "Natural" morality was probably the only thing left for him to discover, and a writer who knows everything is no longer in need of expressing his conflicts. He has merely to spread the light. Yet the discovery is identical with all the other discoveries Tolstoy had made about education, literature, and warfare. Levine learns natural morality from a peasant. Like all the other great discoveries, it is the exclusive possession of the anonymous mass.

And yet when we turn from *Anna Karenina* to *Resurrection*, we find that the discovery has completely altered Tolstoy's outlook as a novelist. *Resurrection* is much more like the old-fashioned novel than *War and Peace* or *Anna Karenina*. To begin with, it has a formal unity that they lack. It is a work of art conceived about one character who is sufficiently strong to maintain the weight of an extended narrative. It is lacking in all the contradictions of emotion in which the earlier work is rich. Everything is grouped in masses, and those masses are significant even if oversimplified. All priests and lawyers and judges do the things they do because they wish to continue drawing their monthly salaries, and, as a result, innocent people are murdered, tortured, and imprisoned. Of course, the picture is overdrawn; the masses are now grouped on too large a scale; the characters are too important; yet the interesting thing to me is that they *are* important, and that I am deeply moved by the things that happen to them.

The secret is, of course, that now Tolstoy's detail is relevant to something and the contradictions in Nekhludov's character are not, and he suppresses them to create the effect he wishes to create as the classic masters of the novel have always done. There are even times when I wonder if *Resurrection* may not prove to be the most enduring of Tolstoy's novels, as it is certainly the most gripping.

chapter 11

Trollope the Realist

Trollope's reputation has suffered so much from the results of his own senile fatuity that it is now almost impossible to define his proper place in English fiction with reasonable accuracy. He left behind him a posthumous autobiography in which he described his method of work and attempted to decry the element of inspiration in literature. Although he merely showed that he was incapable of recognizing it in himself, he has been taken at his word. His reputation collapsed and has never been restored. When his admirers praise the "honesty" of the *Autobiography*, they do him little service; there is a difference between honesty and uncouthness, and as far as the business of literature is concerned, one paragraph of Flaubert's letters is worth everything that Trollope wrote.

Yet it was discovered that young men in England, leaving for the Second World War, were leaving with some novel of Trollope's in their pockets. Though a writer of no great reputation, he was, as Lord David Cecil remarks, "almost the only Victorian novelist whom our sensitive intelligentsia appear to be able to read without experiencing an intolerable sense of jar." Elizabeth Bowen traced the young people's interest to the stability of the world he wrote of—and, being a natural Tory, Trollope certainly wrote of the most stable part of his world and paid small attention to its firebrands and crackpots. Lord David traces his popularity to a "realism" that has kept his work fresh while the less realistic work of his great contemporaries, filled with the burning questions and great ideals of their day, has dated. For those few kind words in favor of realism, one can forgive Lord David much, but even he will not admit Trollope among the greatest of the Victorians. He argues that Trollope's creative imagination is weak; that his characters have not the "preternatural vitality" of Dickens's; that his style is bad by comparison with Hardy's, whose words "at their worst . . . manage to convey their author's temperament; at their best convey it with supreme force and beauty"; and that his power of visualizing a scene—witness Johnny Eames's attack on Crosbie—is slight when we compare it with Troy's exhibition of swordplay in *Far from the Madding Crowd*.

All this is so very convincing that I almost convince myself in recording it, but there is another side to the story. Hugh Walpole, too, uses the illustration of Troy's swordplay, but it seems to me a most unfortunate example. It is a remarkable and beautiful bit of writing, which might well have strayed into Hardy's novel from some romance of Stevenson's, and might equally well have strayed out again without anyone's noticing its absence. Nor do I desire characters to have the "preternatural vitality" of Mr. Pecksniff or Mr. Punch, for this seems to me to degrade them to the level of puppets. The only thing I am sure of is that Trollope's style is weak compared with Hardy's or Dickens's. He had little or no feeling for poetry, and, what is considerably worse from my point of view, he also had little feeling for prose; his writing at its best never rises to the level of Stendhal's or Tolstoy's, which is Continental prose without benefit of poetry. Yet I think Trollope was as great a novelist as either, and a far greater novelist than Hardy.

This is something difficult to establish because there is no one novel of his which is outstanding. *The Last Chronicle of Barset* is, to my mind, a masterpiece as great as *The Red and the Black* or *Anna Karenina*, but it is disgracefully and inconsequentially padded, and I find it necessary to ask my students to make a rough reconstruction of it before making a final judgment. But Trollope's enduring popularity is evidence that needs to be examined. Lord David, as I say, ascribes this to Trollope's "realism," but, in spite of his careful definition, it still seems to me a vague term in this particular context. For Jane Austen is likewise a "realist," but her popularity is of a very different kind.

If one compares the realism of the two writers, one finds, I think, the quality that has kept Trollope so popular. She writes from a preconceived idea of conduct, where he does not. She is a moralist; Trollope is whatever the opposite of a moralist may be. Though Cecil declares that his standards were those of "the typical mid-Victorian gentleman," and though the statement could be liberally documented from the pages of the *Autobiography*, I do not for an instant think it is true.

If there is one phrase more than another which identifies a novel by Trollope it is a phrase like "With such censures I cannot profess that I completely agree." His favorite device is to lead his reader very gently up the garden path of his own conventions and prejudices and then to point out that the reader is wrong. This is not very like the behavior of a typical mid-Victorian gentleman. On the contrary, it is an original and personal approach to conduct, and I think that it is Trollope's approach, rather than his treatment, which pleases intelligent people in our time.

I do not mean that Trollope was a revolutionary figure. In fact, he was a pernickety and crusty conservative who distrusted all new views and methods. But, unlike most English novelists, he did not start out with a cut-and-dried system of morals and try to make his characters fit it. Instead, he made the system fit the characters.

For instance, to take a slight example, one of the conventions of the English novel is that of "one man, one girl," and such is the power of artistic convention that, whatever our own experience may have taught us, we never question this as we read. We could not conceive of Mr. Knightley in love with Harriet Smith as well as with Emma. We certainly could not believe that, having been rejected by Emma, Mr. Knightley would ever immediately propose to Harriet. But Trollope's characters usually behave in that way. One of his principal characters is an Irish politician, Phineas Finn, who is engaged to a very nice County Clare girl called Mary Flood-Jones. But when Phineas comes to London, he immediately forgets all about Mary and falls in love with a society woman, Lady Laura Standish. When Lady Laura rejects him for a dreary Scottish fanatic named Kennedy, Phineas at once transfers his affections to an heiress called Violet Effingham, and when she, in turn, marries a mad nobleman named Chiltern, he toys with the affections of a Jewish widow, Madame Max Gessler. Her he finally does marry, but not until he has become the widower of Mary Flood-Jones. And if the reader, forgetting his own errors, denounces Finn as a heartless rogue, Trollope, in that maddening way of his, chimes in with his pet phrase: "With such censures I cannot profess that I completely agree." Literature is one thing, life another.

If it were to be asserted here that a young man may be perfectly true to a first young woman while he is falling in love with a second, the readers of this story would probably be offended. But undoubtedly many men believe themselves to be true while undergoing this process, and many young women expect nothing else from their lovers.

Not only is Trollope not a moralist in Jane Austen's sense; he even loathes the sort of moral consistency she admires. This, I feel sure, goes back to something in his own youth and early manhood. His childhood was gloomy with the desperate gloom that poverty imposes on people of gentle birth. He grew up ignorant and a bit of a waster, and was pushed into a Civil Service job for which he was not qualified. It is probably significant that he could never reconcile himself to the principle of competitive examination, for had there been such a thing in his own youth, he might never have made good. "I was always in trouble," he says mournfully. The dun who haunts Phineas Finn's lodgings with his perpetual "I wish you would be punctual" was the same who haunted Trollope at his office. It was in despair of his own future that the poor wretch decided to become a novelist at all, for it was the only career his miserable education seemed to have left open to him. There is something almost heartbreaking in his admission that he became a writer only in default of something better, and a novelist because the "higher" branches of literature were closed to him.

Poetry I did not believe to be within my grasp. The drama, too, which I would fain have chosen, I believed to be above me. For history, biography or essay writing, I had not sufficient erudition. But I thought it possible that I might write a novel.

"*Only* a novel!" one can hear Jane Austen retort. "Only some work in which the greatest powers of the mind are displayed, in which the most thorough knowledge of human nature, the happiest delineations of its varieties, the liveliest effusions of wit and humor are conveyed to the world in the best chosen language."

It was only after Trollope's transfer to a miserable job in Ireland—perhaps by contrast with people worse off than himself—that he acquired command of himself and finally became the model of steadiness and probity we meet in the *Autobiography*. It is more than probable that when he diverts criticism from his characters, he is really diverting it from himself. He had endured more than his share, and proved its hollowness by his ultimate success.

But, whatever the reason, he expresses again and again his dislike for men of strong character. "The man who holds out," he says in *The Duke's Children*, "is not the man of the firmest opinions but the man of the hardest heart." ("Heart," incidentally, is a key word with him.) "He has probably found himself so placed that he cannot marry without money," explains an old lady in *The Eustace Diamonds*, "and has wanted the firmness, or per-

haps you will say the hardness of heart to say so openly."
And here is the same thing in an even more striking passage:

In social life we hardly stop to consider how much of that
daring spirit which gives mastery comes from hardness of heart
rather than from high purpose or true courage. The man who
succumbs to his wife, the mother who succumbs to her daughter,
the master who succumbs to his servant, is as often brought to
servility by the continual aversion to the giving of pain, by a
softness which causes the fretfulness of others to be an agony
to himself as by any actual fear which the firmness of the
imperious one may have produced. There is an inner softness, a
thinness of the mind's skin, an incapability of seeing or even of
thinking of the troubles of others with equanimity which produces a feeling akin to fear; but which is compatible not only
with courage but with absolute firmness of purpose when the
demand for firmness arises so strongly as to assert itself.

There, in a paragraph, is the essential Trollope, the
message of Trollope, if such a writer can be said to have a
message; and there, unless I am grievously mistaken,
speaks a man who had himself been badly mauled by life
and who experienced an almost physical terror of doing
the same to others. I suspect that this, too, is the real key
to his conservatism in religion and politics. He detested
reformers like Carlyle, Dickens, and Ruskin because they
were men of strong principles, and strong principles were
things that he associated with hard hearts.

It is not merely that Trollope sympathized with so-
called "weak" people in situations that were merely
ambiguous. Though he wrote within very strict taboos
and his love stories are usually as conventionalized as

the plots of seventeenth-century French comedies, he had the same sort of understanding of irregular relationships. One of the most delightful characters in English fiction is Lady Glencora Palliser, yet we find her in *Can You Forgive Her?* on the point of eloping with a penniless adventurer, Burgo Fitzgerald, and hindered only by the arrival of her husband to bring her home. The two lovers are at a dance, where they are being closely watched, and the whole episode is so characteristic of Trollope that one cannot ignore it. Here, better than anywhere else, one can see what importance he attaches to what he calls the "heart."

> The Duchess of St. Bungay saw it and shook her head sorrowing—for the Duchess was good at heart. . . . Mrs. Conway Sparkes saw it and drank it down with keen appetite . . . for Mrs. Conway Sparkes was not good at heart. Lady Hartletop saw it and just raised her eyebrows. It was nothing to her. She liked to know what was going on as such knowledge was sometimes useful; but as for heart—what she had in such matters was neither good nor bad.

This, then, rather than realism, represents Trollope's true quality as a novelist. Not merely loyalty to the facts, but loyalty to a certain attitude to the facts, to a humility and passivity in the face of life. I do not wish to suggest that artistically this is an unmixed blessing. When Trollope is not inspired by his subject, it gives his work a flabbiness and lack of energy that leave the reader feeling very flat indeed. Even on the trivial plane of "one man, one girl," it results in a lack of incisiveness; Phineas Finn would have been as happy with Lady Laura as with Madame Max; Lord Silverbridge would have done as well

with Lady Mabel as with the American girl, Isabel
Boncassen. Stendhal would have been inspired by these
things to some sweeping generalizations about men and
women, but Trollope merely notes that they are so and
that to pretend otherwise would mean being false to one's
experience.

2.

But it is important to remember that this very humility
gives Trollope a quality not possessed to a similar degree
by any other English novelist. That quality is range, and
by range I do not mean merely the ability he shares with
Tolstoy of handling great masses of material while keeping its elements distinct. I mean primarily the power of
exploring his characters fully, of so understanding their
interior perspective that by a simple change of lighting he
can suddenly reveal them to us in a different way; as, for
instance, in the scene in *Can You Forgive Her?* where
Burgo Fitzgerald, the penniless and desperate adventurer
whose only hope is to seduce Lady Glencora for her
money, buys a meal for a prostitute. It is a most remarkable scene. In any other novelist of the period it would
prove that Fitzgerald had a heart of gold, or, alternatively,
that the prostitute had a heart of gold, or that both had
hearts of gold. In Trollope it is merely one of those minor
shocks by which he reminds us that life is not simple; it
indicates to us that Lady Glencora is not altogether a fool,
and that Fitzgerald, for all his faults, retains a capacity for
spontaneous behavior which endears him to women.

But the best illustration is the wonderful scene of the death of Mrs. Proudie in *The Last Chronicle of Barset*. It is also the best example of the fatuous attitude adopted by Trollope to his own work. In the *Autobiography* he tells us that one day, sitting in the Athenaeum Club, he overheard two clergymen denounce his work, particularly the character of Mrs. Proudie.

It was impossible for me not to overhear their words and almost impossible for me to hear them and be quiet. I got up and, standing between them, I acknowledged myself to be the culprit. "As to Mrs. Proudie," I said, "I will go home and kill her before the week is over." And so I did. The two gentlemen were utterly confounded, and one of them begged me to forget his frivolous observations.

"Simple-minded" is too feeble a word to describe such a passage. Trollope fails to tell us what he could have done with Mrs. Proudie if the two clergymen had not spoken. Of course, intuitively, if not intellectually, he had already known that Mrs. Proudie had to die because Mr. Crawley, the central figure of the novel, is drawn on such a scale that she and her henpecked husband could no longer be treated as figures of fun. You cannot be merely funny at the expense of Lear, and from the opening of the book we know that Mrs. Proudie has at last met her match and that sooner or later she will be broken. She is broken, and leaves the room, knowing that her husband hates her. And then—

In spite of all her roughness and temper, Mrs. Proudie was in this like other women—that she would fain have been loved had it been possible. She had always meant to serve him. She was

conscious of that: conscious also in a way that although she had
been industrious, although she had been faithful, although she
was clever, yet she had failed. At the bottom of her heart she
knew that she had been a bad wife.

"Industrious, faithful, clever"—how subtly the woman's character has been deepened before she goes upstairs
to die. Perhaps only a story-teller can realize the miracle
that takes place in those chapters; the miracle of elevating
two characters of low comedy to the plane of high tragedy
without a single false note. Only one who understood his
characters completely even in their absurdities could have
changed the lighting so impressively and revealed the real
perspective of their souls. The lines about Mrs. Proudie,
like the passage in Jane Austen's *Emma* where the heroine
denounces Mrs. Elton's vulgarity, are written on three
different levels. On the conscious level, Mrs. Proudie
knows that she had always meant to be a good wife. On
the semi-conscious level (notice the phrasing, "conscious
also *in a way*") she knows that she has failed. But in her
feelings, in her "heart," the only ultimate tribunal that
Trollope recognizes, there exists the knowledge, not yet
permitted to reach consciousness, that she has been a bad
wife.

But there is another sort of range which Trollope also
had, and that is the power of describing extreme psychological types, types that are pathological or bordering on
it. The principal character in *He Knew He Was Right*—a
bad novel by Trollope's own standard—is a masterly
presentation of pathological jealousy. Now, Proust can
describe pathological jealousy with similar mastery, but

Proust was the victim of what he described, and the fact that he described it so well meant that there were scores of other psychological states that he could not describe at all. Balzac could describe a variety of extreme psychological states, but his romantic imagination made it impossible for him to treat them from the point of view of simple normality, so that ultimately they fail to impress us. Trollope, because his capacity came from the passiveness and humility with which he contemplated people, could describe scores of such types, but each one rises simple and sheer from a flat plain of normality. Mr. Kennedy, the Scotch puritan in *Phineas Finn*, is an example, as is "the mad lord," Chiltern. But Mr. Crawley of *The Last Chronicle* is the supreme example. He rises out of the commonplace and placid plane of the story, a giant figure who, even when we are looking elsewhere, still magnetizes us like some mountain peak. And of all these characters it is almost impossible to say when they pass the limits of sanity, so closely have they been observed, so carefully has each step been recorded.

The Last Chronicle is the final volume in the Barchester series, and I do not think anyone has ever analyzed the strange development in the works. This is the timetable:

1855	*The Warden*
1857	*Barchester Towers*
1858	*Dr. Thorne*
1861	*Framley Parsonage*
1864	*The Small House at Allington*
1867	*The Last Chronicle of Barset*

In the manuscript of the *Autobiography*, Trollope deliberately deleted *The Small House at Allington*. This leaves us with five novels, of which four deal almost entirely with clerical life. The fifth, *Dr. Thorne*, is a book I find extremely dull. It was written to a plot of Thomas Trollope's, and even Trollope himself thought badly of it. Leave it in, and you have a panorama of English provincial life, centered on a cathedral city; take it out, and you have a saga of clerical life, all sections of it dealing in different ways with the same problem, the problem that in Mr. Crawley is presented to us in its most complex and tragic form.

The saga begins in a very interesting way. *The Warden* deals with a contemporary controversy—that of clerical sinecures. English liberals, aiming at the abolition of feudal privileges, had exposed a succession of scandals concerning sinecures, and Trollope took advantage of this in an astute journalistic way. Trollope took a strong High Church line and satirized very cruelly and cleverly both Carlyle and Dickens, whom he disliked as reformers. He pokes fun at his own reformer, John Bold, who was so mad on the subject that he took up the cause of an old woman who had been overcharged at a turnpike by another old woman, "rode through the gate himself, paying the toll, then brought an action against the gate-keeper and proved that all people coming up a certain by-lane and going down a certain other by-lane were toll-free." John Bold was, in fact, another of those moralists whom Trollope disliked because their firmness of principle seemed to him to express a hardness of heart.

But Grantley, who is Bold's clerical opponent, is

equally unfeeling. It is interesting to watch Grantley's development through the series. In this book he is very harshly handled. Though the son of a saintly bishop, he is a money-grubbing, success-worshipping man who reads Rabelais when he is supposed to be attending to his religious duties.

The Warden is a charming book. It has the quality of the best English novels, of entertaining in a civilized way, but it has no other outstanding quality, and I suspect that if it stood alone, it would be read only by fanatic admirers of Trollope like myself. The important thing is that it does not stand alone. For some reason, Trollope's imagination continued to linger about the cathedral close—as it was later to linger about the British House of Commons—and to ponder the problem of worldliness and sanctity in the Anglican Church. The result was *Barchester Towers*, an infinitely better book, and one that would have been outstanding, whoever had written it, even if it had had no successor. Once again, it has a background of newspaper controversy. For the cruel Whigs, who had attacked clerical sinecures, were attacking High Church bishops and replacing them by nominees of their own who would work with the Low Church and dissenting groups that were the backbone of the Liberal party. Trollope had as great a dislike for Low Church clergymen as he had for reformers. The book opens with the death of old Bishop Grantley, and after his son the Archdeacon has failed of his hopes, there arrive a Liberal, Low Church bishop, Proudie, his preposterous wife, and his greasy chaplain, Mr. Slope. The book is a lament for the good old days when the church was the preserve of English gentlemen.

Few things are more interesting than the sudden change of attitude we feel toward the Archdeacon in those first brilliant chapters. He is as worldly as ever; all his hopes are centered on getting the see for himself; we feel that there is little to be said in his favor, even as opposed to the Proudies and the Slopes, but suddenly Trollope pulls us up with that phrase which I have already quoted, "With such censures I cannot profess that I completely agree."

Our archdeacon was worldly—who among us is not so? He was ambitious—who among us is ashamed to own that "last infirmity of noble minds"? He was avaricious, my readers will say. No—it was for no love of lucre that he wished to be bishop of Barchester. He was his father's only child, and his father had left him great wealth. . . . He would be a richer man as arch-deacon than he could be as bishop. But he certainly did desire to play first fiddle; he did desire to sit in full lawn sleeves among the peers of the realm; and he did desire, if the truth must out, to be called "My Lord" by his reverend brethren.

Even more interesting is the character of Grantley's friend, the scholar-priest Arabin, whom Grantly intro-duces into the diocese to gain an ally against the Low Church faction. Arabin is one of Newman's colleagues, so steeped in church history that he has already been tempted in the direction of Rome and saved from it only by the counsel of a half-crazy parson in a remote West Country village. This is the first hint we get of the character we later learn to know as Crawley, an extraordinary example of the way in which Trollope brooded over his creations.

Barchester Towers is a fine book, spoiled, as Longman's

reader pointed out, by the introduction of the Stanhope family, who are an alien and jarring note. The intention is right, as showing the queer fish High Church discipline introduced into English religious life, but Trollope failed to allow for the fact that they tempt one to take a Low Church view of the whole situation. There is no such fault in *Framley Parsonage*. Once more the conflict is between piety and worldliness, but though Mark Robarts has led an irregular life and got himself badly into debt, Trollope comes out on his side in a much more outspoken way. It is all to the same tune: "We are all the same. Life is like that. Don't be too censorious."

It is no doubt very wrong to long after a naughty thing. But nevertheless we all do so. One may say that hankering after naughty things is the very essence of the evil into which we have been precipitated by Adam's fall. When we confess that we are all sinners, we confess that we all long after naughty things. And ambition is a great vice—as Mark Antony told us a long time ago—a great vice no doubt if the ambition of the man be with reference to his own advancement and not to the advancement of others. But then how many of us are there who are not ambitious in this vicious manner?

Sanctity in this book is represented by Mr. Crawley, whom his friend Arabin has brought to the neighborhood, but even in him the issue of worldliness is not left out. Far from it; for, whether or not he realized it, Trollope had at last found the perfect character through whom he could express the essence of the conflict. Crawley is a saint, but a saint with a wife and family and only a hundred and thirty pounds a year to keep them on. Crawley's sanctity has had to take a terrible beating from his vanity.

He had always at his heart a feeling that he and his had been ill-used, and too often solaced himself at the devil's bidding with the conviction that eternity would make equal that which life in this world had made so unequal; the last bait that with which the devil angles after those who are struggling to elude his rod and line.

There is one very curious thing about the character of Crawley on which no one has, I think, commented. His vanity is a writer's vanity, the same that Trollope described in the *Autobiography*, apparently unaware that every word he wrote could be applied with equal force to his greatest figure.

The author's poverty is, I think, harder to be borne than any other poverty. The man, whether rightly or wrongly, feels that the world is using him with extreme injustice. The more absolutely he fails, the higher, it is probable, he will reckon his own merits; and the keener will be the sense of injury in that he whose work is of so high a nature cannot get bread, while they whose tasks are mean are wrapped in luxury. "I with my well-filled mind, with my clear intellect, with all my gifts, cannot earn a poor crown a day, while that fool, who simpers in a little room behind a shop, makes his thousands every year." The very charity to which he too often is driven, is bitterer to him than to others. While he takes it he almost spurns the hand that gives it to him, and every fibre of his heart within him is bleeding with a sense of injury.

It is Lord David Cecil who lumps Mr. Crawley with the Archdeacon, Miss Dunstable, and Mrs. Proudie as "simple and positive, absorbed in the avocations of average human beings, devoid alike of psychological complexities and abstruse spiritual yearnings, made up of a few strongly marked qualities and idiosyncrasies." I do not think this describes Trollope's characters very well, and I certainly do not think it describes Mr. Crawley at all. He is one of the subtlest figures in all literature, and even between *Framley Parsonage* and *The Last Chronicle* Trollope continued to make discoveries about his character, and they still continue to astonish us. All the manifestations of his stern and ill-regulated piety we are familiar with, but who would suspect the sly and brutal humor or the childish pleasures of the true scholar?

And there was at times a lightness of heart about the man. In the course of the last winter he had translated into Greek irregular verse the very noble ballad of Lord Bateman, maintaining the rhythms and the rhyme, and had repeated it with uncouth glee till his daughter knew it by heart.

How good that "uncouth glee" is! It is like the playfulness of a rhinoceros.

3.

But the problem for the critic remains—why the Church? The answer should be in that dull *Autobiography*, but it isn't, at least on the surface. Why is Trollope so obsessed by the conflict between sanctity and worldliness? Why does he come down again and again on the side of worldliness? Is it perhaps a personal conflict that he never consciously dealt with, a relic of those bitter early days of his?

In some way, the Church in these four novels represents vocation, and Trollope seems to be fighting off the admission of his own vocation and the responsibilities it imposes.

His character remains something of a mystery. He had the dual character of the perfect Civil Servant and the author, and he must frequently have wondered which was the true Anthony Trollope. The thing that hindered him from being a great writer and that makes the *Autobiography* so unrevealing was the same thing that made him the great novelist he certainly was: lack of self-consciousness. The only character this patient and humble observer could never observe was his own, and one element in that character was certainly the Reverend Josiah Crawley.

chapter 12

Flaubert and the New Romanticism

Turgenev's revolt against Gogol, and Trollope's against Dickens were nothing beside the intensity of Gustave Flaubert's repudiation of Balzac and all that he stood for. Perhaps it is something in the French character; perhaps it is something in the character of the French middle classes; but, whereas "middle classes" in English is a neutral term and "intelligentsia" in Russian a positive term of approval, "bourgeois" is a term of abuse, and in every language when agitators wish to concentrate the fury of the mob against merchants and stockbrokers they must have recourse to French. Flaubert himself laid it down as a principle that "hatred of the middle classes is the beginning of wisdom" and compiled with loving detestation over many years a dictionary of the accepted ideas that he regarded as their particular code.

We cannot ignore this attitude of his, for Flaubert was one of the saints of literature. I once discussed with an American friend a book of criticism I proposed to write called *The Artist in Spite of Himself*, which would deal with four great writers who, I felt, should never have been writers at all. At that moment I could think of only three: Ben Jonson, Flaubert, and Joyce. The fourth name eluded me. "It's all right," he said sadly. "It's Henry James." It was.

But as well as being one of the most passionate of artists,

Flaubert was also a French romantic at precisely the point in the nineteenth century when romanticism was turning into what Mario Praz calls decadence and I call symbolism. Not that I would for a moment dispute his claim that romanticism was turning bad. It was, if you will, the point at which romanticism ceases to believe in itself, and begins to caricature itself. Flaubert's friend Le Poittevin, having lost faith in love, proposed to bring a prostitute to the three places in which he had first believed in it and indulge in a ritual defilement of them. "It will give me great pleasure to take her to the places where as a child I *believed* in love," he wrote. "Then after the three days I will pay her off." Flaubert himself laid it down that "the most beautiful woman is scarcely beautiful on a table in the dissecting room, her bowels draped over her face, one of her legs peeled to the bone, and a half-extinguished cigar lying on her feet." It is, of course, only an adolescent phase that most of us have gone through in one form or another, but it tends to become permanent with Flaubert, for his one great book is a formal repudiation of romantic love. In him, as in so many of his contemporaries, that repudiation is linked with an acceptance of cruelty and death. His mind, his friend Goncourt noted, was "haunted by Sade."

And with the name of Sade we are back once more in the world of *Northanger Abbey* and of late eighteenth-century romanticism which Jane Austen so vehemently repudiated. We are far from the passion of Dickens raging at the American judge who had defended slavery that "men who spoke of it as a blessing, as a matter of course, as a state of things to be desired, were out of the pale of reason; and that for them to speak of ignorance or prejudice was an absurdity too ridiculous to be combated"; far from the humanitarian passion of Tolstoy and Turgenev; far from Chekhov, who is ill for two nights after witnessing a flogging. This is the tone, brilliant and apparently only slightly insane, of the kindly old gentleman in a superior lunatic asylum.

We talked bastinado with the nazir. When a man is to be killed, four or five blows suffice—his thighs and neck are broken. When he is only to be punished, he is beaten on the buttocks: four to five hundred blows is the usual number; the patient is sick for five or six months after—it takes that long for the old flesh to be replaced by new. The effendi laughed as he added the last detail. In Nubia the bastinado is usually given on the soles of the feet. The Nubians greatly dread this punishment, as after it they are never again able to walk.

You do, I hope, notice the detached and unemotional air, so different from the crude and vulgar fulminations of people like Dickens and Balzac. This is a very superior lunatic asylum indeed—but an asylum just the same.

Praz has shown brilliantly how this type of romanticism derives from Sade. But other causes need to be considered. One in particular was the change in cultural centers which was taking place as a result of the development of industry and finance. Until the end of the eighteenth century, the center of civilization was always somewhere about the Mediterranean basin, and from this all other centers of culture ultimately drew their life. But with the great advances in science, the center shifted, and by the beginning of the nineteenth century at least London and Paris were more important in determining cultural standards than any Mediterranean city—just as today, by an extension of the same principle, the Caucasus and the Middle West have more real say in man's destiny than either London or Paris. Materially this has led to enormous improvements in human conditions, but historically and climactically these new centers are no substitute for Rome and Athens, and their civilization is full of neuroses. Flaubert, who was a very profound thinker, well understood this, and realized that his philosophic calm in face of the bastinado had nothing to do with similar brutalities in the great classical civilizations.

You would like to make me into a Pagan [he wrote to Louise Colet], you who have Roman blood in your veins. But try as I might, any effort towards that would be useless, for at the very bottom of my soul are the mists of the North, which I have breathed since birth. I carry within me the melancholy of the Barbarians, with their instinct for migration and their innate disgust for life—which made them leave their own country as though by so doing they could take leave of themselves. They loved the sun, all these Goths who went to Italy to die; they had a frenzied longing for light, for the blue sky, for a warm, vibrant existence. I have always had a tender sympathy for them as one might for one's ancestors. But alas, I am no man of antiquity; men of antiquity did not have sick nerves like mine. Nor you, either. You are neither Greek nor Latin; romanticism has touched you too.

Praz identifies—correctly, I think—two stages of romanticism. The first, which lasted until the middle of the century, was Byronism, or the Romanticism of the Fatal

Man. The second, which he identifies largely with Flaubert, covers the rest of the century, and was the Romanticism of the Fatal Woman: Cleopatra, Salome, Pater's Mona Lisa. It is at this point that we begin to notice a growing tendency toward homosexuality.

Flaubert's first work, the early version of *The Temptation of Saint Anthony*, was an accumulation of romantic horrors—not that the later version is very superior. It was listened to in despair by his two friends Du Camp and Bouilhet the poet. When he had finished, Bouilhet argued that he must write a realistic novel—in the manner of Balzac.

Du Camp's account of this whole episode is highly amusing. Bouilhet, who seems to have been a man of strong character as well as a fine critic, persisted. It was he who later impressed on Flaubert that the story of the Delamare family was the ideal subject for such a realistic novel.

Delamare, a student of Flaubert's father, had not been clever enough to qualify as a doctor and practiced merely as a local health officer. He had married a romantic young girl who soon came to despise him, took lovers, got into debt, and finally committed suicide. Delamare, who had known nothing of her conduct and was still in love with her, found life without her unendurable and also committed suicide.

Bouilhet's methods of persuading Flaubert to adopt the theme are also very amusing. He had to sugar the pill of realism as best he might, so he assured Flaubert that there was no necessity for him to deal with the subject of money in Balzac's way. Undoubtedly Mme Delamare had got

into debt, but this was only because of her innocence of
money matters, while as for Flaubert's hatred of the
middle classes, where could he find a better subject than
Delamare on whom to vent all his indignation? All the
same, it was something of a comedown for a serious author
who was contemplating a work in which a lady fell in
love with a god.

Sometimes I cannot help wondering who the real author
of *Madame Bovary* was: Flaubert, who wrote it, or
Bouilhet, who realized that it was the only way in which
his friend could become a great writer. It was Flaubert's
only real book, his undoubted masterpiece, and unquestionably it was so because someone with a good critical
sense had selected for him a subject in which he could not
go wrong and had told him how to write it. It was the only
occasion when Flaubert took the advice of someone with a
better eye for a subject than he possessed. Turgenev
warned him that *Bouvard and Pecuchet* could never be
developed into a novel, but Flaubert paid no heed to him.

Madame Bovary is possibly the most beautifully written
book ever composed; undoubtedly it is the most beautifully written novel. But it is a book that invites superla-
tives. Historically, it was the most important novel of the
century, for about it gathered the new movement in
fiction, naturalism. Naturalism was to realism what
symbolism was to romanticism, the exaggeration of a
tendency. Both symbolism and naturalism were a withdrawal from life. "As for living, our servants will do that
for us." Villiers de L'Isle-Adam's phrase summarizes the
gospel of Symbolism, while Joyce's picture of the artist,

"like God, paring his nails," summarizes the theory of naturalism. In neither case does the artist live or become involved in the business of living. And because at bottom the two creeds were identical in their withdrawal from life, they tended to alternate in the same person. When Flaubert wasn't writing about Homais, the druggist, he was writing of Salome, and even when he wrote of one, half his mind was diverted to the other.

As a result, there is a contradiction between the style and the material. The story itself is intensely ugly and depressing, far more than it need have been, for there is genuine pathos in the theme, a pathos of which Flaubert became aware only when the book was near its close. The pathos is entirely missing from the first three fourths of the story. The style, on the other hand, is extravagantly beautiful; it is the style of a poet who should, one feels, have had a beautiful subject. Instead, there is something in the combination of material and style which suggests a drain on a winter's day when ice has covered everything and reflects the bare trees and brilliant sky. The style is almost that of a romance.

Once, during a thaw, the moisture was oozing out of the trees in the courtyard, the snow melting on the roofs of the out-buildings. She was on the threshold; she went to look for her parasol; she opened it. The parasol, of silk coloured like a pigeon's breast and pierced by the sunlight, lit up with shifting reflections the white skin of her face. She smiled beneath it at the damp heat, and the drops of water could be heard falling, one by one, upon the stretched silk.

If there is any relationship whatever between style and content, then it could be argued—it has, indeed, been argued, though very unconvincingly—that this is a bad style. It is certainly an inappropriate one, but it marks the beginning of a new attitude to style which becomes particularly noticeable in Joyce and Faulkner, in which style ceases to represent a relationship between the author and the reader and becomes a relationship between the author and the object. This may seem paradoxical, but it is what Flaubert meant by *le mot juste*, and the right word applied to the object is frequently neither the word required by the nature of the object nor the word that conveys that meaning to the reader. Instead, it is a glorified form of onomatopœia, like the sound of the falling stream in *Ulysses* or the idiot's monologue in *The Sound and the Fury*, where the timelessness of the idiot's world is supposed to be conveyed in a timeless prose that has neither past, present, nor future.

Flaubert also anticipates Faulkner and Joyce in the use of certain literary devices that take the place of plastic treatment. The method is not being adapted to the characters, if there are any characters in the strict meaning of the word; instead, the characters are being adapted to the methods. Flaubert's principal device is the typical romantic one of antithesis. When the lovers sit together at the agricultural show, their passionate conversation is interrupted antithetically by the voice of the chairman announcing the prizes. Mr. Martin Turnell suggests that the antithesis is not really antithetical, but analogical, and intended to represent the animal nature of the lovers, but this seems to me doubtful, considering the way in which antithesis is used in other chapters.

"Good general farming," cried the President.

"Recently, for instance, when I came to your house . . ."

"M. Bizet of Quincampoix."

"Did I ever guess that I'd come with you?"

"Seventy francs."

"A hundred times I wanted to leave you, and yet I followed you. I've stayed."

"Manures—."

"As I'll stay tonight, tomorrow, for the future, all my life."

"M. Caron, of Arguil, a gold medal."

"Because I was never so charmed in the company of any other woman."

"M. Bain, of Givry-Saint-Martin—"

"I too will keep the memory of you."

"For a merino ram—."

In the same way, when Emma is in a state of spiritual despair and goes for advice and consolation to the parish priest, Father Bournisien, their dialogue turns into straight antithesis.

"Yes," she said, "it is in your power to relieve all wretchedness."

"You mustn't say that, Madame Bovary. Only this morning I was sent for to Bas-Diauville, to look at a cow with wind— they thought it had been bewitched, and not just one cow only, but the whole herd—how on earth it happened, I don't know. . . . Farmers have a good deal to complain of, too."

"So have other people," she rejoined.

"I should be the last to deny it . . . workmen in the large cities for instance."

"They're not the ones. . . ."

"Believe it or not, I have known cases of poor mothers of families, thoroughly good souls, all of them real saints, actually going without bread. . . ."

"But how about women who have bread, but no . . ."

"Fuel in winter, you were going to say?" broke in the priest.

Most of Flaubert's principal effects are of this sort; the scene at the Opéra when Charles, the dull husband, is contrasted with the romantic hero of *Lucia di Lammermoor*; Emma's deathbed, when the two old clowns, the priest and the druggist, argue across her body about Voltaire; and, of course, the cathedral scene where she comes to make her peace with God and ends up fornicating madly in a cab that tears through the city with its blinds drawn. And, whatever one may say of Tolstoy's view that intrigue makes the interest in events dominate over interest in details of feeling, when we come to this monolithic technique there simply is no room whatever for any details of feeling. The parish priest in the scene I have quoted may or may not have been as dull a creature as he appears, but the fact remains that, dull or interesting, no detail of his character could break through the antithetical mold in which the scene is cast. And though it may be argued that by the time of the cathedral scene Emma's degradation has proceeded so far that her romantic soul was no longer capable of being roused to any form of fastidiousness, the argument in fact never arises. Having created his antithesis, Flaubert does not care a rap whether it is psychologically convincing or not; he is a literary man with a method, and because the method of antithesis lends itself most readily to irony, he is quite satisfied that the effect he produces is an ironic one. It is a curious criticism of naturalism that the withdrawal of emotional sympathy with the characters which it demands should produce rhetoric instead of the detachment it sought.

The truth is that this particular theory of literature originated in a painter's studio, for it has all the marks of painters' illiteracy, an occupational disease too rarely fatal. That Manet can paint a pub or Lautrec a pair of Lesbians and produce masterpieces is no reason at all why an author should expect to be able to do the same. Literature is a frightfully impure art. Its medium is words that change their meaning from generation to generation and ideas that are never still, and it has been tied up from the beginning with philosophy and morals. A painter may paint a picture of a Borgia without worrying his head about whether or not he approves of poisoning in principle, but a writer who attempts to do this is violating the terms of his charter. When Flaubert describes himself discussing bastinado with the nazir and ends his story of Herodias with the lines: "And all three, having taken the head of Iaokanann, went off in the direction of Galilee. As it was very heavy, they carried it in turns," he reminds me of a small boy crying: "See me ride no hands, mummy," and of Miss Liza Doolittle's drawing-room manner as she inquires: "What call would a woman with that strength in her have to die of influenza? What become of her new straw hat that should have come to me? Somebody pinched it; and what I say is, them as pinched it done her in."

When used as a purely literary device, as Chekhov mainly uses it, naturalism acts as a useful barrier between author and public; it keeps the former from indulging in Thackeray's fatal trick of lecturing us about his characters, and clears the medium of impurities so that we can really see the object as we may suppose it to be; but when it is used to imply that the subject in literature is of no more significance than the subject in painting, it ceases to be a literary device and becomes a bastard æsthetic.

Turgenev, Flaubert's old friend and admirer, who loved literature with a passion as deep as Flaubert's, saw the flaws in his theory and, as usual with him, translated them into political terms. He planned a novel about "a Russian girl who has accepted the ideas held by the Nihilists, leaves her native country and settles in Paris. There she meets and eventually marries a young French socialist. For some time all goes well in the household, which is united by a common hatred of all laws and ceremonies. But at length the young wife meets and has much confidential talk with one of her own countrymen, who tells her about all that the Russian socialists are thinking and saying and doing in the land of her birth. She recognizes to her horror that the ends and aims, the aspirations and yearnings of the Russian revolutionists are widely different from those of the French and German socialists, and that a great abyss divides her, so far as her thoughts and feelings are concerned, from the husband with whom she used to fancy herself entirely in accord." For "socialist" read "naturalist" and you will begin to see what Turgenev was getting at, which, as he makes plain himself, was the need for an "ethical absolute." He had realized that, for all the love of literature he shared with old Father Flaubert, Flaubert's faith had nothing of the religious passion of his own.

And, of course, we must admit that this link with politics was really there. When the century opened there were only two effective political attitudes possible, conservative and liberal, and only two literary attitudes, romantic and realistic. By the time Turgenev wrote, it was becoming apparent that the liberal group was splitting and producing a new type of extreme radical or communist, while the conservative group was beginning to produce its strong-arm men, who were later to be known as fascists. There is far too close a link between the extreme realists, who are the naturalists, and the extreme radicals, who are the communists on the one hand, and between the extreme romantics, who are symbolists, and the extreme conservatives, who become fascists, on the other, for us to ignore the possibility that they are basically identical. Communism projects everything into the external world, reducing the individual to a shadow, and this is remarkably close to the literary theory of naturalism. Fascism, on the other hand, tends to see the external world as a mere projection of a personal vision, and that is merely what Villiers de l'Isle-Adam is saying when he tells us that "as for living, our servants will do that for us." "When I want to know what Ireland is thinking, I look into my own heart," said Mr. de Valera, to the great indignation of his political enemies—all but the symbolist Yeats, who asked me: "Where else could he look?" But it was Yeats who made his hero, Cuchullain, say: "I make the truth." The one is fascist, the other symbolist, but surely they are at bottom the very same statement.

part IV

The Desolation of Reality

chapter **13**

Dostoevsky and the Unnatural Triangle

The strangest and, judged by later results, the most significant novelist of the late nineteenth century was Fyodor Dostoevsky. When the end of the classical period came, somewhere about 1880, it was his works which were made into texts for later writers. Yet no novelist less typical of the century could be imagined.

He was born in 1821, the son of a hypochondriac doctor. His father had foolishly bought a small estate, which he managed himself, and where he made himself hated by everyone. One day when his son was eighteen he was murdered by his indignant serfs.

In 1846, when Dostoevsky was only twenty-five, his first novel appeared and created something of a sensation; and in the same year it became apparent that he was suffering from some disease that resembled epilepsy, though neither he nor his doctors seem to have been certain that it was.

In 1849 he read aloud at a gathering of friends interested in social matters the correspondence between Byelinsky, the liberal critic, and Gogol, whom Byelinsky attacked for his reactionary views. Later he and others of his group were arrested. They were taken to the Semyonov Square, where, in the presence of troops and populace, their sentences were read out. All were to die by shooting. A priest preached to them on the text "The wages of sin is

199

death." They were then stripped to their shirts in the icy December morning, and the first three were bound to posts before the firing squad. At that moment a courier drove up with reprieves. The whole proceeding had been a brutal farce of the authorities, and at midnight on Christmas Eve, when the whole Christian world was celebrating the birth of Christ, the irons were clamped on Dostoevsky and he set out on his long march to the Siberian "deadhouse."

When he returned after nine years of torture and misery, he was not, as one might have expected, a revolutionary of the most violent kind. Instead, he was a Tory, almost a toady of the Imperialist regime, and his ideal form of government was a dictatorship of Emperor and Church, the two sets of buffoons who had staged his mock execution. Dostoevsky's reactions were not easily predictable. He hated Turgenev—who was a Liberal, and who had lent him money—caricatured him savagely, and appears to have tried to denounce him secretly as an atheist. Turgenev retorted by calling him "a Russian Marquis de Sade," a significant re-emergence of the name after Flaubert and before Proust.

For Dostoevsky's contemporaries it had another meaning. A wild legend was going the rounds that Dostoevsky had raped a child who had later hanged herself, and that Dostoevsky had confessed or been told to confess to Turgenev. The story itself is clearly a legend. It originates in the fact that all through Dostoevsky's work we come across allusions to the rape and suicide of a child, but those who invented and circulated the legend obviously had good grounds for knowing that it was not for nothing that Dostoevsky was obsessed by the theme. His friend and biographer Strakhov, writing to Tolstoy, indulged in an outburst about Dostoevsky's "bestial sensuality" and compared him to certain characters in his own works like Svidrigailov in *Crime and Punishment* and Stavrogin in *The Possessed*. "He was drawn to abominations and he boasted of them," wrote Strakhov. "Viskovatov began telling me how he boasted that in a bathhouse he —— a little girl brought him by her governess."

I am not greatly concerned with the credibility of Viskovatov, or even of Strakhov. All that does concern me is that this is how a number of people regarded Dostoevsky, and that both Tolstoy and Turgenev accepted this view of him. Except for the purpose of understanding his work, it does not matter a button whether or not the statements are true, for no one in his senses can possibly believe that a man so mentally sick could be responsible for his actions, and if they could be proved, their truth would merely add to our admiration of a genius that transcended afflictions more terrible than those we already know he endured.

At the same time, I do not think we shall understand his work at all unless we agree that it is the work of a neurotic. "Neurotic" is a vague word, but it is not half so vague as "prophetic," "mystic," or "religious." Nor, applied to Dostoevsky, is it really vague. The vagueness of the word arises from the fact that neurosis is a question of degree rather than of kind, and there can be no doubt as to the degree of Dostoevsky's abnormality.

Neurosis, as best I can understand it, is a disease arising from the superimposition of a logical structure on a basis of analogical impressions and sensations. In adults it is characterized by outbreaks of a childish character and reversions to childish and adolescent patterns of behavior. In this sense we are all neurotics. The term has meaning only when the outbreaks cause damage to the logical superstructure. One way by which we can tell that is has been damaged is when the sick man consistently fails to distinguish between object and subject. This is a characteristic of the basic analogical mind, what psychologists call the Unconscious or the subconscious mind. We can see it for ourselves in dreams, because the principal difficulty in their translation is the lack of an accusative case. An object in a dream may be both subject and object. "I struck John," for instance, may mean that in attacking John I am really denouncing that quality in myself which I associate with him.

This dream quality of behavior is very obvious in certain extreme forms of neurosis like exhibitionism and voyeurism and sadism and masochism. Almost invariably, each pair is related; the exhibitionist is also a voyeur and the sadist also a masochist, and the one moves into the other with the monotonous persistence of an emotional pendulum. There are plenty of examples in Dostoevsky's work, as in the neurotic girl Lise in *The Brothers Karamazov.*

"There's a book here in which I read about the trial of a Jew who took a child four years old and cut off the fingers from both hands, and then crucified him on the wall, hammered nails into him and crucified him, and afterwards, when he was tried, he said that the child died soon, within four hours. That was "soon." He said the child moaned, kept on moaning, and he stood admiring it. That's nice."

"Nice?"

"Nice. I sometimes imagine it was I who crucified him. He would hang there moaning, and I would sit opposite him, eating pineapple preserve. I'm awfully fond of pineapple preserve. Do you like it?"

It is quite clear from a passage like this that the object is not a real object, and when the sadistic phase moves into the masochistic one there is no question about it. Notice in particular the analogical relationship between the imaginary crime and the punishment Lise inflicts on herself.

As soon as Alyosha had gone, Lise unbolted the door, opened it a little, put her fingers in the crack, and slammed the door with all her might, pinching her finger. Ten seconds after, releasing her finger, she walked softly, slowly to her chair, sat up straight in it and looked intently at her blackened finger and at the blood that oozed from under the nail. Her lips were quivering, and she kept whispering rapidly to herself:

"I am a wretch, wretch, wretch, wretch!"

We can have no difficulty in saying of the character to whom these incidents are ascribed that the logical superstructure of the mind has been damaged, and that Lise is incapable of distinguishing between object and subject. There is yet another characteristic of the neurotic to be distinguished from the episode. Not only is her offense not a real one, but her repentance is likewise unreal. In theory, the offense should be pleasurable and the repentance painful, but in fact it is quite clear that the appropriate emotions have likewise been switched and are as unreal as object and subject. Her pleasure is painful, her pain pleasurable. On the fantasy level where she exists, it is very difficult to distinguish them.

Without an understanding of this, it is almost impossible to understand Dostoevsky's work. Critic after critic has pointed out that he has only one theme: crime and punishment, guilt and repentance. But we have also seen that it is not at all easy to grasp what Dostoevsky means by either, for in him, as in Lise, the logical superstructure of the mind has been damaged, and what he presents to us as crime may prove not to be crime, while what he presents to us as repentance may well prove to be its opposite. For the rational man, however irrational his premises may seem, crime involves an object. Let us say there is a five-pound note lying on my desk, and that my friend John steals it. Jane Austen, if treating this as material for fiction, would probably coldly and deliberately analyze John's character to discover what faults induced him to commit such an act. Trollope would be interested to find out if there were extenuating circumstances and, if there were, to discover how John purged his guilt toward me. Balzac would be so enthusiastic over what could be done by an intelligent man with five pounds that by the time the story ended, John would probably be a millionaire with a priceless collection of furniture and works of art and with a really pretty moral problem on his hands.

For Dostoevsky, all this would be childishness and

logic. John, of course, was madly in love with some woman to whom he wished to give a dinner, and as I was his best friend he naturally stole from me. There is guilt, of course, but then John has never been free of guilt. I know he stole the money, and he knows I know. He longs to burst into tears and confess to me, but I, indulging the natural cruelty in me, which I disguise as morality, refuse him the opportunity. He is thus reduced to compromises and partly confesses by telling me of the wonderful dinner he gave his sweetheart, which cost five pounds. I retort in kind with the story of my maid, who stole two pounds and then went and hanged herself. When, in a fit of desperation at my cruelty, he tries to cut my throat, I am still in a difficult position, for John will insist on being punished in order that he may forgive himself, and I, having already behaved so brutally, have no desire to punish him. Yet, even at the cost of increasing my own guilt, I am compelled to try to diminish his. By the time the story ends—if it ever ends, short of a mutual suicide pact—it will be highly doubtful who stole what from whom. The whole subject-object relationship will have been violently upset. It will be rich in imaginative quality, as no single action can be other than symbolic, and it may even be closer to the truth than the mere series of facts recorded by Jane Austen, Trollope, and Balzac, as there is much in both John and myself which could not be elicited in a court of law. But just because it does not stick to the facts, it must inevitably lack something of those "common feelings of common life" which Jane Austen herself spoke of with approval.

This, I know, sounds like a humorous sketch, but in fact it is a fairly close description of a short novel like *The Eternal Husband*. This is a novel to which Gide rightly attaches great importance, though for me it is important principally because, as far as I know, it is the first example in literature of what I call "the unnatural triangle": the eternal triangle of husband, wife, and lover, or husband, wife, and mistress, as it presents itself to the mind of the adolescent and neurotic. And this is a very striking example of the importance of the subject-object relationship in fiction.

In its adolescent form, it is something that many people have experienced, for two boys who are fast friends frequently fall in love with the same girl, and I suspect that two girls who are fast friends probably also tend to fall in love with the same boy, without ever being aware that they are really being attracted by one another or that the jealousy they feel of one another is really jealousy of the third party. Though this often gives rise to bitterness and heart-searchings, it is a perfectly normal development of the principle of differentiation, and full of poetry and tenderness. The same adolescent reactions when they occur in later life are of a very different kind.

When the novel opens, Velchaninov, the Don Juan, is being haunted by a mysterious figure with a black band round his hat who appears rather like a hallucination. As the story begins in the manner of a fantasy, the reader is not sure but that he is a hallucination. Then, one morning at the peculiar hour of three o'clock (numerals in Dostoevsky are full of interest to those who concern themselves with numeral symbolism), the stranger calls on Velchaninov and reveals himself as Trusotsky, the husband of a woman with whom Velchaninov had an affair some nine years previously. He is in mourning for his wife, and has come accompanied by his daughter, Lisa, aged eight, who is clearly Velchaninov's child, to look up his wife's old lovers, Bagautov and Velchaninov, whose relationship with her he has learned of only since her death. Bagautov gives him the slip by dying, but Trusotsky does have the melancholy pleasure of attending his funeral. He is drinking heavily and taking out his humiliation on the child. Velchaninov has her removed for safety to the house of some friends, but she is so attached to the man she believes to be her father that she pines away and dies. Then, in an extraordinary scene Trusotsky induces Velchaninov to drink with him.

"But now it's not enough that we've drunk together, Alexey Ivanovitch. I must have something else to be satisfied."

He laid his hat on a chair and gazed at him, gasping for breath a little as he had done just before.

"Kiss me, Alexey Ivanovitch," he suggested suddenly.

"You're drunk," Velchaninov declared, stepping back.

"Yes, but kiss me all the same, Alexey Ivanovitch. Oh, kiss me! Why, I kissed your hand just now."

Once more, as in the scene from *The Brothers Karamazov*, the subject-object relationship has been disturbed, and we begin to realize that, just as Lise's pleasure in her sadistic reverie is fictitious, Trusotsky's humiliation is partly delight. Later Trusotsky's attitude becomes even plainer.

"I loved you, Alexey Ivanovitch," Pavel Pavlovitch articu-
lated as though he had suddenly made up his mind to speak,
"and all that year at T—— I loved you. You did not notice it,"
he went on in a voice that quivered, to Velchaninov's positive
horror. "I was too insignificant compared with you to let you
see it. And, indeed, there was no need, perhaps. And I've
thought of you all these nine years, because there has never been
another year in my life like that one."

Trusotsky is on the point of remarriage, but nothing
will satisfy him except to introduce Velchaninov to his
future wife. She, it turns out, is only fifteen—one of the
many indications of Dostoevsky's interest in immature
girls, and it is a weakness he shares with his character.

"That's what bowled me over; that she was still going to
school with the satchel on her arm full of copy books and pens—
he-he. That satchel fascinated me. It's innocence that charms
me, Alexey Ivanovitch; it's not so much beauty of face, it's
that. She giggles in the corner with her school friend, and how
she laughs, my goodness!"

Velchaninov accompanies him to the girl's house, and
there, to his own astonishment, notices himself singing a
love song in a passionate way that attracts attention. Not
only is Trusotsky seeking a repetition of his own humiliation, but Velchaninov, against his will and apparently
against his inclinations, for he does not seem ever to have
been attracted by children, is being forced into the position of supplanting him. The women involved seem to
have nothing to do with the male characters, who merely
use them as an excuse for their own performance. They
seem to have no real subject-object relationship, and are

treated almost as parts of one another, like the murderer and the examining magistrate in *Crime and Punishment*; people who at an unconscious level are necessary to one another for the performance of a particular action, to such a degree that there exists between them a real homosexual attraction and that at certain moments they can even exchange functions. This is shown in the climax when Trusotsky, having nursed Velchaninov through a dangerous liver attack, suddenly tries to cut his throat. At one moment Velchaninov is the subject, at the next he is the object.

This is the story to which Gide rightly attached so much importance, for it is a situation that occurs in his own work, particularly in *The Counterfeiters*, where it is complicated with incestuous feelings; in Proust's work, between Marcel and Albertine's lovers; in Joyce's *Exiles* and *Ulysses*, and in Lawrence's *Sons and Lovers*, as well as in several of his short stories like *Jimmy and the Desperate Woman*. This is how Lawrence summarizes the situation in the latter story.

And as he sat in the taxi, a perverse but intense desire for her came over him, making him almost helpless. He could feel so strongly the presence of the other man about her, and this went to his head like neat spirits. That other man! In some subtle inexplicable way he was actually bodily present, the husband. The woman moved in his aura. She was hopelessly married to him.

In Dostoevsky's novel it is a love affair on the level of fantasy in which the husband or someone in a husband's position connives at his own deception for the sake of a certain abnormal pleasure he derives from the situation;

where, in fact, he actually identifies himself with the lover and compels the lover to join in the identification so as to alter the subject-object relationship and confuse the emotions appropriate to it, it being obvious that where subject and object tend to change places, pleasure and pain must do the same. In Proust's work at least, and possibly in the work of others, it is somehow related to modern idealistic philosophies that make no clear distinction between subject and object.

2.

Dostoevsky was fascinated by the problem of the lesser neuroses. He was himself a pathological gambler and wrote a very interesting novel on the subject. *Crime and Punishment* began as a novel entitled *The Drunkards*, describing the life of a dipsomaniac, Marmeladov, and his family. By a subconscious process of attraction, this drew in the story of a student, Raskolnikov, who murders and robs an old money-lender and her sister, and the second theme gradually dominated the novel. There is no contradiction between the two plots because, as Dostoevsky originally conceived the theme, there appears to be no real distinction between murder and alcoholism. Both, as he presents them, are compulsive acts for which the murderer and the drunkard are not really responsible. The student, a man who has thought a great deal on the subject, comes to this conclusion independently.

According to his conviction therefore, it would seem that this eclipse of reason and loss of will-power attacked a man like some disease, developed gradually and reached its climax a short time before the crime was actually committed; it continued in the same way at the moment of the crime and for a short time afterwards, according to each individual; then it passed off like any other disease.

The two themes are linked in the persons of Marmeladov's daughter, Sonya, who prostitutes herself for her family, and Raskolnikov's sister, Dunya, who, having had an unpleasant experience with a Mr. Svidrigailov, agrees to marry a man called Luzhin entirely for her brother's sake. A letter from his mother announcing the marriage throws Raskolnikov somewhat off balance. Passing through the street, he sees a girl "of about sixteen, or possibly only fifteen," drunk and with her clothes torn. She has been made drunk and then raped, "for the first time," Raskolnikov thinks. An elderly man is watching her greedily, and Raskolnikov quarrels with him, calling him "Svidrigailov," implying the identification between the violated girl and his sister.

After this, Raskolnikov has a terrible dream in which he is still a small boy and, while out walking with his father, sees a peasant beat an old mare to death. He rushes through the crowd to kiss the dead horse on the muzzle, the eyes, and the lips. Raskolnikov himself, like Dostoevsky, apparently takes this dream to refer to the forthcoming murder of the old woman, though in fact it appears to be a parricide dream in which the horse represents the father. Conceivably it could be a dream immediately preceding an epileptic attack and symbolizing its symptoms, but it has nothing to do with the old woman.

After the murders Raskolnikov feels the need for confession and atonement. As with Lise, the sadistic fit is
followed by the masochistic one, but whereas the drunkard, owing to the public nature of his guilt, can enjoy this
relief almost at once, Raskolnikov is cut off from it, and
accordingly cut off from humanity, represented by his
mother and sister. He is then driven to the neurotic expedient of exhibitionism, and symbolically parades his
crime before the police officer and the examining magistrate, the latter of whom understands him perfectly,
being, indeed, only Raskolnikov himself in the aspect of
voyeur. For with exhibitionism and voyeurism, as with
sadism and masochism, there is no real subject or object;
the exhibitionist can expose himself only to himself, and
the voyeur can see only what he already knows.

"And that's not all," says the examining magistrate. "He will
get too enterprising; he'll start poking his nose where he isn't
wanted; he'll talk incessantly about things he ought never to
have mentioned. Talking in all sorts of roundabout ways—
allegorically, ha, ha!"

It is not only Raskolnikov who is betraying himself.
When the examining magistrate and he discuss the nature
of crime, and the former defends the socialist view of it
as a protest against bad and abnormal social conditions,
Raskolnikov breaks in with "A forty year old man
violates a ten year old girl—was it environment that
drove him to do it?" Dostoevsky, too, is talking too
much about things he should never have mentioned.

Now, up to this point the novel is regular enough; at
least, it has nothing like the complication of later books

like *The Idiot* or *The Brothers Karamazov*, which become progressively wilder and more metaphysical. But then the magistrate begins to reveal something that was only hinted at in the opening of the book. Raskolnikov turns out to be the author of an article on crime in which he had argued that exceptional people had the right to break the moral law. Raskolnikov, in fact, is not a sick man at all. "A Roman Caesar is held down under this hump." Like Julien Sorel, he is a Napoleon repressed by poverty.

"No, those men are not made like that," Raskolnikov thinks in despair. "A real *ruler of men*, a man to whom everything is permitted, takes Toulon by storm, carries out a massacre in Paris, *forgets* an army in Egypt, *wastes* half a million men in his Moscow campaign, and gets away with a pun in Vilna."

With the name of Napoleon we are off into metaphysics. In the nineteenth-century novel he plays an almost symbolic part. Stendhal and Balzac exalt him in different ways as the hero, the man whose will and energy triumph over every obstacle, but in Russian literature— and not for nationalistic reasons only—he appears as a villain, a representative of the triumphant Western will as opposed to the Oriental dream of passivity. This is his part in *War and Peace* and *Crime and Punishment*. But in Dostoevsky's work he represents less the will than the intellect, and what is opposed to him is less the wisdom of nature than religious faith. Faith for that part of the Russian mind which leans toward the East is associated with the idea of surrender, and hence with the instincts, whereas among Western writers it goes side by side with good works, self-control, and judgment.

Now, though Dostoevsky was lacking in intelligence, a quality that cannot exist side by side with nervous disease, he had a very fine intellect, which distinguishes him beyond comparison from the romantic writers whom he succeeds and who influenced his work: Sade, Sue, Hoffmann, Lytton, Hugo. It enabled him to confine his work mainly to the field of his own observation—his own sick soul and the souls that resembled it—and it acted as a control to prevent his work's degenerating into idle fantasy. But more and more, as his work develops, he attributes greater significance to the manifestations of the analogical mind, and as these aspects of the personality become clearer before him, it becomes clearer that the villain of the piece is the intellect.

Even more interesting is the fact that it is precisely at this point of the narrative that a new character, Svidrigailov, is introduced. Svidrigailov is the employer who had tried to seduce Raskolnikov's sister, and he is one of the figures who, according to Dostoevsky's biographer, most resembled their author. This I find hard to believe, but undoubtedly he represents an aspect of Dostoevsky's character which must have been visible to his friends.

But I find it impossible to believe that the examining magistrate's revelation about Raskolnikov's views has not produced Svidrigailov's appearance at this point, or, alternatively, that Svidrigailov's impending appearance has not produced the revelation about Raskolnikov. The two things are linked; Svidrigailov is only another version of Raskolnikov (as, in a more limited sense, the early

Raskolnikov is only another version of Marmeladov), the Raskolnikov of the newspaper article, who had argued that everything is permitted to the superior man. His relationship to Raskolnikov resembles that of Smerdyakov to Ivan Karamazov. He is the shadow cast by the intellect on human affairs, and it is he, and not the murderer Raskolnikov, who has committed the real crime with which the novel deals; the crime about which one is compelled to ask if it can be forgiven.

"A woman called Resslich had a distant relative living with her, a niece, I believe, a deaf and dumb girl of fifteen, or even only fourteen, whom this Resslich woman hated like poison, grudging her every morsel she ate. She also beat her mercilessly. One day she was found hanging in the attic. The verdict was suicide. After the usual formalities, the case was closed, but afterwards certain information reached the police to the effect that the child had been cruelly—interfered with by Svidrigailov."

"To me," says Svidrigailov, almost in the words of Trusotsky in *The Eternal Husband*, "a girl of sixteen—those still-childish eyes, shyness, and tears of bashfulness —to me all this is much better than beauty." And Raskolnikov replies: "In fact, it is this monstrous difference in years and mental development that arouses desire in you."

The image of the violated child haunts the whole book, as it haunts so many other novels of Dostoevsky. She appears for a page or two in the passage I have quoted from the early part of the story and reappears in a dream to Svidrigailov, first in her human despair, then as a caricature of the child-love he had once innocently enjoyed—for Svidrigailov is quite sincere in saying that he loved children—and can never enjoy again. Thereupon he kills himself.

There are not, I believe, two novels in *Crime and Punishment*, but three. There is *The Drunkards*, centering on Marmeladov; the novel about the murder, centering on Raskolnikov, who begins as a sort of reflection of the drunkard, but develops into something more sinister; and the third novel, which deals with Svidrigailov. It is not so much a change of purpose as a deepening of the author's idea of guilt. Alcoholism and murder are merely allegorical forms of the real crime that has been committed. We fail to read *Crime and Punishment* correctly unless we recognize that at the end the problem of neurotic guilt is no more resolved than it was when the book opened. It is not resolved in the later novels, though there it is attacked with all the resources of metaphysics. It cannot be resolved because fundamentally it is associated in Dostoevsky's mind with unnatural crime, which his intellect tells him cannot be forgiven, though his instinct suggests to him that it should. As a neurotic, he cannot accept the verdict of the intelligence, which is that since there has been no full responsibility there cannot have been real crime. This is liberal doctrine, Turgenev's doctrine, and, apart from the philosophical objections to it, Dostoevsky rejected it because it deprives the neurotic of his greatest treasure, his illusory feeling of uniqueness.

But Dostoevsky's dilemma is even more complicated than this, and the complications are so much part of the analogical nature of a great deal of his thought that it is exceedingly difficult to describe them objectively. Svidrigailov and the Raskolnikov of this part of the book both represent the intellect, and the intellect, in Dostoevsky's scheme, is atheistic. Now, there is, as well as the intellectual form of atheism, a neurotic, instinctive form, which is the only one that Dostoevsky really understands. The neurotic, in revolt against his father, finds himself in revolt against all accepted forms of authority, culminating in God the Father. But he cannot stop here. Just as an adolescent, in revolt against his father's authority, will need to testify to his own belief in himself by doing things that his father believes wrong, the neurotic atheist is compelled to act against the moral law. It is not only that "everything is permitted to the superior man"; it is that the superior man, in order to prove his superiority, is compelled to behave criminally. There is a world of difference between the two attitudes, but Dostoevsky either does not see it or ignores it. What he does see with great clarity is that the neurotic criminal cannot escape from the sense of his own guilt and the need for repentance and forgiveness. And thus we arrive at a typical Dostoevskian paradox, which becomes much clearer in *The Possessed*, that his favorite characters believe in Christ without believing in God, in mercy without believing in justice.

"I believe in Russia. I believe in the Greek Orthodox Church. I—I believe in the body of Christ—I believe that the second coming will take place in Russia—I believe—" Shatov murmured in a frenzy.

"But in God? In God?"

"I—I shall believe in God."

On the fantasy level, the paradox does not really exist. The instincts, represented as the feminine, maternal side of the character, and the judgment, representing the father, are always shown as struggling not to conquer each other, but to produce a reasonable balance, and they sometimes do this by means of a compromise figure that is at the same time both feminine and masculine. The figure is sometimes homosexual, which leads to a great deal of misinterpretation by psychoanalysts; sometimes it is Christ or someone representing Christ—for instance, a man called Christopher or a woman called Christine. Christ is the symbol of the mediator: "None comes to the Father except through me." In Dostoevsky's metaphysics, which are largely analogical, this compromise figure takes on the attributes of God.

The Possessed again is haunted by the figure of the violated child, but the publishers disguised this by the suppression of three chapters dealing with Stavrogin's crime, which is identical with Svidrigailov's. Stavrogin, in a confession of which he has had three hundred copies printed (again there is some sort of numeral symbolism) tells how he had been lodging in a house where the family had a daughter of fourteen. He had complained about the loss of his penknife; the child had been blamed, and, though in the meantime he had found it, he permitted her to be cruelly and wrongfully thrashed in his presence.

Every unusually disgraceful, utterly degrading, dastardly, and, above all, ridiculous situation in which I ever happened to be in my life always roused in me, side by side with extreme anger, an incredible delight.

By this time Stavrogin had already made up his mind to rape the child, and during the next few days stole some money from a poor official who was too scared to charge him. After the rape, he tells us, the child became delirious and repeatedly cried: "I killed God." She hanged herself while Stavrogin was actually in the house, aware of what she was doing, and only when he was satisfied that she was dead did he go to a party, where he behaved in a gay and lighthearted manner. But since then, he says, he is haunted by the dead child.

I saw before me Matryosha, emaciated, with feverish eyes, in every point exactly as she was when she stood on the threshold of my room and, shaking her head at me, threatened me with her tiny fist. Nothing has ever been so agonizing to me. The pitiable despair of a helpless creature [*of ten years* struck out] with an unformed mind, threatening me—with what? what could she do to me, O Lord?—but blaming, of course, herself alone! Nothing like that has ever happened to me. I sat till night came without moving, having lost count of time. Is this what they call remorse or repentance? I do not know, and even now [*the recollection of the deed itself is perhaps not loathsome to me. Perhaps the memory of it even now contains something which is gratifying to my passion* struck out] cannot say. [1]

Once again, here we have a crime that is not a crime, and remorse that is not remorse because it so obviously contains more pleasure than pain. I find the greatest difficulty in making up my mind about the nature of the

---

[1] *Stavrogin's Confession* (Hogarth Press).

crime that Dostoevsky's heroes confess to. The details are always elusive. The age of the child is always changing, as here from fourteen to ten, or the form of the suicide changes, as in *Crime and Punishment*, from hanging to drowning. Essentially, as it is presented, the crime is too perfect, too Germanic, too literary. It may be compared with a later gimmick in sensational fiction in which a woman overcome with grief for the death of a child or a mother she loves (*cf.* Somerset Maugham and Aldous Huxley) immediately has sexual relations with the first man she meets. It conveys no conviction to me. A neurotic woman will sometimes confess to it, but it is not necessarily true, and sometimes, at least, represents a mere wish-fulfillment. But we cannot mistake the meaning of the child's "I have killed God." This is the real purpose of the intellectual neurotic's crime, the murder of the Father.

And it is not for nothing that, as Freud has pointed out, this is precisely the subject of *The Brothers Karamazov*. This is the most metaphysical of the Dostoevsky novels. The three brothers are a typical dream image of the total personality—not characters from real life, but aspects of the personality: Ivan, the intellect; Dmitri, the senses; and Alyosha, the soul. Alyosha and Dmitri are simply Prince Myshkin and Rogojin from *The Idiot* under different names. Rogojin had actually committed the offense of violating the heroine at the age of twelve, and in the original plan of *Karamazov* Dmitri was to have committed it.

The fourth figure—usually in personality dreams a

shadow who represents death—is the illegitimate half-brother, Smerdyakov. He, like Svidrigailov, is the shadow of the intellect represented in action, and so the actual murderer, but all three are to some extent guilty of their father's murder. Ivan's guilt is the greatest because his, like Raskolnikov's and Stavrogin's, is a proud, presumptuous intellect that has taught to Smerdyakov the lesson that there is no moral law. Yet, at the same time, it is Ivan who is obsessed by the crimes of sadistic maniacs, who lists all the horrors committed on innocent children and denies the right of anyone to forgive them.

"I don't want the mother to embrace the oppressor who threw her son to the dogs! She dare not forgive him! Let her forgive him for herself if she will, let her forgive the torturer for the immeasurable torture of her mother's heart. But the sufferings of her tortured child she had no right to forgive; she dare not forgive the torturer even if the child were to forgive him. And if that is so, if they dare not forgive, what becomes of harmony? Is there in the whole world a being who would have the right to forgive and could forgive? I don't want harmony. From love for humanity I don't want it. I would rather be left with the unavenged suffering. I would rather remain with my unavenged suffering and unsatisfied indignation, *even if I were wrong*. Besides, too high a price is asked for harmony; it's beyond our means to pay so much to enter on it. And so I hasten to give back my entrance ticket, and if I am an honest man I am bound to give it back as soon as possible. And that I am doing. It's not God that I don't accept, Alyosha, only I most respectfully return him the ticket."

This wonderful scene is the profoundest statement of Dostoevsky's dilemma, but on his terms it cannot be resolved. So far as I understand it, the responsibility for unnatural crime still rests on the intellect, but, by a paradox, it is only the intellect which, holding God responsible, can repudiate God. Alyosha's reminder to Ivan that Christ, because of His sufferings, is entitled to forgive, is neither theologically nor philosophically sound, for mercy without justice seems to involve a contradiction, as does the enthronement of Christ and the abolition of God.

The truth is that probably once again Dostoevsky is trying to solve his problem on the level of fantasy, and is failing because he fails to distinguish between subject and object. It is almost as though, in the switching of poles which we have already noticed in other, less metaphysical, dilemmas, he is transferring to the intellect the guilt of the instincts. If this be so, it was a difficulty he cleverly anticipated, for, though the real murderer is Smerdyakov, and the morally guilty party Ivan, it is Dmitri who innocently suffers for their crime, and it is to him, rather than to them, that the new life is promised.

chapter 14

Transition: Henry James

To students of the novel, James is interesting principally as the transition figure between the classical novel and the modern novel. Somewhere in his work the change takes place between the two; somewhere the ship has been boarded by pirates, and when at last it comes into harbor, nobody could recognize in its rakish lines the respectable passenger ship that set sail from the other side of the water. The passengers would seem to have been murdered on the way, and there is nothing familiar about the dark foreign faces that peer at us over the edge.

In the beginning it is all plain sailing. A novel by James looks like a classical novel because it follows the traditions of the classical novel. It derives directly from the novel purified of its Dickensian excrescences and irrelevancies by Flaubert and Turgenev, and even bears a family resemblance to the naturalistic novel of Zola and the Goncourts. It appears to deal with real people in real situations, and yet, when one comes to examine them, people and situations cease to be real in any sense in which a nineteenth-century novelist would have understood the word. As James's work develops—still on the best naturalistic principles of observation and documentation—we become aware that the impression of reality the novels convey is rather like that conveyed by a Kafka allegory. They are held together not by any process of comparison with external models, but by some sort of interior logic, by the internal relations of characters and incidents.

Now, this is a condition to which every work of art aspires. When the novelist has looted some residential area, he no longer concerns himself with its fortunes, but occupies himself cheerfully in the rearrangement of his loot in the manner that best displays its charms. But he still attaches value to the loot, and his rearrangement takes note of the quality of sterling silver and antique furniture. Glancing over his shoulder at Henry James, he perceives in astonishment that James is much more concerned with his private arrangements than with the value of the loot and that, in fact, he is quite content to use any old gim-crack chair or pot as a stand-in. The arrangements are impeccable and rigorous, but at times they resemble those of a magpie of genius rather than those of an artist. He also begins to realize why people do not call on the Master. He gives them the jumps.

There was a general reason for this which I can best describe by linking his name with the names of Ben Jonson, Flaubert, and Joyce, other great literary men who seem to me to have loved literature too well; who cared more for its form than its content and adopted toward it the fetichistic attitude of impoverished old maids inheriting ancestral mansions. Of their devotion there is no doubt. One has only to hear Jonson.

> *I who spend half my nights and all my days*
> *Here in a cell, to get a dark pale face,*

> *And come forth worth the laurel or the bays,*
> *And in this age can hope no better grace—*

But devotion is not enough. There is a human thing to
which, it seems to me, they do violence. Ordinary human
love was something that none of them could describe because literature was their one true love. As an artist,
Jonson was greater than Shakespeare, for at least he saw
to the printing and preservation of his work, but at the
same time there is a decent indifference to one's progeny
not unbecoming to any father, for, as the Spanish poet
puts it, "Life is short, and art is very long and besides,
it doesn't matter."

2.

But there is also a particular reason why the common
reader has never liked James. Of the two great influences
to which he constantly refers, Turgenev and Flaubert,
there is in his work little trace of the former, much, very
much indeed, of the latter. He praised Flaubert finely as
"a powerful, serious, melancholy, manly, deeply-cor-
rupted, yet not corrupting, nature." His choice of epithets
is significant in the light of what we already know of the
direction the novel was taking, and the re-emergence of
sadistic romanticism in the work of Flaubert and Dostoevsky. This is the period in the history of the novel when
the pull of the submarine current of fantasy becomes apparent. What used to be called the *fin de siécle* attitude of
Wilde and the other symbolists makes its way into fiction,

and much of James's work is closer in spirit to Wilde's
Picture of Dorian Gray than he himself would have cared
to admit. Its subject is evil, but not tangible evil as Dickens
would have recognized it, cruelty, greed, or license. The
evil of the novelist influenced by symbolism has no real
concrete manifestation, for it is the evil of Sade and of
the German romantics, a product of the fantasy for which
there is no satisfactory objective equivalent, at least in the
sort of novel which James believed he was writing.

We can see this in *The Turn of the Screw* (which may
be compared with Stevenson's *Dr. Jekyll and Mr. Hyde*,
as both have a dreamlike quality and obviously imply a
great deal more than they state). On the surface, it is a
straightforward ghost story, a German horror tale the
theme of which was given to James by the Archbishop of
Canterbury. The editors of James's notebooks take this
as disproof of the Freudian implications that have been
read into the tale. The Freudian reading seems to me irrelevant, but it is not disproved by a fact of this kind, for
the themes that attract us when we hear them told are
just as capable of analysis as those we create for ourselves.

It describes through the narrative of a governess, improbably placed in charge of the entire upbringing of a
boy and girl, a growing awareness on her part that the
children are being corrupted, and that those who are
corrupting them are the ghosts of their previous governess
and a valet with whom she had had a love affair. The
children know of the love affair, which ended in an abortion and two deaths, and the narrator—to whom the two
villains are visible—struggles with them for the children's

souls, but instead produces the sudden death of the boy, who has leanings in the direction of virtue.

As a work of art, this Ode on the Intimations of Immorality in Childhood seems to an old-fashioned realist like myself as foolish a performance as Stevenson's. As a key to James's work it is, of course, invaluable.

The first thing to observe is James's characteristic difficulty, which is equally characteristic of Stevenson and of other romantic story-tellers in the period before Freud. To carry any real conviction, the story must make evil real to us, as Dostoevsky makes it real in *The Possessed*. But the tradition in which James is writing requires him to prevent the evil ever becoming tangible to us. Like Flaubert as he himself saw him, James must be corrupted but not corrupting. This, as I see it, is the real meaning of the repeated cry in his notebooks that he wants "to let himself go," but cannot. For, though it represents a considerable advance on his early attempts at externalizing what he calls "evil," a love affair between a governess and manservant, even if it is followed by an abortion, is not necessarily evil at all. As readers, we may be permitted to argue that, on the contrary, to have been friendly with the victims of such a human tragedy might well have been to the benefit of two precocious children.

But this, of course, is not what James means; the love affair and the abortion are only a symbol of what he is really getting at, and as he cannot tell us what that is, he can only fall back on his style to persuade us of what is not apparent from the facts. This style, intermediate

227

between the lucid style of the early novels and the turgid
one of the later, already shows a block, a stylistic im-
pediment that embarrasses us like a bad stammer. In the
later novels, for all that James had taken another step in
the direction of "letting himself go," the stammer has
become so acute that they are much more comfortable
to read in the eloquent summaries of F. W. Dupee than in
James's own words. This is the penalty for having something to say which, as a moral man, you do not feel entitled to say. To be deeply corrupted yet not corrupting,
one must develop a stammer.

3.

The main theme of James's work, then, was that of
innocence and corruption, and it formed an antithesis
about which his whole literary personality shaped itself.
Even in an early novel like *Washington Square*, the principal characters are an innocent rich girl and a corrupt
and heartless adventurer in quest of her money. This is
the same theme he used at the end of his life for *The
Wings of the Dove*.

But there, as in other works of the intervening period,
he complicated the subject enormously by extending the
antithesis to govern his own attitude to Europe. He was
fascinated by Europe, and to him Europe spelled corruption, and, like the ingenuous girl in *Washington Square*, he
was in love with corruption. Nationalist criticism has
elevated his choice of residence and citizenship into something like national apostasy, but one must be very simple-

minded indeed to take James's "America" and "Europe" literally.

To do so, one must assume that for James the virtue of innocence was best represented by a Wall Street tycoon. That would seem to be the theme of *The American*, which presents the pattern in its simplest form. Innocence, represented by an American businessman, Christopher Newman, the source of whose wealth is not defined, falls in love with a member of the Bellegarde family, who represent corruption because the girl's mother and brother had murdered her father in order to bring about her previous marriage to a M. de Cintre. Clearly, this is the same theme as *The Turn of the Screw*, for the Bellegardes are being themselves corrupted from beyond the grave, by history.

It also represents another peculiar aspect of James's antithesis, for, as usual, he portrays innocence as rolling in money and corruption as seedy and hard-up. Though it is almost a contradiction in terms, it seems as if James were incapable of imagining any form of innocence which did not involve parting with hard cash or any form of corruption which was not broke.

It represents another form of the process by which James was being caught in the octopus of metaphor, almost unknown to himself and at a period when he seriously believed himself to be an objective writer working in the great tradition of the novel. To take him literally, one would have to treat him as the most materialistic and venal writer who ever lived. If, as seems plain to me, he was nothing of the sort, we must treat "money" as meaning something other than it means in the text. It is a frightening thought, for it means that even at this period the work of an exceedingly self-conscious writer is already out of his own control. In the Freudian sense "money" should mean love, and at the deepest level it may perhaps mean that James's work should be regarded as a struggle between his own lovelessness and some ghost of tender feeling, but on a more conscious level, a level on which James could have handled it at all, it seems to mean "freedom" as opposed to "necessity." I do not think it necessarily means freedom in any material sense, but rather freedom of choice, freedom of will, and that this is what the "European" tempters are trying to steal and replace with something determined. One might almost describe the antithesis in terms of "election" and "grace." But though this helps me to understand what the Bellegardes want from Newman, I am not so clear as to what Newman wants from the Bellegardes. It may be knowledge; it may be experience. If this be so, one would assume that James's problem was to acquire the experience of Europe without the historic limitations imposed by it, to learn but remain free, to be ultimately "deeply corrupted but not corrupting."

As James's work develops, it tends to become more and more disembodied. The murder in *The American* is a metaphysical murder like the murder in *The Brothers Karamazov*, but, even so, it was too physical for the mature James, and after this he concentrated more on suggesting the evil that he could not state. In *Portrait of a Lady* it is built up by hints, little by little, but as he has never really defined what he means by evil, the hints almost escape us, and we listen and strain, feeling deaf and shortsighted, wondering what on earth it is about Osmond and Madame Merle that makes them different, if different they are, from the Touchetts and Lord Warburton.

In the treatment of the theme in *The Wings of the Dove* James reaches the climax of evasiveness. Why the theme should have been intruded on the novel at all is not clear, for the original subject was conceived round the death of his brilliant cousin Minny and her will to live. But because his heroine's will to live is really a will to love, he rapidly switched the emphasis from her to the man she loves, Merton Densher, and Merton's betrothed, Kate Croy, who persuades him to make himself loved by Milly Theale in order to inherit her wealth. Densher agrees to the last stages of the plot only on condition that Kate becomes his mistress, which she does while he pays his respects to Milly. The conspirators' mean plot is revealed to Milly by the wicked Lord Mark, whereupon the woman with all the wealth in the world—James cannot stop being enthusiastic about the vast size of the Theale fortune—in the reiterated pomposity of James's Mandarin style, "turns her face to the wall" and dies of a disease as unnamed as the source of her wealth. Yet by a supreme generosity she leaves Densher a wealthy man, though a most unhappy one, for he realizes too late that he loved her, and now he can marry Kate only if she agrees to sacrifice the fortune, which Kate, of course, will not do.

At the same time, the fortune is supposititious, for not only do the conspirators destroy Milly's deathbed letter to

Densher, but also they do not open the letter from her New York lawyers, which, we are given to understand, makes Densher a wealthy man. Evasiveness could go no further. "The truth was doubtless that really, when it came to any free handling and naming of things, they were living together the five of them in an air in which an ugly effect of 'blurting out' might easily be produced," the author says blandly, but no such ugliness ever intrudes. "Necessary" scenes are suppressed and reported much later at third hand and in Mandarin style: Lord Mark's cruel revelation; Densher's final twenty-minute interview with the dying girl he is deceiving; Milly's death, of which no single detail reaches us. And in the grave, owlish, theatrical scenes information is withheld to the last gasp of extracted dialogue, as when Densher has his interview with Kate with the dead girl's letter unopened in his pocket, the letter that is to make him a rich man, the letter that is burned unread.

It is too much for the mere reader, but one can understand James's fascination for the critics in a novel like this, all but divorced from reality, all but autonomous and self-sustaining, scene giving birth to scene and metaphor to metaphor, as in a dream. And, without recourse to the notebooks, which gives birth to what is more than the reader can imagine. Does Venice give birth to the word "palace," which gives birth to the metaphor of Milly as the "princess," or does she die in Venice because the word "princess" came first into James's mind? Local color, the physical body of the novel, which had never been very strong in James's work, becomes as disembodied as the elaborate metaphors he plays with. One ends up on tiptoe, straining, straining to catch those last whispers coming from farther and farther offstage as incident and background retreat further into the labyrinth of the author's mind.

4.

Once more, one has to ask what "money" in these novels means, because what James has gained in his development is a freedom that belongs more properly to the theater than to the novel. The sense of freedom belongs to the dramatist as the sense of necessity belongs to the novelist. In the theater the presence of an audience and its consent to the conventions of the art make it necessary for a character to appear when he is needed and from whatever remote regions he must be brought. In the novel, which is made for the solitary reader, the less contrived the action is the better, and from that absence of contrivance the novelist must make a new sort of grace. Now, not only does James impose his action on his characters as though they enjoyed complete liberty, but he also turns it into pattern. This is good theatrical practice, for in the theater an action that is effective the first time is many times more effective when repeated, and James deliberately duplicated his effects in this way.

The notebooks, in particular, show him at it. Assume, he says, that a society girl gives her socially unpresentable mother out for dead. This, as he recognizes, is a good theme if treated from the mother's point of view. But by

the time he has mulled it over, it becomes the story of a socially unpresentable mother ditched by her society daughter and a socially unpresentable man likewise ditched by his society wife. This does not multiply the effect of the theme as it would in the theater; it diminishes it by robbing the characters of their uniqueness. They have simply become aspects of a pattern.

So, in one of the later stories, *Julia Bride*, we find a girl of obviously "unsteady" character whose mother has had three divorces while she herself has had six broken engagements. As she is now proposing to marry money, Julia approaches her onetime stepfather to ask him to accept full responsibility for his divorce from her mother. But the stepfather himself is proposing to marry money, so, instead of agreeing to Julia's proposal, he wants *her* to acquit *him* of responsibility for the divorce. This, one feels, ought to have been duplication enough for anybody, but James is only beginning to warm up to the possibilities. This time Julia turns to an old sweetheart to ask him to accept responsibility for their broken romance (that something more than this was involved is implied but not stated). For a change, she finds him enthusiastic, the reason being that he too is marrying money, and not only is he anxious that his wife-to-be shall learn that there was nothing between himself and Julia, but, as Julia's young man has breeding as well as cash, and his intended is a social climber, he wishes to give her an item for her collection! With intrigue of this sort, there is no possibility of character-drawing in the sense in which the story-teller understands it.

It may be because of the light it throws on James's own problem as an artist that I have always had a soft spot in my heart for *The Tragic Muse*. The novel has emotion of a type that James, like Jonson, understood: the love of the artist for his art. But art, as he describes it, is quite different from art as any other of the great nineteenth-century novelists understood it. It is an art like a religion—not merely an alternative way of life, but an alternative to life. Like the evil on which it is frequently predicated, it is an absolute, and its pursuit is an esoteric cult.

And again we are faced with James's difficulty, for the art he writes of is something that demands the ultimate from its devotees, and James finds it impossible to describe a character who can give in that way. There is no place here for a Gauguin or a Van Gogh. This, of course, is not a criticism of James, for in fact the novelist is closer to society than any other artist, and it was not until the poets had shown the way behind the mirror—above all, not until scientists like Freud had given qualified approval to the experiment—that novelists began to explore the resources of their own medium.

Art, then, has become a new thing, but Nick Dormer's sacrifice of his political career to follow it is futile because his well-bred wife, Julia Dallow, will, as Gabriel Nash predicts, turn him into a society painter. The only figure who has the capacity for living the artistic life with all its implied sordidness is the Jewess Miriam Rooth, and even she will never become a really great actress because, whatever interest the diplomat Peter Sherringham may have in her art, he will marry little Biddy Dormer, who has nothing of the makings of an artist in her. He will not marry Miriam and join her in the gutter. He will not write the sort of plays that would enable her to give new life to the theater. Like James himself, he and Nick Dormer stand on the edge of the marsh, looking longingly at the sunlit meadows beyond, the meadows where Proust will one day walk, but which they will never reach.

chapter 15

Thomas Hardy

By 1882, when Trollope died, the novel as the nine-teenth century knew it was already done for. In Russia, Chekhov had begun to be known; in France, Maupassant. Both were short-story writers rather than novelists, and both had affiliations with naturalism, the literary theory that evolved about *Madame Bovary*. In England, naturalism was still almost unknown, and was finally introduced by an Irishman, George Moore. In fact, the social ground-work for naturalism had never been laid, and writers and public were still wedded to the idea of the novel as enter-tainment. But the tendency to symbolism had already shown itself in the form of a revived romanticism, and novels and tales were being largely written by poets who managed to sustain their dual identity. Hardy and Mere-dith are good early examples, as Stevenson and Kipling are good later ones. Both Hardy and Meredith were fine poets, and Hardy, at least, was a great one.

At the same time, poets do not make great novelists. Theirs is an interior world, to begin with. The novelist's is an exterior world that he tries to assimilate to an interior world. Their characters are nearly always more than life-size; they act with extraordinary boldness in landscapes of surpassing beauty, and the accidents that befall them, while picturesque, are rarely of human significance. They are also more easily influenced by general ideas than the novelist, whose thoughts have to be passed through human channels not remarkable for their powers of retention. I have already quoted the anonymous critic who suggests that the teaching of philosophy in German universities may have something to do with the fact that Germany has never produced a great novelist.

Thomas Hardy and George Meredith were both influenced by the Darwinian theory. Hardy was very deeply influenced by it. Already, before Darwin, there had been among the educated classes in England a decline in religious belief. Among the working classes both Arnold and Florence Nightingale noticed that the decline took the form of atheism. Atheism is the poor man's agnosticism, and the Darwinian theory hastened the process.

Up to this point it might have been said that in the novel science and art were working together toward a more rational picture of human existence, but Darwin left the poor artist's part in this far behind. In his field, tradition seemed useless, for this was something unknown to the thinkers of Greece and Rome. It opened up a vast and frightening panorama of cosmic history, put a new edge on the conflict that people like Dostoevsky were portraying between science and religion, and even divided the rationalists themselves.

In fact, there were two ways in which they could accept Darwin's world-picture. One was the way of the optimists, who merely regarded it as fresh and incontrovertible evidence of a supernatural force operating through all life, whether they called it God, the First Cause, the World Spirit, the *élan vital*, or the Life Force. It was something they shared and could help to direct. This was largely how Shaw and Wells regarded it, and for them there was no essential difference between it and the ordinary nineteenth-century creed of progress. Things were obviously getting better, and now it turned out that they had been doing so from the beginning. One could rely on Nature. As Meredith put it,

> *Into the breast that gives the rose*
> *Shall I with shuddering fall?*

To which Hardy would have replied: "Emphatically." For there was a darker interpretation possible: that these changes in the forms of life followed no laws but their own, and that human consciousness, instead of being part of the process, was merely an accident. One might have to postulate the existence of a First Cause, but not of any concern on its part for the development of its handiwork. "We have reached a degree of intelligence which Nature never contemplated when framing her laws," he wrote, "and for which she consequently has provided no adequate satisfactions." "Thought," he wrote in *The Return of the Native*, "is a disease of the flesh." In other words, God created a world containing an accidental element of intelligence which he was not intelligent enough to anticipate or provide for. It is a view that differs only slightly from Shakespeare's after his study of Montaigne, and which I once defined as putting the Almighty on trial for murder and then faking the evidence. It seems to me a peculiarly British view. The insular temperament has reserves of idealism unknown to the cynical Latin, and the shock experienced by an Englishman when he discovers that God does not play cricket is often an overwhelming one.

It was among the working classes that Arnold and Florence Nightingale discovered atheism, and Hardy belonged to these. Nor, English society being what it was, was it ever possible for him to leave them. He died a wealthy man, but long after his death, when I asked a Dorchester man if he had known the great writer, I realized that I had failed to insult him only because I was a foreigner and knew no better. He explained with great patience and gentleness that *"Mister* Hardy was what is known in this country as a self-made man," but admitted that his wife knew Hardy's wife "socially." There is an embarrassing passage in Mrs. Hardy's reminiscences which describes Hardy's mother being wheeled down to the roadside by her daughter to see the guests departing from her son's garden party, and the vain attempts of the younger woman to prevent the old lady from cheering.

Darwinism affected Hardy more deeply than it affected other novelists because he was essentially simpler than any of them. He was driven to atheism because he was unaccustomed to the agnosticism of the educated classes, and remained till the day of his death, at least with a considerable portion of his mind, religious and even superstitious. "Half my time," he says, "(particularly when I write verse) I believe—in the modern use of the word—not only in the things that Bergson does but in spectres, mysterious voices, intuitions, omens, dreams, haunted places, etc., etc." The qualification is particularly revealing. Superficially his mind is critical and pessimistic, but in that part of him which writes poetry, it is still the mind of the folk at any age in any part of the world.

He is a fascinating example of historic schizophrenia, standing on the frontier of two cultures, watching traditions older than the Celts, whose barrows topped the neighboring hills, disappear as the extending railway line brings in the latest music-hall song, the latest melodrama, the latest scientific theory. When two cultures clash in this way, what happens at the time is not that the more sophisticated one triumphs, but that the less sophisticated takes refuge in the depths of the heart. This is what he means when he says that half his time he believes in "spectres, mysterious voices, intuitions, dreams, haunted places, etc., etc." At the same time he is slightly ashamed of his own weakness. What takes place in the conscious part of a mind like that is the spread not of sophistication, but of naïveté. Hardy as a thinker is naïve because he thinks with only half his mind. His feelings, on the other hand, are profound.

The problem for the critic is to distinguish between the two Hardys. If one considers him as a novelist in the way in which one considers Tolstoy or Trollope, it soon becomes plain that he is not a novelist at all. More than any other novelist who ever lived he is socially limited and naïve. Naturally, he is a genius, but his genius is akin to that of the *douanier* Rousseau or an American primitive. Not only has he no notion of how men and women other than the working classes of Dorset live and think, but also when he tries to apply to these people the romantic conventions of the novel he has no idea of how they would behave. "Can a man fooled to utter heart-burning find a reason for being merry?" asks one lovelorn farmer. "If I have lost, how can I be as if I had won? Heavens, you must be heartless quite! Had I known what a fearfully bitter sweet your love would be, how I would have avoided you and never seen you and been deaf to you." This has the genuine quality of the American primitive, delighting us not because it resembles anything in the created world, but because it so plainly does not resemble anything while passionately attempting to do so.

The only characters in Hardy who can be described as satisfactory (apart from the character of Henchard in *The Mayor of Casterbridge*, which has a certain rough consistency) are the choruses of rustics, and this is not because he understood rustics any better than he understood other classes, but because he did not attempt to treat them as characters. The idea that humble and inarticulate people could be treated as characters probably occurred to him as little as the idea that his mother could be invited to a garden party. The rustics in Hardy are considered not from the point of view of the novelist, but from that of the poet, as part of an anonymous, idyllic rural background. Accordingly, he was able to give them a richness and quaintness of vocabulary which he would have felt it improper to give his more articulate characters.

All Hardy's faults are faults of simplemindedness. His invention is largely meaningless and frequently highly embarrassing. The plot of *Far from the Madding Crowd* is as stagy as anything in Dickens, but it is unsatisfying because, unlike Dickens and, indeed, unlike most Victorian novelists, Hardy is not in the least a stagy man. He writes in this way only because he has read and seen too many melodramas and is lacking in the critical insight that would enable him to see how far removed they are from those things which came natural to himself.

The Mayor of Casterbridge is easily his best-planned novel, but even in this the plotting is unnecessarily complicated. Consider it for a moment. Henchard sells his wife to a sailor at the fair while he is drunk. When he comes to his senses and realizes that his simpleminded wife believes in the legality of the sale and has gone off with the sailor, the shock is so great that he vows to give up drink for twenty-one years, and as a result makes his fortune as a grain-dealer. His wife returns with their daughter, Elizabeth Jane, and to avoid scandal he marries her a second time. At the same time he takes as partner a young Scotchman, Farfrae, who falls in love with Elizabeth Jane. But in the meantime he has had a love affair with a comparatively wealthy woman, Lucetta (the name alone is ominous), who comes to live near him, in Casterbridge. Gradually, Farfrae, a younger and more brilliant man, pushes Henchard from his high place in the business life of the town. Mrs. Henchard dies, and he then discovers that Elizabeth Jane is not really his daughter, but that of the sailor, Newson. He forces her to leave his house, and she takes up residence with Lucetta, as her companion. By this time Lucetta has fallen in love with Farfrae, and she eventually marries him. By a coincidence, the gossips of the town get hold of Lucetta's correspondence with Henchard and she is held up to ignominy at a time when she is pregnant. Farfrae is away and Henchard follows him to give him warning, but Farfrae does not trust his rival's message, and, as a result of this, his wife dies. Farfrae then marries Elizabeth Jane, but not before her real father, the sailor, has returned from the dead and revealed the imposture of Henchard, who by this time is clinging frantically to Elizabeth Jane as the only creature life has left him to love.

The plot is intended to strip the proud, emotional Henchard of everything and send him to die in the wilderness, but it overshoots the mark. It is needlessly complicated, and it is not complicated for the purpose of demonstrating Hardy's thesis that we are mere flies to the gods who "kill us for their sport," but for the modest purpose of providing serial entertainment for Hardy's readers, who liked surprises at proper intervals. It gives us an embarrassing picture of a simpleminded, meditative man doing his best to say things he does not really wish to say in an involved manner that does not come naturally to him when what he does wish to say is something as simple, clear, and poignant as an old song.

2.

On the other hand, it must be said in Hardy's favor that much of this melodrama revolves about old beliefs, old customs, old buildings, and old crafts. At the worst, this diminishes the commonness of the contrivance; at its best, it gives the contrivance a new life by withdrawing its conventionality and replacing it by the description of things timeless and beautiful in their very nature. Any Victorian writer who had heard of it would have used the sale of the wife for the sake of its dramatic quality. Only Hardy was interested in it as the survival of a whole world of belief regarding the marriage bond.

It may even be said to justify itself because, in fact, the second and greater Hardy had little or nothing of the true novelist in him. In *Under the Greenwood Tree* he wrote the only novel of his which does not depend on meretricious coincidence and melodrama; which is absolutely authentic; and, enchanting as it is, it is clearly not a novel at all. It is an idyll that will be remembered as long as fiction is read, not for the sake of its characters or their emotions, but for its picture of life in rural England before it was swamped by railway culture.

This was the real inspiration of the second Hardy, Hardy the poet. Whenever he looked forward, he saw only chaos and gloom; whenever he looked back, his memory filled with enchantment. He was not only one of the great folklorists and historians; he was also the greatest master of local color that the nineteenth century had seen, greater even than Dickens.

Here, whether or not he knew it—and probably he did not—Hardy was affected by the naturalists, and we can trace in him the development of a purely pictorial kind of writing which must ultimately derive from Flaubert. Unlike Flaubert, he never allows it to settle into neat little miniatures, and long before the cinema he had invented a technique that anticipates it, as in the wonderful chapter of *The Mayor of Casterbridge* where the two women see the

town for the first time. Hardy begins in the air high above
the town as it lies in evening light; fades to a horizon view
of it, far away and flat upon the plain; and then tracks
slowly toward the tree-lined rampart that surrounds it and
down the Main Street, pausing now and again to give a
close-up view of bow windows, shutters, or inn signs.

The lamplights now glimmered through the engirdling trees,
conveying a sense of great snugness and comfort inside, and
rendering at the same time the unlighted country without
strangely solitary and vacant in aspect, considering its nearness
to life. The difference between burgh and champaign was increased too by sounds which now reached them above others—
the notes of a brass band. The travellers returned into the High
Street, where there were timber houses with overhanging stories
whose small-paned lattices were screened by dimity curtains on a
drawing string, and under whose barge-boards old cobwebs
waved in the breeze. There were houses of brick nogging which
derived their chief support from those adjoining. There were
slate roofs patched with tiles, and tile roofs patched with slate,
with occasionally a roof of thatch.

Consider the difference between the tempo of such a
passage and the tempo of the plot of *The Mayor of Casterbridge*, and you will almost feel the difference between
the two Hardys; the one whose mind slides through
character and event like a knife through butter, and the
other whose mind crawls blindly and lovingly over the
surface of things like an old spider weaving his web of
enchantment about them. To read him is like looking at a
Cotman drawing in which one can identify the very quality
of materials, wood, stone, and tile, from the draughtsman-
ship. The second Hardy is a matchless describer of all

natural phenomena, and of all objects and characters to which time has given the patina of natural phenomena; old inn signs, roofs, walls, church pews, old tools, old customs, old people chattering in the twilight as they chattered in the time of the Celts. He dismisses Lucetta's house with a phrase because it was Georgian, either not old enough in his day to have acquired the historic patina or because in its conscious symmetry it sought to impose itself upon the landscape.

Because he does not read himself into what he describes, Hardy is not a realist, but though, like Flaubert, he may be said to read himself out of it, he is not a naturalist either. Flaubert reads himself out because he believes that an artist must not become involved with his subject matter, but Hardy does so for a different reason. One can see it in the way he frequently intrudes an observer on the scene, and the observer is present even when not mentioned. He is present in the use of the passive voice: "were heard," "were found," "were to be seen," "were to be discovered," "was apparent," and in phrases like "a close examination revealed," "the inside of the hut as it now presented itself," "that stillness which struck casual observers," "we turn our attention to the left-hand characteristics," "his face now began to be painted over." Curiously, Leon Edel points out that exactly the same device occurs in Henry James.

Partly this is due to a pictorial imagination of almost unnatural sensitiveness which is not always easy to distinguish from naturalism, a style of writing deeply influenced by painting. But naturalism cannot explain why the observer—the watcher and listener—is so often obtruded where no such obtrusion is necessary or even desirable. *Far from the Madding Crowd* opens with Gabriel Oak watching from cover while Bathsheba Everdene looks approvingly at herself in the mirror. In the second chapter he sees her again, through a crevice in the wall of the cowshed where she and her aunt are working by night, and in the third he observes her once more, as she practices tricks on a horse, unaware of being watched. So too, in *The Return of the Native*, we have the great opening in which the reddleman watches from a hollow while Eustacia Vye climbs on the barrow to look for signs of her lover's return.

There the form stood, motionless as the hill beneath. Above the plain rose the hill, above the hill rose the barrow, and above the barrow rose the figure. Above the figure was nothing that could be mapped elsewhere than on a celestial globe.

It is not as though Hardy were excluding himself from the scene. Rather, it is as though he were being excluded and returning as a sort of disembodied presence, a *revenant*, someone of different substance who cannot mix with the human materials he observes, and happy only in the contemplation of their physical surroundings or in the presence of rustics to whom he is invisible; who are, as it were, only portions of the landscape made visible and audible; men and women who are eternal only because, like the animals, they remain dumb and patient and uncomprehending.

"Joseph Poorgrass, are you there?"

"Yes, sir—ma'am, I mane . . . I be the personal name of Poorgrass."

"And what are you?"

"Nothing in my own eye. In the eye of other people—well, I don't say it; though public thought will out."

"What do you do on the farm?"

"I do do carting things all the year, and in seed time I shoots the rooks and sparrows and helps at pig-killing, sir."

"How much to you?"

"Please nine and ninepence, and a good ha'penny where 'twas a bad one, sir—ma'am, I mane."

There is a curious passage in Hardy's journals which seems to me to throw a great light on this attitude.

For my part, if there is any way of getting a melancholy satisfaction out of life it lies in dying, so to speak before one is out of the flesh; by which I mean putting on the manners of ghosts, wandering in their haunts, and taking their views of surrounding things. To think of life as passing away is a sadness; to think of it as past is at least tolerable. Hence, even when I enter into a room to pay a simple morning call I have unconsciously the habit of regarding the scene as if I were a spectre not solid enough to influence my environment; only fit to behold and say, as another spectre, said: "Peace be unto you."

This was no mere chronic pessimism or passing mood, for again and again in his poetry he speaks as for the dead, for "the Squire and Lady Susan" as well as "poor Fanny Hurd." If Hardy is not a realist like Dickens, it is that he is "not solid enough to influence his environment," but neither is he a Flaubert or Joyce, "like God, paring his nails." He is a ghost; a ghost that finds the spectacle of passing life intolerable, and can contemplate it only as if it were already gone by, its sufferings ended. All his characters are treated as though they were already dead, and even among the shadows he evokes he will turn from any face too fair or venturesome to contemplate some Celtic fort or fifteenth-century cottage that has already outlasted generations of such eager souls. It is almost impossible for the artist to evade the spirit of an age, and even in the west of England, far from the bustle of James's society world, the novel was closing in on itself and the novelist being pushed to the extreme periphery of experience. Hardy was as incapable as James of placing himself again where Trollope and Tolstoy stood, in its burning center.

chapter 16

Chekhov

It is hard to trace the collapse of the classical novel without first realizing how the educated classes themselves were split during the eighties and nineties of the last century. If one takes England, there are, on the one hand, the scientific optimists like Shaw who believed that scientific progress was the real key to man's continued existence; and on the other hand the symbolists like Wilde and Yeats who had no belief in progress. The latter were bored by the novel as they were by the tendentious poetry of the late Victorians, and the alternative was there, in their own fantasies. Jane Austen had drawn back in horror from the romantic excesses of Northanger Abbey; the young writers at the end of the century were bored and disgusted by the tedium of Mansfield Park. So Northanger Abbey came back. Literature is forever swinging between Northanger Abbey and Mansfield Park. Neither can ever die. Northanger Abbey is in all of us from our earliest dreams of pleasure and power; the Gothick castles are not in history, but in our imaginations.

All through the nineteenth century they had hovered about the novel, changing places with science in Balzac's scheme, emerging finally into daylight in Flaubert and Dostoevsky. By that time they had been taken over by a great poet, Baudelaire, and passed on to other poets until at last they influenced Yeats and Rilke. In England they

may be said to have begun with Ruskin's disgust at the
architecture of the midland industrial towns and with the
enthusiastic medievalism of the pre-Raphaelites until they
passed into the work of a genuine sexual maniac like Swin-
burne and thence into that of Wilde and the symbolists. At
their finest, they represented the protest of the human
imagination against the brutal materialism and ugliness of
the age, now enormously fortified by science; at their
worst, they were merely the sickly vapors in the brains of
impotent men. As religion declined, the passion for magic
grew, and in people like Alistair Crowley we see a recrudescence of black magic and the Black Mass. And everywhere the fantasy associated itself with symbolism, the
belief that the external world does not exist or may be
ignored, that only the internal world has value. "As for
living, our servants will do that for us."

Meanwhile, the realistic movement attempted to
identify itself more closely with science. The mixture of
fact and fancy in Balzac was taken to be strictly scientific,
and Zola and the naturalists continued what they believed
to be Balzac's work with the fancy left out. In the widen-
ing gap between the two attitudes emerges a new type of
writer, Bourget and Dostoevsky—the Graham Greenes of
their day—insisting on the dichotomy between material
and spiritual, between science and religion, science and art.
The whole conflict seems to concentrate about the Dreyfus
case just at the extreme end of the century. Zola's defense
of Dreyfus, an honest defense of an innocent man, is
magnified into an attack on the army and the Church.
It is the point at which one begins to perceive the close

link between symbolism and fascism. And not religion only, but science as well, is being exaggerated into a sour and brutal fanaticism.

To write of Chekhov at all one must try to understand that background, for he is, in a sense, the last of the liberals, the last writer of fiction to attempt a synthesis of a world that is already falling into chaos about him. Such a synthesis was no longer possible to the novelist, and Chekhov perceives it only by the lightning flash of the short story, and only in solitary lives. The novel by its very nature presupposes a group, a social system that can absorb the lonely figure. The short story is the art form that deals with the individual when there is no longer a society to absorb him, and when he is compelled to exist, as it were, by his own inner light. Hard on Chekhov's heels comes Gorky, the last of the major Russian figures, and his characters are not merely lonely individuals; they are nomads, forever wandering about the fringes of society.

Chekhov's conflict is a vastly intensified version of Turgenev's. Where Turgenev had had to resist the combined pressures of the Slavophiles and the Radicals only, Chekhov has to face attack from the pietists and conservatives on one side and the socialists and materialists on the other. His whole position is adequately illustrated by the delicate balance he was compelled to strike between his two publishers, Suvorin, the conservative, who published his earlier stories, and Lavrov, the progressive, who published his later ones. Chekhov was very far from being a party man. He was obviously deeply attached to Suvorin, as he was to all gentle, intelligent, civilized people. But, though polite, vague, and indecisive to the point of insipidity, he would always, when driven to it, take a stand. He took his stand with Suvorin on the issue of the Dreyfus case.

Lavrov, who must have had a genuine streak of imbecility in him, once called Chekhov "unprincipled," and produced one of the few furious letters that shy, evasive man wrote. Suvorin, an altogether finer character, also needled Chekhov constantly, though in a much more civilized way, and evoked the great series of letters in which Chekhov defends modern science against the "idealists" and refuses to admit any conflict between science and art.

Anatomy and literature have an equally illustrious ancestry, the same enemy—the devil—; and there is no reason for them to fight. . . . If a man understands the circulation of the blood, he is rich; if in addition he also studies the history of religion and knows the ballad "I Recall the Wondrous Moment," he is the better for it; accordingly we are treating of assets only.

Science, religion, and art are all good things; this is Chekhov's lesson, and to quarrel with any of them is merely to cut off your nose to spite your face. The heroes he particularly admires, and who keep on recurring in his stories, are the doctor and the teacher, for each has so much to give that would make the lives of our children, if not of ourselves, more beautiful, and by trying to drive a false dichotomy between them the Bourgets and Dostoevskys are impoverishing rather than enriching the world of thought.

Though his own religious convictions would seem to have been limited to a belief in God and the devil, a God who represents culture and knowledge and a devil who represents ignorance and passion, he was just as irritated by the attempt to decry religion. Merejkovsky describes the old monk in *Easter Eve* as "a failure," and Chekhov in exasperation asks: "How is he a failure? He believed in God; he had enough to eat, and he had the gift of composing hymns." Belief in God, like poetry and anatomy, is also an asset. Why put yourself into one of the warring camps and pretend that the other is a liability? You impoverish only yourself. "Noah had three sons, Shem, Ham, and Japheth," he says amusingly. "Ham only noticed that his father was a drunkard, and completely lost sight of the fact that he was a genius, that he had built an ark and saved the world."

For some years he was affected by Tolstoy's teaching, and even indulged in a little preaching himself, but he finally dismissed it with the remark that "there is more love of humanity in electricity and steam heating than in chastity and abstention from meat." The truth is that he was filled with loathing and distrust of all factions, religious, political, and literary. "The party spirit," he wrote, "especially when it is dull and without a spark of talent hates freedom, daring and initiative." "Freedom" here is the significant word. He was the grandson of a slave; he had by his own efforts freed himself from the residue of that slavery in squalor and pettiness, and had to continue to do so by remaining free of all that resembled it.

255

What might be his summing up of his quarrel with
Suvorin is contained in a crushing little parable called
Rothschild's Fiddle, whose principal character, Yakov
Ivanov, an anti-Semitic coffin-maker, spends his whole life
mourning his losses without once realizing that his own
life is a dead loss; that he has failed in industry and
generosity, and that in terms of his own diabolical account-
ancy, the only thing of which the profit is certain is death.
He has a wife he might have loved and a river he might
have fished in, but his wife dies without hearing a word of
love from him, and he has never caught the smallest fish in
the river. The river—now that we are in the age of
metaphor, with Ibsen and James—is, of course, life.

Yet it was a respectable river, and by no means contemptible;
it would have been possible to fish in it, and the fish might have
been sold to tradesmen, officials, and the attendant at the railway station buffet, and the money could have been lodged in
the bank; he might have used it for roving from country house
to country house, and playing the fiddle, and everyone would
have paid him money; he might even have tried to act as bargee
—it would have been better than making coffins; he might have
kept geese, killed them, and sent them to Moscow in the winter
time—from the feathers alone he would have made as much as
ten roubles a year. But he had yawned his life away and done
nothing.

This little parable is Chekhov at his gravest, for the
meaning is that we are all coffin-makers, all makers of
categories, all refusing to fish in the great river of life and
counting as losses what God had intended us to count as
gain.

2.

It is not enough to think of Chekhov merely as a Russian and a fellow countryman of Dostoevsky, whom, in his irritable way, he described as "good but pretentious." That is the error of nationalist criticism. Chekhov is also the strict contemporary of Shaw, and has a great deal more in common with him than with Dostoevsky. Like Shaw, he is fundamentally optimistic (it is only a very superficial criticism that sees him as a gloomy writer); like him, he is optimistic because he believes in science and thinks that "life in two hundred years' time will be unimaginably beautiful." Where he differs from Shaw is in his insistence on culture. Life cannot get better until people themselves get better, and people cannot begin to get better until they have set themselves free of the devil's snares of ignorance and prejudice and stop talking of capitalists, Freemasons, Jesuits, and Yids. Unlike Shaw, he represents this problem in terms of people. Here he resembles Jane Austen even more than Shaw, because he writes always as a moralist, but his morality is no longer the morality of a group; it is the short-story writer's morality of the lonely individual soul.

Chekhov was originally a writer of skits and vaudeville sketches, and much of what he learned in this branch of writing reappears in his later famous stories in a wonderfully exalted form. Inconsequence and absurdity, originally designed merely to raise a laugh, now represent the essential loneliness of the human soul, and a comic phrase like

257

"I send you a pound of tea for the satisfaction of your physical needs" now becomes a poignant reminder of how impossible it is for the soul to communicate with the souls of others. What makes Chekhov so difficult for some readers is his concentration on the tragedy of inarticulateness and loneliness. One of his most moving stories describes an old cab-driver who tries to tell his rich and busy clients of the death of his son and, failing to get a single listener, goes at last to the stable and tells his old nag instead. One of his funniest describes a priest who finds a well-educated monk to denounce his wayward son in a letter and then ruins the whole tremendous effect by adding a few lines of cheerful, scandalous gossip. And this does not apply only to uneducated people. The tragedy of the dying bishop is that he cannot get his own mother to stop calling him "Your Grace," and joyous people, like sad ones, address themselves to nothing. Probably the most typical Chekhov conversation is a monologue addressed to someone inattentive or half asleep, like that scene in *The Cherry Orchard* in which the lovelorn maidservant tells her romance to the yawning girl by the window. Whether we are good or bad, we are still lonely, but all the same it is better to be lonely and good.

And though he may have argued with Suvorin that anatomy and the arts had nothing to fight about, his own stories show that the fight between them was always going on in himself. Because, though a great artist must have a battlefront of belief, it can be sustained only by the internal battle between judgment and instinct. The heroine of one of his most famous stories is a doctor's wife who becomes the mistress of a painter and neglects her apparently stupid, good-natured husband till he dies after sucking the poison from a child's throat. Only then does she realize that everyone but herself has long recognized him as a great and famous man.

Olga Ivanovna remembered her whole life with him, from beginning to end with all its details, and suddenly understood that he was in real fact a rare and remarkable and, compared with those men that she knew, a great man. And remembering how her late father and his colleagues had treated him, she understood that they had seen in him a coming celebrity. The walls, the ceiling, the lamp and carpet blinked at her sarcastically as though they wanted to say "Missed him! Missed him!"

But it is not enough merely to respect science, for the artist too, though he may appear anything but respectable, has an essential element to contribute to the beautiful world of two hundred years hence. Without him, in fact, it will be impossible. This is the theme of Chekhov's most ambitious work, the short novel *The Duel*, which describes a seedy hanger-on of culture, one Laevsky, and his mistress, Nadyezhda, who are living together in the Crimea, though they have long since grown tired of each other.

"This soup tastes like licorice," he said, smiling; he made an effort to control himself and seem amiable, but could not refrain from saying "Nobody looks after the housekeeping. . . . If you are too ill or busy with reading, let me look after the cooking."

In earlier days she would have said to him: "Do, by all means" or "I see you want to turn me into a cook," but now she only looked timidly at him and flushed crimson.

259

This is not mere naturalistic detail, as it would be in the work of a French writer of the time. It is the detail of a moralist. Like the coarseness of Lydia Bennet and her mother, it is intended to define by implication an ideal of behavior which Laevsky and his mistress cannot aspire to, and which is the real cause of their unhappiness. Nadyezhda is deceiving him with another man, and has so put herself into the other man's clutches that she cannot repel his filthy advances. Laevsky is planning to leave her, and so conceals from her the fact that her husband is now dead and that he is at last free to marry her. The local doctor (a saint, as usual), who runs a little *table d'hôte* for a scientist, Van Koren, and a simpleminded seminarist, would lend Laevsky the money, but he in turn has to borrow from Van Koren, who loathes both Nadyezhda and Laevsky for some stupid criticisms they have passed on science. It is the old conflict between anatomy and the arts, and what Von Koren fails to realize is that, whatever faults Laevsky and Nadyezhda may have, they are still in the eyes of God—the God of culture and knowledge that Chekhov worshipped—sensitive, educated, and artistic, far superior to the mediocrities by whom they are surrounded. In their thoughtless way they may have joined themselves to the faction opposed to science, but Von Koren has committed himself far more deeply to the opposing faction of the materialists. Actually, the danger lies with him rather than with Laevsky, for, as Chekhov perceives, he is ruthless and insensitive and restrained by no feeling of awe or doubt.

Von Koren will not part with the money until Laevsky

agrees to take Nadyezhda with him, and finally maddens
Laevsky into challenging him. The prospect of imminent
death brings out a real element of seriousness and manli-
ness in Laevsky. The duel takes place; the scientist is on
the point of killing him in cold blood when he is interrupted by the good-natured, muddleheaded representative
of religion, so that the shot just grazes Laevsky's neck.
But he has had his lesson, becomes reconciled to Von
Koren, marries Nadyezhda, and settles down to a dull
and useful life with her.

Perhaps *The Duel* is not Chekhov's greatest story,
though it is superbly told; but in it the diffident, irritable
voice is just a shade louder and more articulate, and the
story throws light on all the other mysterious and beautiful
stories that haunt our memory for years like poetry or
music. As in Shaw's *Candida* and Joyce's *Ulysses*, we are
aware that the two contrasted characters are really two
aspects of the same character, which is the author's, and
that they externalize a conflict of aims in himself. We see
that the delicate balance that he was trying to preserve
between himself as doctor and as artist, between his
report on Sakhalin and his stories, between anatomy and
the arts, was a personal balance, and that Chekhov, the
saintly, public-spirited doctor who built schools and endowed libraries, had a shady artistic alter ego who did not
really care a rap for schools, libraries, or progress and
asked no more of life than "to be idle and love a fat girl."

The Duel is a curious farewell to the nineteenth-century
novel with all its passionate strivings, its savage indignation, its burning hopes. "If we respect science and cul-

ture," the writer seems to say, "we shall in the end conquer disease, poverty, and ignorance. Life in two hundred years' time will be unimaginably beautiful because, whatever we may say, there are positive things and negative things, and ultimately the positive things will triumph. I know, because my grandfather was a slave and I am a free man. As a child I was beaten; when I grew up, they stopped beating me, and that is progress. But what use will progress be unless it also means spiritual progress, unless we continue to fight against slavery, our own slavery to brutal fantasies; if we are still disgusting in our family relationships, and have no useful, positive work to keep us occupied and to help on the business of progress? So we must all be more polite and tender and truthful, and work very much harder than we do, and learn to be fastidious and not leave syringes in the bathroom; and then in the remote future, life will really be worth while. But of course we must not be too fanatical even about that because we shall be dead anyway. But still, Afanasey Andreitch, my guinea pig, my little sucking dove [or whatever bit of translator's Anglo-Russian you prefer], we really ought to work harder."

It is the final, unanswerable, doubting restatement of the middle-class creed of the nineteenth-century novel.

part V

Behind the Mirror

chapter 17

The Last Phase: Freud and the Broken Will

Chekhov died in 1904. By that date Maurice Barrès was already writing of how we shall "disengage positive truths situated in our deep *subconscious*." By 1907 Mr. E. M. Forster was referring casually to "the subconscious mind." By 1912 Lawrence was discovering that his love for his mother was really an Œdipus complex that existed in his "unconscious," and by 1914 Proust was speaking of "the involuntary memory" that exists in our unconscious and is triggered into momentary consciousness by some familiar sensation, like the taste of a pastry dipped in tea. Already the modern novel is under way, and there is no doubt whatever as to one main source of it. That is Freud's *Interpretation of Dreams*, published in 1900.

There was already a vast interest in the subject. The recrudescence of the romantic revival had stirred people's interest in the esoteric, in magic and in dreams. Stevenson's *Dr. Jekyll and Mr. Hyde* was a dream. So was Chekhov's *Black Monk*. Naturally, Dostoevsky's work is full of dreams of a fascinating kind. The psychologists had tapped an area of the mind which did not react in the same way as the rest of it, and which they described in various ways, and dreams were obviously related to the operations of this area.

Finally Freud not only showed how they were related to the area, but he taught people how to translate the dreams themselves. Stevenson's darling little "brownies of the brain," to whom he attributed his best creations, now turned out to be most unfairylike creatures. *Dr. Jekyll and Mr. Hyde* represents an exceedingly dangerous state of mind on the part of the author rather than of the characters. Freud's theory did not escape devastating criticism from his own students and colleagues, and his technique for translating dreams is much more likely to produce nervous disease than to cure it, but his book represents one of the great achievements of the human mind, and in its main tenets his theory has lasted and has continued to exert an increasing influence over literature and art.

This is most obvious in the use of dream images— "symbols," as Freud rather loosely calls them. "Symbols" in this sense had been used pretty freely through nineteenth-century fiction, and very freely indeed in the latter half. They were used by writers like Melville and Hawthorne to give prose the rich metaphorical texture of verse, and in the writing of old and tired men they always have a tendency to crop up as an alternative to analysis. As Yeats remarked with a sneer, Ibsen's later work is full of "the odour of spilt poetry," and the odour in James's later novels is quite overpowering. But even in Chekhov we are likely to run across parables in the manner of *Rothschild's Fiddle*, in which the "coffins" represent categories, the "river" life, and so on.

Wherever they do appear, they are always in conflict with the objective and analytic tradition of European prose. If Jane Austen were writing *Pride and Prejudice* in the modern way, the hero would never need to reveal his arrogance by all those subtle touches which Jane Austen analyzed. He would have been satisfied with a peacock on the lawn, and Elizabeth Bennet would ultimately have wrung its neck. Lawrence's *Wintry Peacock* goes very close to doing this. The main thing is that the character would be represented by an image corresponding to the author's view of his principal obsession or the author's view of his part in a poetic phantasmagoria. Either way, his character and role are determined, and his part in the story is more metaphorical than real. As time goes on, and the novel heads more obviously in the direction of allegory, it is entirely metaphorical. The characters in *Finnegans Wake* and in Kafka's *The Castle* are metaphors.

One serious effect of this on the novel has been in the conception of what an individual is. Freudian theory has linked up with the determinism of the mechanists and suggested to the average educated man that he has no control whatever over his own destiny; that all the significant events in his life took place in early childhood when he was incapable of either appreciating or influencing them, and that he is, in every sense, a creature of his heredity and environment, conditioned from the womb to the grave. Now, in Victorian fiction there is undoubtedly an exaggeration of the freedom of the individual, but there is a much more serious exaggeration in modern fiction of his lack of freedom, and the characters of Joyce, Proust, and Faulkner are entirely dominated by circumstances, too feeble in will ever to be able to detach themselves from their own treadmill. We never find them resisting, striving, seeking; they are borne down by the women (or the men) to whom some blind instinct attaches them, and some form of suicide seems to be the only fate open to them. It is the twilight of the conscious mind.

Less serious, though still important, is the influence of Freudian theory on the attitude to sex. The romantic revival, gone more or less underground, had reveled in semi-pornographic fantasies. In the book of Professor Praz to which I have already referred, he traces from the late eighteenth century onward up to Gide and Barrès certain obsessions of a sexual character. These are partly homosexual and, after Flaubert, mainly homosexual, though the homosexuality is not of a type that is familiar to us from classical literature, for it is invariably associated with the principal perversions of normal sex: sadism, masochism, voyeurism, and exhibitionism, and sometimes with incest as well. These were the subject matter of the pornographers and the *poètes maudits*, and Freud's theory domesticated them by showing that we all have similar tendencies, and that they are in fact no more abnormal than the conventional relationships of son and mother, husband and wife.

This is the reason for the enormous influence of Dostoevsky on later European literature, because Dostoevsky had actually treated those subjects in that particular way, and Freud had shown his attitude to be scientifically correct.

Much of the literature that follows the Freudian theory might be described as "permissive romanticism"—Northanger Abbey treated as though it were Mansfield Park, and without that shudder of guilt which always accompanies it in the work of the early romantics. Much of the strangeness of modern fiction comes from the fact that when you examine the material, it is not in the least novel, any more than Dostoevsky's is novel; it is really the old romantic claptrap treated from the realistic point of view.

Besides—and this may be the most significant difference of all—the Freudian theory, by dwelling almost exclusively on the imagination, had made the modern novelist doubt the existence of an objective reality behind what he writes. The subconscious mind does not distinguish between subject and object; it is the main difficulty in the translation of dreams. No such doubt was possible to Jane Austen or to Trollope. If Turgenev and Tolstoy had doubted it, they would have run the risk of being seized by what did not exist, or what, if it existed, could not be apprehended, and of being confined in a dungeon to learn the elements of Aristotelian philosophy. A modern French writer, Marcel Aymé, says that when the Allied troops burst into Belsen and Buchenwald, what they saw was a poem by Baudelaire, and if, as I think, the work of this whole period has become history, it is because, after Belsen and Buchenwald, the romantic novelist has nowhere to go. The future is with the Aristotelians.

chapter 18

D. H. Lawrence: Sons and Lovers

When we look at the last complete period of the novel, we find such names as Marcel Proust, James Joyce, André Gide, D. H. Lawrence, E. M. Forster, Thomas Mann, and Virginia Woolf.

And we are at once pulled up because at least four of the principal figures did not write novels at all. They wrote autobiography more or less thinly disguised as fiction. Another characteristic of this quartet is that none of them seems to have been sexually normal. All fell deeply under the influence of their mothers; Gide and Proust remained homosexual for their entire lives; Lawrence showed strongly marked homosexual tendencies, while Joyce's work covers practically every known form of sexual deviation. The only subject that none of them could apparently treat was normal heterosexual love.

Now, this can scarcely be a coincidence, and when we examine their work and find that even the types of deviation resemble one another, we are forced to the conclusion that there must be a common element that makes their authors react in this particular way.

Let us look first at Lawrence's *Sons and Lovers*, which is particularly interesting because, though it ends as a novel of the modern type, it begins as one of the classical kind, made familiar to us by nineteenth-century novelists.

To begin with, we have to notice that it is the work of

one of the New Men who are largely a creation of the Education Act of 1870. Besides, we must note that it comes from the English Midlands, the industrial area. Naturally, the two facts are linked, and they represent a cultural shift not only from the middle to the working classes, but also from the area of wealth to the area of industry. The young people in the book are full of literary allusions that are not merely the self-conscious showing off of a young literary man, but represent the whole struggle of the working classes for culture. There is the same atmosphere in C. P. Snow's *Strangers and Brothers*, and for a similar reason.

It indicates too the dangers of such a shift of attitudes, for the Midlands, at least to a foreigner like myself, seem to be a different country altogether from the South of England, and even at times to resemble Ireland more than England. They are dissenting in religion, socialist in politics, and with a way of life which—again to a foreigner —seems full of dignity and even beauty. And, again, it is worth remembering that one of Lawrence's best stories, *Odour of Chrysanthemums*, which describes a miner's death, is not only quite unlike any other English story: though the critics have failed to notice it, it is also a very careful pastiche of Synge's *Riders to the Sea*. It suggests that young people of Lawrence's period did apparently recognize that in some ways their life was closer to Irish than to English ways, and that if it was to be given its full dignity, it had to be approached from an Irish standpoint.

But—and this is Lawrence's tragedy—it reminds us too that, unlike Ireland, the Midlands have no cultural capital, and that a young man of genius is necessarily driven to London, where he may learn only too quickly to despise the standards of his own people. This is not true of everybody, but of Lawrence it certainly is true. London acquaintances thought him something of a bounder and a cad. The family described under the name of Lievers in *Sons and Lovers* certainly did not think him either. It is the tragedy of William in the same novel. In later years Lawrence is the homeless, rootless man of letters drifting from country to country, continent to continent, writing with unfailing energy and brilliance, but never with the intensity displayed in *Sons and Lovers* and some of his early stories.

The break with his roots occurred during the writing of the novel, and it is plain for anyone who will take the trouble to read it carefully. Absolutely, the opening half is the greatest thing in English fiction. It has all the brilliance of *Pride and Prejudice* and the opening of *Middlemarch* with the tragic power of certain scenes in *The Last Chronicle*. Put in its simplest form, it is the dilemma of a sensitive boy between the conflicting claims of mother and sweetheart. This adds a new element of tragedy to the novel, for, despite the universal quality of the theme, it is an element that could only have come from the New Men and the industrial areas, for it is only in those surroundings that a boy is forced to recognize the spiritual achievement of motherhood. A hundred pounds a year would have been sufficient to mask the whole achievement and tragedy of Mrs. Morel. Even a difference in class would have done so, for, greatly as Mrs. Crawley is drawn by Trollope, her struggle is presented as it appeared to a member of the upper classes: a sordid, unnecessary, *imposed* ordeal. In Lawrence, poverty is treated as a necessary condition of life, and it is by means of the explicit exiguous budgets that we are made to appreciate the full significance of Mrs. Morel's attempts to create order and beauty about her, and the delight and anguish these could bring to a sensitive boy. We *respect* Mrs. Crawley's struggle to find necessities for her family; we *rejoice* in the glorious scene in which Mrs. Morel gives rein to her wicked extravagance and comes home clutching a pot that cost her fivepence and a bunch of pansies and daisies that cost her fourpence.

Again it is the Midland background that gives significance to Miriam's passion for culture, this, too, a struggle toward the light, though of a different kind. As we are made to feel the weight of Morel's physical violence and the brutality of the mines crushing us down like a leaden sky, so too we feel with almost agonizing intensity the upward movement in chapel, school, and home, the passion of desire to "build Jerusalem in England's green and pleasant land." Nature is not, as in Hardy, a dark background to a gloomy fate, but an upward surging like music, poetry, religion. No other novel is so filled with flowers. When in a novel for the leisured classes someone talks of Rilke, or a Picasso print, or carnations, one's tendency is to groan: "Holy Smoke, he's off again!" But we rejoice in Mrs. Morel's little triumph over the pot-man, in Miriam's algebra lesson, in Mrs. Morel's three little bulbs under the hedge. These are no longer the

negatives of dandyism or the neutrals of an educated
class, but the positive achievements of a life with a sense
of purpose and direction, lived by people who are complete moral entities. Joyce, too, had known the same
thing, and in the terrible little scene in *Ulysses* when
Dedalus's ragged sister covets the secondhand French
grammar, he makes us feel it, but we feel it rather as an
icy clutch on our hearts than as a moment of rejoicing in
man's passionate desire to transcend himself. Joyce's
Dublin was a place without signposts. Again, his poverty
is pathetic rather than tragic.

It is hard to criticize this matchless book, yet there *is*
something wrong with it, and, whatever it may be, it is
the same thing that is wrong with Lawrence himself and
that turns him into a homeless man of letters, and it is
here, under our eyes, that the smash occurs if only we
could see what it is. What I mean is not a literary fault,
or is so only in a secondary sense. It would be only
natural that a young man's book should contain shifting
planes, particularly when all the significant scenes are
written with such explosive power that it is a miracle
when he recovers any sense of direction at all. No, the
smash is a psychological one and inherent in the situation
that he describes rather than in the technique he uses to
describe it. It is inherent in the situation of the young
man torn between his mother and Miriam, both of whom
want the same thing from him.

There is almost certainly a false note in the chapters
describing Miriam as Paul Morel's mistress. I do not
know if in real life Lawrence was actually the lover of the

girl he describes as Miriam, nor am I greatly concerned about the question. But the situation of the novel implies that they could never have been lovers, and that this was in fact the thing that drove Paul to Clara. The trouble with the Œdipal relationship is that it specializes the sexual instinct. Sexual contact is the only thing lacking between the boy and his mother, and he tends to seek this in a form where it implies nothing else, where it does not produce an actual feeling of betrayal of the mother—in Gogol in the form of self-abuse, in Proust in the form of homo-sexuality. Human love—the type represented by Miriam —is bound to represent a betrayal of the mother, because the love is identical except for this one slight specialized thing. Miriam is his mother's rival because the love that she offers is human love; Clara is not because the love that she offers is in fact a non-human love.

Clara is non-human in the same way as every single woman whom Lawrence described after the writing of this book is non-human. None of them is allowed to challenge the image of his mother in humanity. And this is where we come to the really pathological streak in the book. Clara is a married woman whose husband is a smith in the surgical-appliance store where Paul is employed, and immediately she appears in the novel her husband appears also. He hates Paul long before Paul becomes the lover of his wife. When Paul and she become friendly, Paul presses her with questions about her relations with Dawes. He even has a fight with Dawes, and later goes to visit him in the hospital and makes friends with him. The two men have a peculiar relationship centered on their common possession of Clara, and finally Paul brings about the reunion of husband and wife.

Now, these chapters, which occupy a considerable part of the last half of the book, have nothing whatever to do with the subject of the novel—at least on the surface. They might easily belong to an entirely different novel. Indeed, they might be about different characters, for from this point onward Paul is referred to as "Morel," a name which has so far been associated only with his father, so that we even get superficially confused in our reading. Lawrence's original intention is fairly clear. It was to present Miriam not as a type of human love, but as a type of spiritual love, Clara as a type of sensual love, neither of which can satisfy the heart of the young man who loves his mother. This design has been obscured by the irrelevant physical relations with Miriam on the one hand, and on the other by the emphasis laid on Clara's husband as opposed to Clara herself. But that is only part of the trouble. The real trouble is that Paul Morel is not in love with Clara, but with Dawes. Subject and object have again changed places, and we are back with the old extraordinary theme of *The Eternal Husband*. That this is not merely a personal and perverse reading of the strained melodrama imposed on a young man of genius by his lack of experience will be clear to anyone who knows his Lawrence, for the theme occurs again and again in his later work. The most interesting example is an early story, *The Shades of Spring*, in which the girl we have come to know as Miriam is shown after her young man's desertion of her. She has now become engaged to a second man, and the story describes the odd attraction that the first feels for him. It is most explicit in *Jimmy and the Desperate Woman*, where Lawrence recognizes in the person of another man of slightly effeminate tastes the attraction of a physically powerful husband transmitted through the wife. The biographers tell us that the hero of the story is Middleton Murry, which merely indicates how incapable Lawrence became of drawing any character objectively: he can only attribute to him his own peculiar weakness. The whole passage is worth considering again in context.

And, as he sat in the taxi, a perverse but intense desire for her came over him, making him almost helpless. He could feel, so strongly, the presence of that other man about her, and this went to his head like neat spirits. That other man! In some subtle, inexplicable way he was actually bodily present, the husband. The woman moved in his aura. She was hopelessly married to him.

And this went to Jimmy's head like neat whiskey. Which of the two would fall before him with a greater fall—the woman, or the man, her husband?

It is hard to know what the real origin of this perverse attraction in Lawrence represents. That it existed in him in real life we may safely deduce from Murry's remark—made in all innocence of the meaning of the texts I have quoted—that Lawrence was attracted to Frieda's husband almost as much as to Frieda. Obviously the attraction is homosexual, but that word is so loosely and coarsely abused that it can scarcely be applied without misgivings to a noble and refined personality like Lawrence's. It is certainly linked with his adoration of his

mother, and it seems as though the link must be a specialized form of sexuality which excludes the spiritual element
merely because it would then become a rival to mother
love. At the same time, the figure of the father, consciously excluded by the boy, would seem to return in an
unrecognizable, unconscious form and take its place in the
relationship with the woman. If one accepts this reading
of it (and it is as tentative as any reading of an analogical
situation must be), Dawes is really Paul's father, and
Paul, through his relationship with Clara, which gives
him the opportunity of probing Dawes's relations with
his wife, is not only able to repeat the offense against his
father by robbing him of his wife, but is also, in the
manner of a fairy tale, able to undo the wrong by reconciling them. It is a beautiful example of the dual function
of such analogical relationships.

Whatever the origin of the situation, it is the key to
Lawrence's later work. His rejection of Miriam is a rejection of masculinity in himself, and after it he is condemned to write only of those things which the feminine
side of his character permits him to write of. He is an
intuitive writer by sheer necessity. To Edward Garnett
he defended his new, non-human form of writing by the
pretense that the old sort of realistic writing which
Garnett understood was out of date, but that his own
choice of this sort of writing took place only after *Sons and
Lovers* is clearly untrue. The choice was made during the
actual writing, and the result is the Clara-Dawes section,
the end of the old Lawrence and the beginning of the
new.

Not that he may not have felt the necessity, for all over Europe the old human conception of character was breaking down. Character in Turgenev and Trollope exists as an extension, by virtue of its predictability. All their great characters have been lived with. They are regarded, rightly or wrongly, as being essentially knowable. When Joyce uses the word "epiphany," "a showing forth," for the themes of his own stories, he indicates already that the temporal, objective conception of character no longer exists, and that it can be apprehended only in moments when it unconsciously betrays itself. Virginia Woolf, too, insists on this moment of revelation, and, like Joyce, she writes the typical one-day novel of the period. The day itself is regarded as an epiphany. Proust's characters are all perceived in such moments, and nothing that we have learned about them at one moment gives us the least indication of what they may be like in another. It is, of course, a view, deeply influenced by Freud's theories, which make the character unknowable except to the analyst; it is even, in many of the writers of the time, a view motivated by the furtiveness and secrecy of the homosexual, yet in the light of history it is so much a response to all that has gone before that one cannot help wondering whether even Freud and the homosexuals are not themselves mere symptoms of something taking place entirely in the mind.

chapter 19

Proust

Proust's *A la recherche du temps perdu* is another of the great books of the period, and one that continues to grow on me at least in the same way as *Sons and Lovers*, though, like this, it also raises problems that did not even seem to exist when I read it first in my early twenties.

First let me describe what those first volumes seem to be about and see what comes clear in the description. It begins with the narrator's waking from sleep and recalling his childhood. He remembers the visits of a neighbor called Swann, a man of no great importance in the neighborhood, and the anguish these had caused him because of his mother's failure to give him a goodnight kiss. As though in passing, the narrator describes the sudden vivid recollection of childhood roused in him when he tasted a pastry dipped in tea. Among the neighbors we meet the parish priest, who visits the boy's great-aunt and discusses with her in the most inappropriate way the meaning of local place names, which with him seem a hobby and even a mania. We meet also a man called Legrandin, who appears to be an artist and a radical, though on closer acquaintance he turns out to be a hopeless snob.

Then—very clumsily introduced—there comes a dramatic incident. An old music master named Vinteuil, a nobody, as everybody in the neighborhood presumes, has a daughter who is a homosexual. After her father's death, the boy most improbably eavesdrops on a scene in which the Lesbian and her friend spit on the portrait of the father who had so adored her.

Then—even more clumsily linked to the main narrative, if narrative it can be called—comes the episode of "Swann in Love." Swann, it now turns out, far from being the nobody the boy's family had believed him to be, is a prominent figure in the international society of Paris. He starts a love affair with a courtesan named Odette de Crécy, a familiar figure at the home of a family named Verdurin, wealthy, semi-artistic climbers who run a salon where the "new" painters are received and the "new" music is played. Swann in love identifies his passion with a phrase from a beautiful modern sonata written by someone called Vinteuil, the old music master of the opening section. Swann, who has the entry of the most brilliant houses in Paris, is enchanted by the Verdurins, though they are far from being enchanted by him. He falls passionately in love with Odette, but she continues to deceive him with other men. Not only does Swann lacerate himself about these infidelities; he also does the same about her past love affairs. By means of an inquisition he elicits from her the admission that she is not only a courtesan, but also a Lesbian. In one very peculiar scene she brings him home to sleep with her while another man is apparently concealed in the room. And this woman, whom he later marries, and of whom he wearies, is the mother of Gilberte, the narrator's first sweetheart. Odette still continues to deceive Swann, and

we are given to understand that her accepted lover is a
M. de Charlus, one of the great Guermantes family that
haunts young Marcel's imagination.

Now, without even considering the rest of the book,
we have here enough material for a complete work on
Proust. Because we do not have to read very far before
we realize that M. de Charlus is not the lover of Odette
at all. M. de Charlus, in some respects the principal
character of the novel and certainly the most entertaining
one, is the type of all homosexuals. Why, then, does
Proust emphasize the legend of his love affair with Mme
Swann?

And what about all the other misconceptions we have
been compelled to nurse? We have been deliberately
misled as to Swann's position in Paris society, and nobody
has told us that Vinteuil, the old music master, is really
the great composer of that name about whose work we
are later told so much. Even a well-informed man like
Swann is unaware of his identity. "Someone of the same
name as himself, one of his relations," he supposes. It
may, of course, be true. Perhaps cultured people can live
next door to an old farmer called Robert Frost and never
ask: "Not *the* Frost?"

It is not convincing, but it is necessary to the plan of
the book, as illustrated, for instance, by the parish
priest's derivations of place names. His amateur errors
will later be corrected at even more inordinate length by
Brichot, and this, in fact, is the pattern that runs through
the whole texture of the book. Like the rumors that con-
nect Odette with a distinguished old gentleman who in

his whole life never laid hands on a lady, the notions regarding Swann's position in society, and Swann's own
guesses about the old music master, they are merely
aspects of a general atmosphere of error in which the
whole novel is intentionally bathed, and which it will
ultimately be the task of the artist to dissipate when he
discovers his true vocation.

The drift of the book now begins to come clear. You
think Legrandin is an artistic soul and a radical. On the
contrary, he is a vulgar snob. You believe the woman
traveling on the train with you, whose appearance and
behavior you have so skillfully analyzed, is a brothel-
keeper? Not a bit of it. She is the Princess Sherbatoff.
Error appears as a principle of nature. Even the errors
of the parish priest, Bloch's assumption that every Englishman is called "Lord," and the malapropisms of the hotel-
manager are all forms of this universal principle. The
gardener of Mme de Cambremer is faithful to her until
his death and venerates her for her goodness, but nothing
on earth will ever rid him of his erroneous belief that she
has been guilty of treason. In one of the funniest scenes
in Proust, M. de Verdurin explains to Charlus why he
must yield precedence to M. de Cambremer, who is
practically a nobody.

"But don't you see, since we happened to have M. de Cambremer here, and he's a Marquis, while you're only a
Baron . . ."

"Pardon me . . . I am also Duc de Brabant, Demoiseau de
Montarges, Prince d'Oleron, de Carency, de Viareggio and des
Dunes. However, it is not of the slightest importance. Please

do not distress yourself," he concluded, resuming his subtle smile, which spread itself over those final words: "I could see at a glance that you were not accustomed to society."

But then we are faced with the question of what the reason is for such an attitude, and here we can only fall back on the sexual attitudes of the novel for enlightenment. There is some enlightenment in the scene between the homosexual girls which Marcel observes, for Proust himself calls the scene "sadistic." It is interesting because it represents one of the ways in which our old friend of the romantic revival works his passage to modern literature, but it is not quite accurate. There is undoubtedly a sado-masochistic element in the scene, but primarily— like the scene in which Odette brings Swann home with her while another man is concealed in the room—it is exhibitionist-voyeur. In fact, one of the things that become clear from the study of Proust is that we use the word "homosexual" in a very loose and unscientific way. In modern literature there is not, to my knowledge, any such thing as homosexuality; there is only a perverted form of sex which combines voyeurism and exhibitionism, sadism and masochism with something that *resembles* homosexuality. This is sex with human love left out, as in Gide's extraordinary marriage, where love was reserved for the virgin wife and sexual satisfaction for streetboys.

The whole problem of what this sort of sex really is is raised by the section called "Swann in Love" because, in fact, this is the pattern for all the other love affairs, homo- and hetero-sexual, that Proust describes, and a very queer pattern it turns out to be. In this sort of love the

Lover is nearly always rich, cultured, and sensitive; the Beloved a person of little breeding, usually a prostitute. The Lover expects from the Beloved no more than what his wealth can buy, and the Beloved tries to cheat him even of this. The relationship of rich and poor, generous and venal, makes it necessary for Proust to argue that love is not as the intelligence perceives it to be—partly subjective and partly objective—but exclusively subjective, without any possibility of reciprocity, and disappearing completely with the cessation of the subjective infatuation of the Lover. "In love one seeks before everything else a subjective pleasure." Consequently, the more subjective the pleasure, the more satisfactory the relationship, so that the *type* of love is best represented by the antics of an old gentleman who finds all beauty under a bus-conductor's cap.

This has about as much relationship to human love, at least as the intelligence perceives it, as a zoologist's notebook, but, of course, it is characteristic of a great artist that he should be able to persuade us that an abnormal relationship is really the most normal thing in the world, and indeed is what we ourselves have always been accustomed to.

2.

But at once Proust finds himself in a difficulty from which he was never able to rescue himself entirely. To this subjective pleasure of love all objective or semi-objective pleasures are subordinate, including the pleasure we find in great art. But is there any objective pleasure in great art, or is that too wholly subjective? Watch how Proust describes Swann's identification with Odette's base tastes.

This charm of drawing him closer to her, which her favourite plays and pictures and places possessed, struck him as being more mysterious than the intrinsic charm of more beautiful things and places, which appealed to him by their beauty but without recalling her. Besides, having allowed the intellectual beliefs of his youth to grow faint, till his scepticism as a finished "man of the world" had gradually penetrated him unawares, he held (or at least he had held for so long that he had fallen into the habit of saying) that the objects we admire have no absolute value in themselves, that the whole thing is a matter of dates and castes, and consists in a series of fashions, the most vulgar of which are worth just as much as those which are regarded as the most refined.

Here we see Proust balancing dizzily on the edge of a cliff over which he is in danger of toppling, and over which, in my own belief, he does eventually topple: the denial of artistic values, which would in turn be a denial of any importance to his own work. Here is a man who has devoted himself to Art as a medieval ascetic devoted himself to God, and who still half believes there is no virtue in asceticism and that any voluptuary is as close to, or as far from, God as himself. He does so because the artistic creed that he has picked up from his sexual attitude proclaims that "nothing is but thinking makes it so" and that our thinking is entirely dictated by our passions.

But just as the conversation, the smiles, the kisses of Odette became as odious to him as he had once found them charming if they were diverted to others than himself, so the Verdurins' drawing-room, which not an hour before had still seemed to him amusing, inspired with a genuine feeling for art and even with a sort of moral aristocracy; now that it was another than himself whom Odette was going to meet there, to love there without restraint, laid bare to him all its absurdities, its stupidity, its shame.

Now, of course all this is perfectly true and within the experience of most of us in the sense that we recognize that the subjective element in love tends to transform all the objects and people related to our loves, and we were not waiting for Proust to tell us that "the lunatic, the lover and the poet are of imagination all compact." But that is not how Proust is presenting it to us, fundamentally because that is not how it is being presented to his own mind by his passions. What he is saying is that Verdurin's drawing-room really exists for Swann only through his passions, and that it can only appear beautiful or ugly, clever or stupid. What he gives us is exactly the same inversion of values that he already gave us in the Legrandin episode, and it is characteristic of the whole novel and of his whole attitude to psychology. It is what I call the "either-or" type of psychology. The "passions" of the Balzacian system have disappeared entirely, for in fact there is no such thing as a constant in any character, no single element that is statistically predictable. Everything is a construct of the imagination.

Suddenly Saint-Loup appeared, accompanied by his mistress, and then, in this woman who was for him all the love, all possible delight in life, whose personality, mysteriously enshrined

in a body as in a tabernacle, was the object that still occupied incessantly the toiling imagination of my friend, whom he felt that he would never really know, as to whom he was perpetually asking himself what could be her secret self, behind the veil of eyes and flesh, in this woman I recognised at once"Rachel When from the Lord," her who but a few years since . . . used to say to the procuress: "Tomorrow evening then, if you want me for anyone, you will send round, won't you?"

I realised also then all that the human imagination can put behind a little scrap of face, such as this girl's face was, if it is the imagination that was the first to know it; and conversely into what wretched elements, crudely material and utterly without value, might be decomposed what had been the inspiration of countless dreams, if on the contrary, it should be, so to speak, controverted by the slightest actual acquaintance.

It seems absurd to criticize a passage of such beauty and bring it down to terms of meaning, yet it is necessary to do so if we are to understand where Proust and modern literature are going. For, mark you, Proust is not merely saying that a character has no value other than that which our imagination attributes to it, though he is saying that loud enough for anyone. He is saying too that whatever this act of the imagination evokes in ourselves is also fallacious and must disappear with its source. When we meet Saint-Loup a little later, he is a quite different character, rejoicing in M. de Charlus's reputation as a womanizer, because Saint-Loup as Rachel's lover is chaste, but Saint-Loup, no longer her lover, is a rake. Either saint or devil, beautiful or disgusting, noble or vile; there is no middle way, for if there were, it would represent a core of objective reality and the character would not merely be an occasion of error. And here it seems to me that as an artist he is again treading dangerous ground. He is saying that there is no objective reality in the things we pursue, or if there is, that this must forever remain unknown to us, but also, as a corollary, that the subject itself is illusory since it changes character in response to the stimulus or lack of stimulus offered it by the imagination; that a man who is "good" when pursuing an illusory "good" object will cease to be so when he ceases in his pursuit. Proust's psychology owes nothing to Aristotle. It does not even seem to have crossed his mind that if there is no object, then equally there can be no subject.

3.

One of the principal effects of this on the book is in the shadowy nature of the characters, and their tendency to inexplicable extremes of behavior. Swann, for instance, who has been presented to us as gentle and even ineffectual, suddenly becomes a raging devil and speaks a language we have never heard from him before.

"To think that she could visit really historic buildings with me, who have spent ten years in the study of architecture, who am constantly bombarded by people who really count, to take them over Beauvais or Saint-Loup-de-Naud, and refuse to take anyone but her; and instead of that she trundles off with the lowest, the most brutally degraded of creatures, to go into ecstasies over the petrified excretions of Louis Philippe and Viollet-le-Duc! One hardly needs much knowledge of art, I should say, to do that, though surely, even without any particularly refined sense of smell, one would not deliberately choose to spend a holiday in the latrines so as to be within range of their fragrant exhalations."

The most interesting thing about this interesting passage is that, in fact, Swann himself has ceased to speak and we are listening to the voice and cadences of Charlus, the homosexual. One has only to compare this with any of Charlus's tirades. Swann's knowledge of art—now apparently quite objective—is the same as Charlus's royal blood; ignorance of architecture has become synonymous with middle-class parentage, and we recognize Charlus's hysterical arrogance in his favorite excretory images. Proust himself seems to have become aware of the similarity while he was writing it, for he makes Swann think of "men whose natures were analogous to his own, as was, so far as the heart went, that of M. de Charlus." But Swann is not only another aspect of Charlus; he is also an aspect of the narrator "in whom I discover the delightful errors of my youth"—the worldly Proust, in fact. Proust is really dealing only with aspects of one single character, and all the different aspects are linked by the monstrous nature of their love—and hate. Because we must not forget that if love is entirely subjective, then hate must equally be so, and if Swann, Marcel, and Charlus need no other attractions in the people they love than those provided by their own imagination, then Odette, Albertine, and Morel might be as faithful as they pleased because their lovers would still have invented reasons for their hate. We see that they have chosen this particular man or woman not because he or she can make them happy, but because he or she can make them *unhappy*, and the unhappiness that these have the power to cause is the real secret of their attraction. Again we return to our old friend the Marquis. The attraction in every love affair Proust describes is sado-masochistic, and so voyeurism and exhibitionism are mainly ways of giving and receiving pain. As I have said about Dostoevsky, where there is no true object and subject, then there is no proper correlation between pain and pleasure. When a character as object hurts us, we naturally feel pain, but when once the object becomes confused with the subject, then we can imagine that the appropriate emotions become equally confused, and we rejoice in our own sufferings as though we were inflicting them on others. Ultimately, it would seem that sexual deviation, at least so far as we can understand it from Proust, is a result of the inordinate use of the imagination. "The nostalgia for the gutter" is the nostalgia for an entirely self-created world.

And there is no doubt that here, as in *Ulysses* and *Exiles*, *Sons and Lovers* and *Jimmy and the Desperate Woman*, we are dealing with the situation that was first revealed in Dostoevsky's *Eternal Husband*, the unnatural triangle of the homosexual, in which the woman is merely used as bait for the man.

The moment we grasp the morbid character of Proust's love and its relation to his work, we also begin to understand a great deal of his great novel which has nothing to do with love. As we have seen, in homosexual relationships like those of Proust, Gide, and Wilde there can be no question of reciprocity. All feeling belongs to the Lover, and he alone creates the reasons for his love and hate. Not only is he not interested in the facts, but also he violently resents the facts as an intrusion on his self-created imaginative world. In the very amusing and tragic scene in the homosexual brothel where Proust loved to install himself as spy, Charlus, who likes to imagine himself the beloved victim of murderers and rapists, congratulates his flogger on the brutal murder of an old woman. When the flogger, who is far too innocent to understand Charlus's perversion, denies in shocked tones that he ever laid a hand on anybody, Charlus irritably shuts him up. The flogger is intruding on Charlus's fantasy. An exhibitionist's victim who only showed amusement at his behavior would drive the unfortunate creature almost insane.

And so, as love is error, then everything must be error. Because there is nothing in the man or woman we love but a fiction created by ourselves, we can never know truth. This is Proust's real debt to Bergson, though in a very disingenuous letter he tries to deny it. Only an idealistic philosophy could provide the framework for such a very peculiar vision of life, and Bergson's suited Proust's book because it makes no attempt to distinguish object from subject. Proust's own philosophical views are none too clear. For much of the time one may read him as saying that objective reality may exist, but that if it does, we cannot apprehend it. At other times he seems to say flatly that there is no reality outside the mind.

It was she [the Duchess] who first gave me the idea that a person does not (as I had imagined) stand motionless and clear before our eyes with his merits, his defects, his plans, his intentions with regard to ourself exposed on his surface . . . but is a shadow that we can never succeed in penetrating, of which there can be no such thing as direct knowledge.

In the great section on the theory of literature he expresses this view even more emphatically: "I had realized that only gravely erroneous observation places everything in the object while everything is in the mind."

"I make the truth." "When I want to know what Ireland is thinking, I look into my own heart." This is symbolist doctrine with a vengeance.

Finally, we come to the last difficulty. How are we to reconcile symbolist doctrine with the novelist's practice? Where is the reality of the work of art, if it has such a reality? And here Proust falls back on his theory of the voluntary and involuntary memories, though the "involuntary memory" he describes is no other than the "deep subconscious" of Maurice Barrès of 1904, Freud's Unconscious of 1900. Reality exists only in the involuntary memory, and can be evoked only by the artist, for the ordinary man perceives it only in flashes of sensory recollection like that in which Marcel eats pastry dipped in tea or stumbles on an uneven surface. And then comes the thrilling description of the artist's vocation.

The artist's labour, of trying to perceive under matter, under experience, under words, something which differs from them, is exactly the inverse labour from that which at every moment when we live diverted from ourselves, self-love, passion, intelligence, and habit accomplish likewise in us, by heaping above our real impressions to hide them from us the names and practical aims of what we falsely call life.

All modern romanticism consists in one long battle with the intelligence, but of all modern romantics, Proust seems to me the only one of whom one can say that the battle results in a draw. Of the others one can say, as I think Faulkner once said, that the measure of their genius was the scale of their defeat.

chapter 20

Joyce and Dissociated Metaphor

Proust and Joyce were the heroes of my youth, but while Proust's work has continued to grow on me, Joyce's has lost its charm. The reason may be that I know too much about it. The reason for that may be that there is far too much to know.

That weakness of Joyce's does not begin with *Finnegans Wake*. It begins with his first book of fiction. It may be that the earlier stories in *Dubliners* are plain sailing; to me the later ones at least are exceedingly difficult to understand, and I can only admire the critics who so blandly profess to interpret them.

Let me begin with one small detail of which I shall have more to say. It is the first paragraph of a story called *Two Gallants*, and I merely wish to point out that the style is unusual.

The grey warm evening of August had descended upon the city and a mild warm air, a memory of summer, circulated in the streets. The streets, shuttered for the repose of Sunday, swarmed with a gaily coloured crowd. Like illumined pearls the lamps shone from the summits of their tall poles upon the living texture below which, changing shape and hue, unceasingly, sent up into the warm grey evening air an unchanging unceasing murmur.

This beautiful paragraph, apparently modeled upon the prose of Flaubert, has a deliberation and self-consciousness exceedingly rare in the work of a young man and, indeed, rare in Flaubert. There is a deliberate repetition of certain key words, sometimes with a slight alteration of form, like "warm," "grey," "change," and "cease" which produces a peculiar effect that is not the result of precise observation, but of a deliberately produced hypnosis.

And here, so far as I can see, that particular experiment ceases for the moment. But in stories like *Ivy Day in the Committee Room*, *Grace*, and *The Dead*, there is a deliberate and self-conscious use of form which produces a similar result. I have read these stories many times, and cannot profess to understand them. I am not impressed by the argument that they should be read "straight." I envy the ability of those who can read "straight" such a passage as that I have quoted, but I cannot emulate it. To me it seems queer, and I cannot help searching for the reason for its queerness.

In *Ivy Day in the Committee Room* we are in the headquarters of a candidate in a Dublin municipal election after Parnell's death. We meet the caretaker and a canvasser whose name is O'Connor and who wears a badge in Parnell's memory. The caretaker complains of his son's drinking habits. Another canvasser called Hynes appears, and they discuss the prospects of their getting paid, as well as the arrival of Edward VII on a visit to Dublin. A third canvasser called Henchy appears; Henchy has approached the candidate—a publican—for payment and had no luck. Even his request for a few bottles of stout seems to have been ignored. There is reference to the publican's father, who had kept an old-clothes shop where he had sold liquor on the side. Hynes goes out, and Henchy indignantly asks what he was doing there. His father was a decent man, but, according to Mr. Henchy, the son is not much better than an English spy. The scene is interrupted for a few moments by an unfrocked priest, Father Keon, who is looking for the publican, and then the dozen of stout arrives and the messenger boy is dispatched for a corkscrew, which he later takes back. Two fresh canvassers arrive: Mr. Crofton, a Protestant and socially a cut above the others, and Mr. Lyons, and as there is no corkscrew, two bottles of stout are put before the fire. Then, after the first cork pops, the men discuss Edward VII—a decent man who likes his glass of grog— and Parnell, till Mr. Hynes, the alleged spy, returns and a third bottle is laid on for him. Mr. Henchy, his former critic, now calls him "Joe" and asks him to recite. He recites a doggerel poem of his own in praise of the dead leader, and the third cork pops. The last lines run:

"What do you think of that, Crofton?" cried Mr. Henchy. "Isn't that fine? What?"

Mr. Crofton said it was a very fine piece of writing.

The story is remarkable for a certain apparent looseness of texture which is almost a new thing in literature. Events seem to occur merely as they would occur in everyday life; people drift in and out; there is no obvious design, and yet the story holds our attention. As a storyteller, I am impressed by the achievement, but at the same time it is clear to me that the casualness is only apparent. To begin with, the form is based upon political comment that emerges from a ground bass of booze. Everybody in the story is thinking or talking of drink, and the crisis, such as it is, when Mr. Henchy's mood mellows and he calls Hynes by his Christian name, is the result of the dozen of stout. The parallelism between King Edward and Parnell, "the Uncrowned King of Ireland," is clear, though the repeated references to "fathers"—human fathers, holy fathers, and City Fathers —I do not understand. But there are other details that show the careful structure of the story. Take, for instance, the bottles of stout. The corkscrew is absent, so one is borrowed from, and then returned to, the nearest public house, which leaves us with three bottles that must be opened by the primitive method of heating them. There is no doubt that this episode has been contrived to suggest the three volleys fired over the dead hero's grave.

The author's brother tells us that *Grace* was intended as a parody of *The Divine Comedy*, the pub representing Hell, the home Purgatory, and the church Paradise, but even this does not seem to me to explain all the peculiarities of the story, which again gives an elaborate impression of casualness. A commercial traveler falls down the steps of an underground lavatory and hurts himself. He is rescued from the police by an influential friend who then organizes a campaign to make him quit the drink, and the story ends in a Jesuit church with a businesslike sermon fit for business gentlemen like Mr. Kernan. There are two long discussions in the story, one dealing with policemen, the other with priests, and these seem to represent the temporal and spiritual powers; but even these discussions have a peculiar quality because each deals with the problem of good and bad types. Like the characters in the story, these seem to be neither very good nor very bad; and the whole manner of the story, which is the mock-heroic, seems to be a denunciation of mediocrity.

But whether or not there is a hidden structure of metaphor in the two stories I have mentioned, there is no doubt of its existence in *The Dead*, the latest to be written and the most elaborate in construction. This metaphor is unique just because it is hidden. Many nineteenth-century writers, particularly the Americans, used metaphor and allegory, but Joyce's metaphor resembles the dissociated metaphor of dreams, which is intended to baffle and deceive the conscious mind.

The story is about a young man with tuberculosis living in the west of Ireland who falls in love with a girl called Gretta. He spends one whole night outside her window, and dies soon after. Years later, at a musical party in Dublin, Gretta, now the wife of a man called Gabriel Conroy, hears the young man's favorite song, "The Lass of Aughrim," and tells her husband of the incident. Then Conroy looks out and sees the snow, death's symbol, drifting down over the city.

In the story the process of recollection is unconscious and is built up of odd scraps of metaphor. The train of allusion is fired when Conroy enters, "scraping the snow from his goloshes." He asks the maid jocularly about her

wedding, and she replies bitterly that "the men that is
now is only all palaver and what they can get out of you."
The repudiation of the living in relation to love and marriage is an anticipation of Gabriel's own feelings at the
end of the story. His aunts, the old music teachers, ask if
it is true that he and Gretta are not going home to
"Monkstown" for the night, and Gabriel replies that
after the previous year's party Gretta had caught "cold."
The reference to "a cold" is deliberate, as is, perhaps,
the reference to Monkstown because the Cistercian
monks mentioned later who are supposed to "sleep in
their coffins" are another metaphor of death. The party
is, of course, a musical one, as the young man had been a
singer. Because the setting of the incident has also to be
placed by means of allusion, one of the guests, Miss
Ivors, who is a Nationalist, talks of going with a party
to the west of Ireland during the summer, and disputes
with Gabriel, who prefers to go abroad. The reference to
marriage at the opening is continued by things like the
old song, "Arrayed for the Bridal," and the imperfections
of "the men that is now" are emphasized by the mention
of Caruso, who, though he may be a good singer, is not
nearly so good as a forgotten tenor named Parkinson,
while in Gabriel's speech he contrasts Miss Ivors with his
aunts and finds her to "lack those qualities of humanity, of
hospitality, of kindly humour which belonged to an older
day." His tribute to the memory of the dead is only
another chord in the theme, which is simply that all love
and beauty and grace are with the dead, and that as hus-

band he himself can never compete with that long-dead youth until the snows cover himself as well.

It is a beautiful story, and perhaps here, at any rate, the mysterious effect of dissociated metaphor is not out of place, though elsewhere I find that it produces something akin to claustrophobia in me. I long to know how Mr. Kernan and Martin Cunningham would really express themselves if released for a few moments from the need to be so damn metaphorical.

2.

Sir Desmond MacCarthy describes in one of his essays how I first came to notice the peculiar cast of Joyce's mind. The incident concerned a picture of Cork in his hallway. I could not detect what the frame was made of. "What is that?" I asked. "Cork," he replied. "Yes," I said, "I know it's Cork, but what's the frame?" "Cork," he replied with a smile. "I had the greatest difficulty in finding a French frame-maker who would make it."

Whether or not this indicated, as I thought, that he was suffering from associative mania, it proved a valuable key in my efforts to understand his work.

It also proved a necessary one, for though in his years of fame Joyce had interpreters galore who propounded his work to the public even before it was completed, we have no such interpreters for the early stories and *A Portrait of the Artist as a Young Man.*

This seems to me an exceedingly difficult book. The

first thing to notice is that the peculiar style used in the opening of *Two Gallants* is now a regular device. It can best be described as "mechanical prose," for certain key words are repeated deliberately and mechanically to produce a feeling of hypnosis in the reader.

The soft beauty of the Latin word *touched* with an enchanting *touch* the *dark* of the evening, with a *touch* fainter and more persuading than the *touch* of music or of a *woman's* hand. The strife of their minds was quelled. The figure of a *woman* as she appears in the liturgy of the church *passed* silently through the *darkness:* a white-robed figure, small and slender as a boy, and with a falling girdle. Her *voice*, frail and high as a boy's, was heard intoning from a distant choir the first words of a *woman* which pierce the gloom and clamour of the first chanting of the passion:
Et tu cum Jesu Galilæo eras—
And all hearts were *touched* and turned to her *voice*, shining like a young star, shining clearer as the *voice* intoned the proparoxyton, and more faintly as the cadence died.

I have italicized a few of the principal words to show how a chain of association is built up, but the reader can see for himself that other words are similarly repeated. The whole structure of the book is probably lost unless Joyce's notebooks give some indication of what it was, but I have an impression that Joyce wrote with a list of a couple of hundred words before him, each representing some association, and that at intervals the words were dropped in, like currants in a cake and a handful at a time, so that their presence would be felt rather than identified. I suspect that a number of those words, like the spot-

lighted word "touch" in the passage I have quoted, are
of sensory significance, and are intended to maintain in
our subconscious minds the metaphor of the Aristotelian
scheme of psychology, while others, like the word
"passed," seem to have a general significance in relation
to the movement of the individual through time and space.
Whenever the emotion overflows, it is represented by
inversion and repetition. The whole subject should be
studied in a few paragraphs like the following:

He was *alone*. He was unheeded, happy and near to the *wild
heart* of life. He was *alone* and young and wilful and *wildhearted*,
alone amid a waste of *wild air* and brackish waters and the
*sea*harvest of shells and tangle and veiled grey sunlight and
gayclad, lightclad figures of *children* and *girls* and voices *childish*
and *girlish* in the *air*.

A *girl* stood before him in mid*stream; alone* and *still, gazing* out
to *sea*. She seemed like one whom magic had changed into the
likeness of a strange and beautiful *seabird*. Her *long* slender *bare*
legs were delicate as a *crane's* and pure save where an emerald
trail of *sea*weed had fashioned itself as a sign upon the flesh.
Her thighs, fuller and *soft*hued as ivory, were *bared* almost to
the hips where the *white* fringes of her drawers were like *feathering* of *soft white down*. Her slate-blue skirts were kilted boldly
about her waist and *dovetailed* behind her. Her bosom was as a
bird's, soft and slight, slight and soft, as the breast of some dark
plumaged dove. But her *long* fair hair was *girlish:* and *girlish*
and *touched* with the wonder of mortal beauty, her face.

She was *alone and still, gazing* out to *sea:* and when she felt his
presence and the worship of his *eyes*, her *eyes* turned to him in
quiet *sufferance* of his *gaze*, without shame or wantonness. *Long,
long* she *suffered* his *gaze* and then quietly withdrew her *eyes* from
his and bent them towards the *stream*. The first *faint* noise of
gently moving water broke the silence, low and *faint* and

whispering, *faint* as the bells of sleep; hither and thither, hither and thither; and a *faint* flame trembled on her cheek.

I find it difficult to transcribe, let alone analyze, the passage because it seems to me insufferably self-conscious, as though Walter Pater had taken to business and commercialized his style for the use of schools and colleges, but those who admire such prose should, I feel, be compelled to consider how it is constructed. I suspect there are at least two movements in a passage of this sort, one a local movement that seems to rise and fall within the framework of the paragraph in relation to the dominant image, and which produces words like "crane," "feathering," "down," "dovetailed," and "plumaged"; and another, over-all movement in which key words, particularly words of sensory significance like "touch," "eyes," and "gazed," are repeated and varied. I fancy that these could be traced right through the book, and that the study of them would throw considerable light on Joyce's intentions.

It is important to note that this is something new in literature, and it represents the point, anticipated in Flaubert, at which style ceases to be a relationship between author and reader and becomes a relationship of a magical kind between author and object. Here *le mot juste* is no longer *juste* for the reader, but for the object. It is not an attempt at communicating the experience to the reader, who is supposed to be present only by courtesy, but at equating the prose with the experience. Indeed, one might say that it aims at replacing the experience by the prose, and the process may be considered complete

when Joyce and his interpreters refer to one chapter in
Ulysses as a canon fugue or, as they prefer to describe it
in their idiomatic way, a *fuga per canonem*, which it is
not and, by the nature of prose and of canon fugues, could
not possibly be.

So far as I understand it, which is not very far, *A
Portrait* is a study in differentiation based on Aristotle's
De Anima and St. Thomas's *Commentary*. The first page,
which looks like a long passage of baby talk, is an elaborate construct that relates the development of the senses
to the development of the arts, a device later used in
Ulysses, when we find the transmigration of souls discussed over an underlying metaphor of the transmutation
of matter. "Once upon a time," the words with which
the book opens, represent story-telling, the primary form
of art. This whole passage is a fascinating piece of exposition. The first external person identified by the child
is his father, whom he identifies first by sight, then by
touch. Himself he identifies with a character in the story
his father tells him, and from the abstract "road" of the
bedtime story constructs a real road containing a real
character whom he identifies by the sense of taste—"she
sold lemon platt." He learns a song, the second of the
arts, which contains the key words "rose" and "green,"
and he unconsciously identifies these with "hot" and
"cold." When, instead of "O, the wild rose blossoms in
the little green place," he remembers "O the green wothe
botheth," we know that he has wet the bed because he
has linked the symbols for hot and cold. From this episode
the unconscious images become conscious, and the sense

of touch, the primary sense, according to Aristotle, is clearly differentiated. "When you wet the bed first it is warm then it gets cold." The metaphor is carried through into the divided politics of the home, for "Dante had two brushes in her press. The brush with the maroon velvet back was for Michael Davitt and the brush with the green velvet back was for Parnell."

As the first chapter develops, we find the boy at school with a high temperature that causes him to feel hot and cold by turn. This is illustrated in the prose by alternations of metaphor. The boy remembers washing his hands in the Wicklow Hotel where there were two taps, hot and cold. At school his class is divided into two groups, York and Lancaster, red and white. When he goes to bed, we know he is shivering violently because he is thinking of ghost stories, of black dogs and white cloaks, of old people and of strange people. We know the bed is warming up when he begins to think of the holidays, of warm colors and familiar faces. Eventually, when delirium overtakes him, the civil war between Davitt and Parnell is also used as a metaphor. The little drama is played out against a background of other antitheses: big, small; nasty, nice; damp, dry. There are no mental or moral antitheses because the boy knows of "right" and "wrong" only in terms of answers to schoolbook questions. He cannot think. As he can only feel, the only quality that can be attributed to him is "heart," the organ to which Aristotle ascribes sensation, and so we get, casually tossed in, the phrase "He was sick in his heart if you could be sick in that place."

In the next section we get a repetition of the words
"good" and "bad," "right" and "wrong," which still have
no true meaning for the boy because mind has not yet
been born in him. Mind emerges only when he has been
unjustly punished, and once more Joyce tosses the casual
reference in—"before he could make up his mind," to
indicate that the miracle of differentiation has taken place.
The soul, though born in all women with menstruation, is
born in males only with mortal sin, so that it is scarcely
mentioned until the boy has been with a prostitute. Then
it overflows the pages.

The differentiation is marked also in the literary forms.
Its æsthetic is propounded to Lynch in the final pages of
the book.

"Art necessarily divides itself into three forms progressing
from one to the next. These forms are: the lyrical form, the
form wherein the artist presents his image in immediate relation
to himself: the epical form, the form wherein he presents his
image in mediate relation to himself and to others: the dramatic
form, the form wherein he presents his image in immediate
relation to others."

This progress is also used as part of the metaphorical
structure of the book to illustrate the differentiation taking
place in Stephen's character. It begins with lyrical forms;
when he goes to college, it turns into epic; and, finally,
when he makes up his mind to leave home (action), it
becomes dramatic—the diary form. "The lyrical form,"
says Stephen, "is in fact the simplest verbal vesture of an
instant of emotion, a rhythmical cry such as ages ago
cheered on the man who pulled at the oar or dragged stone

up a slope." Accordingly, each of the early sections represents an "instant of emotion" and ends with a cry, though the cries seem to be differentiated according to the stage of self-consciousness which the individual has reached. Thus, the first cry, "Parnell! Parnell! He is dead," though supposed to come from a crowd of imaginary figures on a shore, is the impersonal, unindividualized cry of the sick child in a state of delirium, attributing his own suffering to dream figures. In the next section, when Mr. Casey cries: "Poor Parnell! My dead king!" the cry, though impersonal, is individualized and is followed by tears, though the tears are not Stephen's own. It is not until he himself has been punished unjustly that he gives a scream of pain and his tears flow. Again he cries when he goes to the prostitute, but this time with lust, and his tears are tears of relief. He cries once more when terrified by the thought of his sins, and his tears are tears of repentance. Finally, in the scene with the bird-girl, he cries again, but there are no tears, for the artistic emotion is not kinetic.

In reading Joyce, one is reading Literature—Literature with a capital L. The tide rises about the little figures islanded here and there in a waste of waters, and gradually they disappear till nothing is left but the blank expanse of Literature, mirroring the blank face of the sky.

3.

Everything in *Portrait* was, I believe, deliberate, but at the time it was written there was no Boswell to tell the world what Joyce intended, and his is such a curious type of mind that it is not very easy for the reader to see what he is getting at. By the time *Ulysses* and *Finnegans Wake* appeared, Joyce had Boswells galore, and the commentaries even preceded the books. Unfortunately, the commentaries are not always accurate because Joyce had a mania for mystification, and he even amused himself by mystifying those he enlightened.

Ulysses was preceded by a play called *Exiles*, which is absolutely necessary for its full understanding. The play deals with an Irish writer, Richard Rowan, who believes that his wife is playing him false with another man, a sort of disciple. Rowan also finds himself in a tragic position regarding his mother, a pious Catholic. We can see from the notes printed in the second edition of the play that the former theme is autobiographical and is based on the relations between Joyce himself, his wife, and an Italian acquaintance. What makes it most interesting is the way in which Rowan reveals that he himself longs for his own deception and is deliberately making himself a party to it. He is Trusotsky of the *Eternal Husband* in another form. It is also interesting to note in Rowan's character a marked identification with Christ and a tendency to look for Judases among his friends.

This play is the real basis of *Ulysses*, with the part of Richard Rowan divided between Stephen Dedalus, who is haunted by his dead mother, and Bloom, who is haunted by the idea of his wife's infidelity. All the same, when once one grasps the analogical relationships, one realizes that they are the same person and may either be regarded as a man young and old or as two aspects of the same man. The subject of the book is the attempt at reconciling them They pass, they skirt one another, all day, but it is only at night that they meet, and when Stephen becomes involved in a quarrel with some soldiers, Bloom, forgetting his natural restraint, calls him "Stephen" as Henchy in *Ivy Day in the Committee Room* forgets himself and calls Hynes "Joe."

The style is prodigiously elaborate, and even the large volume that Mr. Stuart Gilbert dedicates to it with Joyce's assistance fails to indicate some of its complexities of metaphor. Each chapter is written in a different style, and, as one of my students ingeniously pointed out, the names given to these styles by Gilbert and his author are themselves metaphorical. Mr. Bloom and his wife being intended to represent a modern Ulysses and Penelope, the first chapter shows them discussing the transmigration of souls. The basic metaphor for this is the transmutation of matter, so that the first line informs us that Bloom "ate with relish the inner organs of beasts and fowls." He goes out and buys a kidney for his breakfast, receives a letter from his daughter, Millie, who is improbably employed in a photographer's shop in Mullingar, the center of the Irish cattle industry, and finally, instead of going to the upstairs toilet, which might have upset the metaphor somewhat, he goes to an earth closet outside the house and returns to earth the matter that will come back as food for cattle, and so on in an eternal progression.

Not only is each chapter metaphorical, but also the metaphor is sustained by puns. For instance, in the

"Aeolus" chapter there are frequent references like "raising the wind," and in the "Hades" the idea of death is sustained by words like "mortgage" and names like "Todd." The worst pun I have been able to identify describes Mrs. Bloom looking at two dogs. "And the sergeant grinning up. She had that cream gown on with the rip she never stitched. 'Give us a touch, Poldy. God, I'm dying for it.' " "Dying for it" is characteristic; the reference to "Sergeant Death" and his grin will be caught only by the literary-minded, but "the gown with the R.I.P." is in the realm of the crossword puzzle. At the same time, it is not merely a joke played on the reader. For Joyce, all thought arises from the unconscious and returns to it. The thought that he must "renew" the book from the Capel Street library reminds Bloom of the word "reincarnation," which he is looking for. The simplest way of reading *Ulysses* is by a process of free association, for that is how Joyce himself thinks and how his characters are made to think.

The opening chapters of *Ulysses* are probably the highest development of Joyce's peculiar genius, for this lay with the habitual, the normal, the everyday, and his interest and observation were sustained by an elaborate system of analogy. But analogy will not permit of growth or development, and these have to be foisted artificially onto the book, and as it approaches a crisis, it becomes more and more bogged in tortuous technical devices like the chapter in the lying-in hospital where the development of the embryo is illustrated by the development of English prose from its most primitive forms, and the so-called "canon

311

fugue" where "Blstp" is supposed to represent an empty fifth.

The trouble with it is that it reduces man himself to a metaphor, a step that is openly taken in *Finnegans Wake*, and the Aristotelian philosophy with which we began has gone out the window. From Bloom, who cannot even defecate without illustrating something, it is only a step to H.C.E., who is merely a metaphor in the mind of God and has no personal existence.

Like the atom bomb, this can result only in the liquidation of humanity, and humanity has no choice but to retrace its steps and learn the business of living all over again.

Having grown up in a society in which the nineteenth-century novel was still contemporary, I have lived through two periods of literary taste, and I feel that I may perhaps be in at the beginning of a third. I noticed this first when I had the job of reviewing fiction after the war, and found writer after writer who was obviously in revolt against literary ideas as they were. One of those, C. P. Snow, has since become famous, and has left the literary world in no doubt that he is dissatisfied with the literary conventions of the pre-war period. One of his critics has complained bitterly that Snow, instead of leading the novel forward from Joyce, is attempting to bring it back to Trollope—a position that I fancy Snow himself would be very pleased to maintain. Nobody, I trust, is proposing to continue the process illustrated in *Finnegans Wake*.

I noticed a similar temper, perhaps mistakenly, in some of the work of a rather evasive writer, Marcel Aymé. One little-known book of his postulates the position of the modern writer with French malice and wit. It is called *Le Confort intellectuel*, and in it an old aristocrat tries to tempt a young novelist, who is Aymé himself, to declare in public that literature since Baudelaire has been going badly astray and drifting further and further away from life. It is a not unfamiliar thesis, and has always been popular with those who never seem to care for literature anyway, but it is not often that one hears it argued by real artists. In a series of monologues, the Tempter, who of course is also Aymé, Aymé the critic, tries to convince the young writer of the truth of what he is saying, and the book ends with the writer's indignant refusal to utter such heresies. "Monsieur," he says feelingly, "I should be banned from every literary circle in France." It is a typical French argument with a typical French conclusion, which suggests that the author will do nothing in particular about it.

There is much more dogged determination among the English writers, even if they have not presented their conclusions with quite the same force. But it is certain that C. P. Snow is far from being alone in his views. In the work of Joyce Cary, for instance, there is a revaluation of the whole nineteenth-century position which marks the contrast between him and the pre-war generation. One opens a novel of his and reads:

> It is no good talking to children like Ann because they have no education; only information. They are like wastepaper baskets full of exploded newspapers and fraudulent handbills. They don't mind going to bed with each other, or talking nonsense, or making a pigsty of the world. But they are shocked that a bad child should be punished with the rod.
>
> It would be useless to tell Ann that I and Lucy, whom she pities for our hard upbringing, probably had greater happiness in our childhood than she and Robert, in the same nursery, twenty years afterwards.
>
> They cannot understand the virtue of law, of discipline, which is to give that only peace which man can enjoy in this turmoil of a world: peace in his own soul.

This, of course, is only dramatic monologue, and not to be taken as expressing Mr. Cary's views, but at least the views have been dramatized, and that is something new in our time. As in the nineteenth century, the problem of literature's future is bound up with that of humanity's future. It may be that it has none, for not only are the weapons of destruction outgrowing man's capacity to control them, but also the middle classes, the only group that could conceivably control them, are being steadily crowded out. On the other hand, humanity has faced crises before now, and the middle class has a high standard of adaptability, and it may be that it can create a new age of relative peace and order.

For myself, the only light I have on the subject is a text in St. Mark. This seems to be the only occasion when Christ evaded a direct question. The Doctor of the Laws —a theologian—asked him which was the most important of the commandments, and Christ replied by quoting the first two: "Thou shalt love the Lord thy God" and "Thou shalt love thy neighbor," and added: "There is no commandment more important than these." We are told that the Doctor of the Laws was delighted with the reply—the first in history to express satisfaction with a witness who refused to answer a direct question.

Or perhaps an exceptionally intelligent man. For the problem that the Doctor of the Laws was posing was the age-old one between subjective and objective truth, between faith and good works (the aspect that has been so satisfactorily settled by Graham Greene), between symbolism and naturalism, communism and fascism. On a higher level, it is not at all unlike Chekhov's evasions when attacked by Lavrov and Suvorin. For Christ's reply, if I understand it, means merely that reality is inapprehensible; that if we keep our minds and hearts like clear glass, the light of God shines through us, but that we can be certain of God's presence within us only by the light it sheds on the world outside us. That, in fact, truth is subjective and objective, and that there is no truth greater than this.

index

The page numbers of extended discussions are printed in boldface type.

i

This book was set on the Monotype in *Janson*, a recutting made direct from the type cast from matrices made by Anton Janson some time between 1660 and 1687.

Of Janson's origin nothing is known. He may have been a relative of Justus Janson, a printer of Danish birth who practiced in Leipzig from 1614 to 1635. Some time between 1657 and 1668 Anton Janson, a punch-cutter and type-founder, bought from the Leipzig printer Johann Erich Hahn the type-foundry which had formerly been a part of the printing house of M. Friedrich Lankisch. Janson's types were first shown in a specimen sheet issued at Leipzig about 1675.

Composed, printed, and bound by KINGSPORT PRESS, INC., Kingsport, Tenn.

Paper manufactured by P. H. Glatfelter Co., Spring Grove, Pa.

The typography and binding were designed by Herbert Bayer.